James Fitzjames Stephen

Horae Sabbaticae

Reprint of Articles Contributed to the Saturday Review. First Series

James Fitzjames Stephen

Horae Sabbaticae
Reprint of Articles Contributed to the Saturday Review. First Series

ISBN/EAN: 9783337249892

Printed in Europe, USA, Canada, Australia, Japan

Cover: Foto ©Lupo / pixelio.de

More available books at **www.hansebooks.com**

HORAE SABBATICAE

HORAE SABBATICAE

REPRINT OF ARTICLES CONTRIBUTED

TO

THE SATURDAY REVIEW

BY

Sir JAMES FITZJAMES STEPHEN, Bart., K.C.S.I.

FIRST SERIES

London
MACMILLAN AND CO.
AND NEW YORK
1892

All rights reserved

CONTENTS

ESSAY		PAGE
I.	JOINVILLE AND ST. LOUIS	1
II.	FROISSART'S CHRONICLES .	22
III.	PHILIPPE DE COMINES	55
IV.	MONTAIGNE'S ESSAYS	124
V.	HOOKER'S 'ECCLESIASTICAL POLITY'.	145
VI.	ARCHBISHOP LAUD .	167
VII.	CHILLINGWORTH	187
VIII.	'THE LIBERTY OF PROPHESYING'	209
IX.	JEREMY TAYLOR AS A MORALIST	226
X.	,, ,,	242
XI.	,, ,,	263
XII.	HACKET'S LIFE OF ARCHBISHOP WILLIAMS	286
XIII.	CLARENDON'S 'HISTORY OF THE REBELLION' .	309
XIV.	LORD CLARENDON'S 'LIFE'	329

I

JOINVILLE AND ST. LOUIS[1]

M. DE SAINTE-BEUVE says that Joinville is the best representative 'of the age which we like to represent to ourselves as the golden age of the good old time. If this happy period ever existed in the past, it was in the reign of Saint Louis, during the fifteen years of peace under the shadow of the oak in the forest of Vincennes.' Joinville certainly gives us a vivid glimpse of this past age. It is, however, only a glimpse, and before the figures of the picture can be fully appreciated, it is necessary to sketch slightly the frame in which they must be set.

The forty-four years of the reign of Louis IX. (1226-1270) nearly coincide with the fifty-six years of the reign of Henry III. (1216-1272), and cover one of the great epochs of European history; for during that period the French Monarchy and the English Constitution were founded, and the first great religious crisis of modern Europe—that which included the de-

[1] *Mémoires de Jean Sire de Joinville ou l'Histoire et Chronique du très chrétien roi St. Louis.*

struction of the Albigenses, the erection of persecution into a system, and the crusades—came to an end.

The final conclusion of the Languedocian troubles, and the fall of the independence of the province may be dated in 1244. At the same date the successes of Louis in his war with Henry III., and the additions which his dominions received on the fall of Raymond, extended the French Monarchy from the Scheldt to the Mediterranean and the Pyrenees.

Thus the great events of the boyhood and early manhood of Louis were the extension and consolidation of his own dominions, by the same causes which overthrew the Albigensian heresy and established the Inquisition. This of itself would account for the great space which the question of orthodoxy occupied in his mind. It occupied, however, a similar space in the minds of his contemporaries.

The Church was at that time by far the greatest and most powerful organisation in the world; for though there were several great sovereigns,—Louis IX., Henry III., and the Emperor Frederic II., there was hardly such a thing in the whole of Europe as a nation well defined and thoroughly organised. The Church, moreover, was not only powerfully organised, but was instinct with life in every part. Councils, general, provincial, and national, were still a reality. The clergy of every country, and almost of every church, had their own special rights, which they maintained with the greatest determination. Even at St. Louis's own funeral there was a quarrel, between the clergy of the Abbey of St. Denis and the Archbishop of Sens and the Bishop of Paris, as to the right of the prelates to officiate. It had to be arranged before the funeral could proceed, though the new king, Philip III., with all the aristocracy and clergy of France, was kept waiting with the coffin at the church doors. The political side of religion was thus constantly brought home to everybody.

The intellectual movement, both within and without the Church, was at least as powerful. On the one side, the Albigensians had developed views of which, at this distance of time and with our imperfect sympathy with the feelings of a past age, it is difficult to form a just opinion. They would, however, appear to have involved, on the part of those who held them, not merely a revolt against all the institutions of the age, but a formal surrender of part of human life to the evil principle, coupled with that strange mixture of asceticism and license as to the other part, which is the practically necessary complement of such a view. On the other hand, there was within the Church a movement, or rather a series of movements, in which several of the great questions of religion were debated in a terminology and under conditions strange to us, but most influential over the men of that age.

In the thirteenth century, the Church was rather the friendly and sympathetic ruler, than the enemy of what then passed for reason; and this relation was rendered possible by the scholastic conception of science, and by the universal belief that the method of acquiring knowledge was to argue downwards, from principles generally admitted to be true, either as self-evident, or as notoriously revealed from heaven.

All theology may be divided into two great branches —the process of ascertaining certain facts, and the process of giving form to certain sentiments; at different periods the result of these two processes, and their relation to each other, differ. The degree of completeness, precision, and system which can be given to the religious emotions—in other words, the extent to which feeling can be translated into propositions, depends upon the amount of certainty which is felt as to the facts to which the sentiments relate. In the thirteenth century all the facts were taken for granted. The apparatus for examining or discussing them did not then exist. Hence it was possible to exhibit, in an astonishingly definite and systematic form, what in reality were only conjectures, upon subjects about which religious people felt a curiosity.

For instance, amongst the innumerable subjects on which Thomas Aquinas considered himself scientifically able to pronounce an opinion, were (according to Hallam) such as these: Could God have permitted actions against natural reason? Can he dispense with the law of nature? Did he act in a legislative, or in some, and what, other capacity, in the matter of the sacrifice of Isaac? To us these questions appear insoluble or puerile, but in that age various principles which could be logically connected with them were universal postulates, and the state of religious sentiment was such as absolutely to demand some rational organisation.

It was the age not only of the Albigensians, but of the Pastoureaux, the sect which tried to erect what is called the religion of the Holy Ghost, the time of the Father having ended at the birth of Christ, and the time of the Son at the rise of the Pastoureaux. An immense mass of peasants marched half over France on this strange errand under an unknown leader in 1251. In 1260 the Flagellants scourged themselves through every city in Europe; and the Dominicans and Franciscans, with other orders of less importance, were in the full flush of their early enthusiasm, and afforded a safety-valve for fanaticism.

Their intense sense of the emotional side of religion enabled the monks to take up the logical side of it ardently and successfully. The greatest of all the Dominicans was Thomas Aquinas, a friend, and often a guest of St. Louis, and the work of his marvellously laborious life seems to have been—for it would be presumptuous for any one to speak positively on the contents of eighteen folio volumes known to him only by report—to expand and systematise the premisses which orthodoxy supplied, into a form sufficiently minute and definite to exercise, and, if possible, to satisfy, the reason, and to afford to the religious emotions that food and support, which they find in the intricacy of systems assumed to be strong because they are complex. Long chains of coherent reasoning often confirm the faith by which they are supported, as a number of hurdles will bear up a heavy superstructure on a swampy foundation.

Thomas Aquinas was the architect of the greatest structure of this kind ever erected, and St. Louis's character is an indirect illustration of its practical objects. To use the picturesque language of M. Michelet, who compares the thirteenth century to a pyramid: 'Au sommet le grand bœuf muet de Sicile' (Aquinas's nickname, given on the principle on which the owl at Arundel Castle was called Lord Thurlow) 'ruminait la question.' 'Audessous de l'ange il y avait l'homme, la morale sous la métaphysique. Sous St. Thomas, St. Louis.' The charm of Joinville's *Mémoires* is, that they draw an original picture of a man who might be considered the flower of the age in which these influences were at work. They set in the clearest light his sound intelligence in common things, his passionate religious sensibility, and the wild course of conduct into which he was led by indulging it. They also throw a curious light on the doubts, just sufficiently realised to enable him to look upon faith as difficult and meritorious, which passed through the mind of St. Louis, and no doubt through the minds of many others in that age, for the thirteenth century was an age of doubt as well as of faith. In its history indications are still to be found of a sceptical movement, not the less real because it was secret.

'The Latin writers of those times' (says Mosheim)

'often complain of public enemies of the Christian religion, and even of mockers of the Supreme Being. . . . The Aristotelian philosophy, which reigned in all the schools of Europe, and was regarded as identical with sound reason, led not a few to discard the doctrines commonly held and preached respecting Divine Providence, the immortality of the soul, the creation of the world, and other points.'

'They defended themselves,' adds one of his annotators, 'by distinguishing between theological truth and philosophical,' as many others have done to our own days. The Emperor Frederic II. was, of all the men of his age, the most deeply and widely suspected in this matter. The suspicions of his orthodoxy (which were probably not ill founded) were embodied in the myth of the book *De Tribus Impostoribus*.

Such was the age in which Louis IX. lived and reigned, and which Joinville commemorated. The leading dates of it are few. The first period extends from his accession, in 1226, to the first crusade in 1248. The second takes in the first crusade, from 1248 to 1254. The third consists of fifteen years of peace, 1255-1270; and the fourth consists of the few weeks which were occupied in the second crusade, July-August 1270. Joinville's *Mémoires* contain an outline of the first period, a pretty complete history of the second, some account of the third and scattered anecdotes as to the whole of the reign, for the most part not dated.

The book begins with a division of the subject,

which is soon given up. The first part, it is said, is meant to show in general how the king 'se gouverna tout son temps selon Dieu et selon l'eglise, et au profit de son regne' (p. 1). The second part relates his 'great acts of chivalry and great feats of arms.'

The first part consists of characteristic anecdotes told without arrangement, some of which have become almost proverbial, and of which all are eminently characteristic. The first of these is splendid in its simplicity and magnanimity.

'Il me demanda se je voulais estre honoré en ce siecle et avoir paradis à la mort, et je li diz oyl. Et il me dit, Donques vous gardez que vous ne faites ne ne dites à votre escient nulle riens, que se tout le monde le savoit, que vous ne peussiez congnoistre, je ai ce fait, je ai ce dit' (p. 6).

The most curious of these anecdotes are those which show how deeply the controversies of the day had affected Louis, and what was the view which orthodox men of his age took of the nature of religious doubt. They viewed it as in all cases, a voluntary act to which a man was distinctly tempted by the devil, and for which he was responsible, just as he would be for any other definite sin.

'The holy king did his utmost to make me believe firmly in the Christian law. . . . He said that we ought to believe firmly in the Christian law; when people are dying the devil does all he can to make them die in doubt on points of faith; for he sees that he cannot take away the good works which a man has done, so that he will have lost him if he dies in the true faith. Therefore we ought to guard and defend ourselves against this snare; say to the enemy when he sends such temptations, Begone. . . . He said that faith and belief were such that we ought to believe firmly, although we had only hearsay evidence. He asked how I knew that my father's name was Simon. I said I firmly believed it because my mother had told me so. Then, said he, you ought to believe firmly all the articles of faith to which the apostles testify, as you mean to sing in the creed on Sunday' (p. 13).

He also told a story of a conversation between a 'great master in divinity' and the Bishop of Paris. The theologian said to the Bishop, weeping much :—

'I tell you, sir, said the master, I cannot help weeping, for I fear I am an unbeliever, for I cannot force my heart' (*mon cœur ahurter*) 'to believe in the sacrament of the altar as the Church teaches us, and I know these are temptations of the devil. Sir, said the Bishop, tell me, when the enemy sends you this temptation, does it please you? The master said, Sir, it annoys me as much as possible. I will ask you, said the Bishop, would you take money to avow with your mouth anything contrary to the sacrament of the altar or against the other holy sacraments of the Church? Sir, said the master, I would rather have the limbs torn from my body than I would make such an admission. I will say more, said the Bishop. You know that the King of France is at war with the King of England, and you know that the castle on the march between them is La Rochelle in Poitou. Now, I ask you, if the King had delivered you the castle of Rochelle to keep, which is on the frontier, and had delivered to me the castle of Laon, which is in the heart of France, and in a peaceable country, to which ought the King to be most indebted at the end of the war, to you who had kept Rochelle without losing it, or to me who had kept Laon without losing it? Good God, sir, said the master, to me who had kept La Rochelle. Sir, said the Bishop, I tell you that my heart is like the castle of Laon, for I have no temptation or doubt as to the sacrament of the altar, wherefore, I say that God owes you four times as much for believing with your heart in war and tribulation, as he owes me for believing firmly and peaceably.'

In the same spirit was another story of Louis. De Montfort refused to go and see a miraculous host, which had turned into visible flesh and blood. 'Do you go and see it, who disbelieve. I believe firmly. ... And do you know what I shall gain? In heaven I shall have a crown more than the angels, who see face to face, and so are obliged to believe' (p. 15). There is one more of the king's stories which, well known as it is, will bear repetition, as the comment is usually separated from the facts to which it relates.

There was to be a controversy at Clugny between the Jews and the clergy. A knight begged to be allowed to open the discussion. He asked for the greatest of the rabbis, and when he came, asked him if he believed in the history of the Virgin Mary. The rabbi naturally said No. The knight said 'que moult avait fait que fol'—that he had acted very like a fool, in coming to the Virgin's house, if he neither believed in nor loved her; and so saying, 'he lifted his crutch and hit the Jew near the ear and knocked him down, and the other Jews ran away, and carried off their master all wounded.' The knight, when blamed by the abbot, justified what he had done by saying that there were many Christians present who, if they had heard the controversy, would have gone away unbelievers. 'And I tell you,' said the king, 'that no one, if he is not a great scholar, ought to dispute with them; but a layman, when he hears the Christian law attacked, ought to defend it with the sword only, which he ought to drive into their bellies as far as it will go.' 'De quoy il doit donner parmi le ventre dedens, tant comme elle y peut entrer' (p. 16).

These stories give the keynote of Louis's mind. Faith, in his view, was the act of believing without evidence, or even against evidence. Nay, the greater the objections from a rational point of view, the more merit was there in believing. Whatever made, or seemed to make, against the 'Christian law' was a temptation of the devil, and whoever doubted or denied it was a personal enemy, to be combated by laymen like himself, with the sword; by 'great clerks,' like Thomas Aquinas, with syllogisms; and by the ecclesiastical authorities with the Inquisition backed by the secular arm.

This faith was the fruit of a still deeper feeling.

In his instruction to his daughter Isabelle he says: 'Dear daughter, have in yourself a desire which is never to leave you, that is to say, to please our Lord as much as you can, and give your whole heart to this, so that if you were certain that you would never be rewarded for the good you might do, nor punished for the ill you might do, you would still be obliged to keep yourself from doing anything which could displease our Lord, and would try to do what would please Him as much as you can, solely for the love of Him.'

Joinville tells a story which shows how widely such feelings were spread. At Acre 'brother Yoes saw an old woman crossing the street carrying in her right hand a pan full of fire, and in her left hand a bottle of water. Brother Yoes asked her: 'What do you want to do with this? She replied that she wanted to burn paradise with the fire and to put out hell with the water, so that they should be no more.' 'Why do you want to do that?' 'Because I wish that no one should do good to have the reward of heaven, or for fear of hell, but only to have the love of God, which is worth so much, and which gives us all good.'

With all his piety Louis IX. was the last man to underrate his own position in relation to the clergy. The bishops on one occasion addressed him by their spokesman as follows: 'Sire, the archbishops and bishops here present, have charged me to tell you that Christianity is falling and melting away in your hands, and will fall still more unless you interfere, for no one at the present day cares for being excommunicated. Therefore, sire, we ask you to order your bailiffs and serjeants to imprison those who are excommunicated a year and a day to compel them to give satisfaction to the Church! And the king replied without taking counsel that he would willingly command his bailiffs and serjeants to imprison excommunicated persons as they wished, but that he must take cognisance of the sentence' (*i.e.* of excommunication) 'to see whether it was just or not. Upon this they consulted and replied to the king that they would not give him cognisance of matters relating to the Christian religion. And the king told them that he would never give them cognisance of what belonged to him, nor order his officers to imprison persons excommunicated to force them to get absolution whether right or wrong. 'If I did so I should go against God and against right. And I will give you a proof of it. The bishops of Brittany have kept the Count of Brittany excommunicated for full seven years, and then he got absolution from the Court of Rome, and if I had constrained him' (to get absolved) 'in the first year I should have done so wrongfully.'

Joinville, whose unconscious portrait of himself is only less interesting than his portrait of St. Louis, was a very different kind of man. They were not unlike Sancho Panza and Don Quixote. Joinville admired and reverenced the king beyond all bounds, but he was by no means of the same way of thinking, or rather of feeling. He would appear to have been a model of the orthodox sensible men of the world of that day. He seems to have acquiesced in the creed of the time, to have believed it, and submitted to it, rather as a straightforward matter of prudence than from any special devotional feeling. A strong vein of frank dislike of cant runs through all that he says on such subjects.

The following anecdote is characteristic of them both. 'He once called me and said, I dare not speak to you on account of the sharpness of your wit in things touching God,[1] and therefore I have summoned these monks because I want to ask you a question. The question was this, Seneschal, what sort of thing is God?' (quel chose est Dieu?). 'I said, Sire, so good a thing that better cannot be. Well, said he, that is a good answer which you have made, and is the same which is written in this book which I hold in my hand. And now I ask you, which you would like best, to have the leprosy, or to commit a mortal sin, and I, who never told him a lie, said I would rather commit thirty mortal sins than be a leper. Next day when they were alone, the King gave him a solemn reproof, but Joinville does not seem to have changed his views. Louis asked him if he washed the feet of poor men on Holy Thursday.' 'Sire, dis-je les pieds de ces vilains ne laverai-je ja' (p. 81).

[1] 'Je n'ose parler à vous pour le soutil sens dont vous estes de chose qui touche à Dieu.'

His own religious observations show how straight-forward and simple-minded he was, and in what a direct business-like way the laymen of those days regarded such matters. Speaking of the belief of the Bedouins in predestination, he says: 'It is as much as to say that God has no power to help us; for it would be foolish to serve God (ils seroient fols ceux qui serviroient Dieu) 'if we did not think that He could prolong our lives and protect us from evil and mischief' (p. 79).

On one occasion Joinville knocked down one of his knights for quarrelling with another, saying as he did so : 'Get out of my house; so help me God, you shall not come back.' The knight made great interest to be pardoned, but Joinville says : 'I answered that I could not take him back unless the Legate would absolve me from my oath. They went and told the Legate, and he said he could not absolve me, as the oath was reasonable, and had served the knight quite right. . . . And this I mention to teach you not to take foolish oaths' (p. 176). The directness and simplicity of Joinville's views about prayer and oaths show a contented, straightforward, business-like view of religion which few people possess in our days.

Without reading the whole of Joinville's account of the crusade it would be difficult to form a just idea of the way in which the passionate devotion of Louis and the practical sense of Joinville set each other off throughout. Joinville's prevailing notion seems to have been that it was the right thing to do, and that he and others would or might go to heaven for it. He speaks of those who were killed as martyrs. 'The Bishop of Soissons greatly desiring to go to God, when he saw our troops retreating to Damietta, would not return to his native land, but hastened to go to God. He, therefore, spurred his horse and attacked the Turks all alone. They cut him down, and put him in the company of God, and in the number of the martyrs' (p. 119).

He also distinguished himself by strongly opposing, on the point of honour, a premature proposal to return to France; but when there was a talk of a second crusade he as strongly condemned it. 'I was much pressed by the King of France and the King of Navarre to cross myself, and I answered that while I was serving God and the king beyond the sea (in the first crusade) the officers of the King of France and the King of Navarre had destroyed and impoverished my vassals, so that they and I never were in a worse condition. I said also that if I wished to do God's will, I ought to stay at home and take care of my people; for if I were to risk my body by going on the crusade, clearly seeing that by so doing I should injure my people, I should offend God, who gave his body to save his people. I thought those who advised the king to go committed a mortal sin, for as long as he was in France the whole realm was at peace, at home and abroad, and after his departure things got continually worse' (p. 235).

Notwithstanding his clear apprehension of the plain duties which the King neglected by going on this strange wild-goose chase, no one could feel his piety more deeply than Joinville. He says that to canonise him was not enough. 'He should have been put amongst the martyrs for all he underwent in the crusade. . . . If God died on the cross, so did he, for he went as a crusader to Tunis.'

The actual history of the crusade must be gathered from the book itself. It is impossible for any abstract to do justice to the merit of a story the beauty of which depends so much upon the way in which it is told. But it may be worth while to give, in the most cursory way, the outline of the events which Joinville describes.

Louis IX. took the cross on his recovery from an illness, in December 1244. So difficult was it in those days to make all the necessary arrangements, that he did not sail from Aigues Mortes till the 28th of August 1248. He reached Cyprus on the 17th of September, and stayed there till the following May. He landed at Damietta on the 3d of June 1249, and took the town on the 6th, owing to the panic which the landing caused amongst the Turks. The Nile began to rise, and the crusaders loitered at Damietta till the end of November, waiting for it to fall, and did not appear before Mansourah, the half-way stage to Cairo, or Babylon as Joinville calls it, till the 20th of December. They remained in front of Mansourah till Shrove Tuesday (8th February 1250), when a great battle was fought, in which the Saracens were defeated. There was more fighting on the Friday, which was not so favourable to the French. After this, the armies maintained their positions till early in April, when the Christians, worn out with sickness and warfare, were obliged to retreat. The retreat became a rout, Louis himself being taken prisoner and held to ransom. Early in May the ransom was paid, and the army made its escape to Acre by sea. There, and at Jaffa, Louis remained four years, doing hardly anything of importance, and not even succeeding in entering Jerusalem. He returned to France on his mother's death, early in 1255, and entered Paris on the 7th of September.

Nothing could be more miserable than the generalship of this strange expedition. In just seven years' absence from France there was not much more than three months of fighting (8th February to 8th May 1250); the rest of the time was either wasted in delay or passed in doing nothing at all. The loss was awful. Of 2800 knights who left Cyprus with the King, only 100 went with him to Acre. The whole transaction was a wretched failure. On the other hand, Homer himself is hardly more picturesque than Joinville. Every page has its picture. The following are a few instances of his powers. He thus describes Greek fire :—

'La manière du feu gregois estoit telle que il venoit bien devant aussi gros comme une tonnel de verjus, et la queue du feu qui partoit de li estoit bien aussi grant comme un grant glaive; il faisoit telle noise au venir que il sembloit que ce feust la foudre du ciel; il sembloit un dragon qui volast par l'air; tant getoit grant clarté que l'on véoit parmi l'ast comme si il feust jour pour la grant foison du feu qui getoit la grant clarté. . . . Toutes les fois que notre saint roy voit que il nous getoient le feu gregois il se restoit en son lit et tendoit ses mains vers Nostre Seigneur et desoit en plourant, "Biau Sire Dieu, gardez moy ma gent," et je croie vraiement que ses prières nous orent bien mestier au besoing' (p. 65).

The following is a very Homeric sketch of a bit of a battle: 'There was wounded, Monseigneur Huges d'Escoz with three sword cuts on his face, and Monseigneur Raoul, and Monseigneur Ferri de Loupey with a sword between his shoulders, and the wound was so large that the blood came out of his body as from the bung-hole of a barrel. Monseigneur Erart de Syverey was struck by a sword in the face so that his nose fell over his lip; and thereupon I recollected my lord St. James, and said, "Biau Sire, St. Jacques, whom I implore, help and succour me in this business"' (p. 70).

Take again this picture of St. Louis himself: 'The King came with all his battle and halted on a causeway with a great blast and noise of trumpets and cymbals. Never was seen so fine a man at arms, for he was above all his men from the shoulders upwards, with a gilt helmet on his head, and a German sword in his hand' (p. 71).

I must content myself with one more of these pictures, though the whole history is almost made up of them. On the disastrous retreat from Mansourah Joinville with others fell into the power of the Saracens, who were about to put them to death. Upon this, says Joinville,—

'A number of people were confessing themselves to a monk who was there. For my own part I could not remember any sin I had committed, yet I saw the more I struggled the worse it would be, so I crossed myself and knelt down before one of the Saracens, who had a Danish carpenter's axe, and said, "So died St. Agnes." The Constable of Cyprus knelt by my side and confessed himself to me, and I said, "I absolve you in so far as God has given me power;" but when I got up I could not remember a single thing he had said' (pp. 107, 108).

Joinville was not present at the last Crusade of St. Louis. It formed an appropriate ending to his life. For fifteen years after his return from Syria, he ruled France with exemplary virtue, and with the most resolute and vigorous good sense, asserting his own authority, not only against the nobles but also against the clergy, and, in the case of need, against the Popes; but the strange vein of enthusiastic religion which prompted him to the first crusade was always present in him, as in one form or other it was in most of his family. Exaggerated asceticism was not enough for him. He was devoured by melancholy at not having seen Jerusalem, and he determined on a second expedition. It was even more absurdly planned and disastrously executed than the first. After three years of preparation he sailed on the 1st July 1270 for Tunis of all places in the world. The plague broke out in the army. Louis died there in August, so did his son the Comte de Nevers; so did the Papal Legate, and many others. The French returned to Sicily, and lost eighteen ships in a storm. When they landed, the King of Navarre and his wife, Louis IX.'s daughter, died of the plague caught at Tunis. On the journey home the wife of Philip III., Louis's successor, died, after giving birth to a child who died also. The dismal catastrophe of this crusade, the last expedition which deserved the name, was an appropriate practical comment on the value of the vein of fanatical asceticism which ran through the character of St. Louis. It is impossible to read his history without feeling that nothing but the accident of his age saved him from a full participation in the Albigensian persecution. Whether there was much more moral justification for the crusades, in which he spent so much of the substance of France, is a question too wide, and also too hackneyed, to be discussed here.

II

FROISSART'S CHRONICLES[1]

FROISSART's chronicles probably throw more light on certain aspects of the period to which they refer, than is thrown by any other single writer upon any other period. What Boswell did for the literary society of which Johnson formed the centre, what St. Simon did for the Court of Louis XIV., Froissart did for the military life of the fourteenth century. His history extends over a period of seventy-three years, beginning with the accession of Edward III. in 1327, and ending with the coronation of Henry IV. of England in 1400. He appears to have been born himself in 1337, and he must have lived into the fifteenth century, though the date of his death is not known. His whole life was devoted to the production of his book. He was continually engaged either in collecting materials for it or in making use of them. This appears from many passages in which he describes his

[1] Chronicles of England, France, Spain, and the adjoining countries from the latter part of the reign of Edward II. to the coronation of Henry IV., by Sir John Froissart. By Thomas Johnes Esq. In two volumes. Bohn 1862.

various journeys and their common object—namely, to collect information. 'I, John Froissart,' he says in one place, 'set myself to work at my forge to produce new and notable matter relative to the wars between France and England and their allies . . . which excellent matter I shall work upon as long as I live; for the more I labour at it the more it delights me, just as a gallant knight or squire at arms who loves his profession the longer he continues in it so much the more delectable it appears.'[1]

Notices indeed are scattered over the latter half of his work which show that he had hardly any other occupation in life than that of collecting news. Speaking of one of the attempts made in the time of Richard II. to make a permanent peace between England and France he says, 'I who at the time resided at Abbeville to learn news'[2]—Abbeville being the scene of the treaty. But the most characteristic passage of all is one in which he gives an account of his *modus operandi*: 'I may perhaps be asked how I became acquainted with the events in this history to speak so circumstantially about them. I reply to those who shall do so that I have, with great attention and diligence, sought in divers kingdoms and countries for the facts which have been or may hereafter be mentioned in it; for God has given me grace and opportunities to see and make acquaintance with the greater part of the principal Lords of France and England. It should be known that in the year 1390 I had laboured at

[1] II. 548. [2] 561.

this history thirty-seven years, and at that time I was fifty-seven years old; a man may therefore learn much in such a period when he is in his vigour and well received by all parties. During my youth I was five years attached to the King and Queen of England, and kindly entertained in the household of King John of France and King Charles his son. I was in consequence enabled to hear much during those times, and for certain the greatest pleasure I have ever had was to make every possible inquiry in regard to what was passing in the world, and then to write down all that I had learnt.'[1]

The result of the uninterrupted and sedulous gratification of these tastes for many years of his life together was that he succeeded in producing an enormous historical picture, which, whatever may be its defect in detail, may at all events be trusted to give a vivid general representation of its subjects. I will try to give some indications of the nature of the principal passages. The task is not so formidable as it might appear to be from the extent of the work. Johnes's translation of Froissart contains six thick volumes in common 8vo, or 1500 closely-printed pages in royal 8vo; but by far the greater part of the work is composed of matter so uniform in its character that it is comparatively easy to point out and illustrate the most striking passages.

The first words of the first chapter [2] state correctly the object of the whole book. 'To encourage all

[1] II. 258. [2] I. 3.

valorous hearts, and to show them honourable examples, I, John Froissart, will begin to relate' etc. The one eternal subject of the apparently endless history is war. Other things come in incidentally, but the general impression which Froissart gives is that the age in which he lived was completely given over to fighting, and cared about nothing else whatever.

Besides the great war between France and England which lasted with occasional and very ill-observed truces for about a hundred and twenty years—there were subsidiary wars almost too numerous to mention —wars between England and Scotland, wars between the French and the Flemings, wars between Ghent and Bruges, three-sided wars in Brittany, wars between France and Navarre, wars in Spain, wars in Portugal, wars in Béarn, wars in the different provinces which fell by degrees under the power of the Duke of Burgundy, wars in the county of Foix, wars, in a word, wherever there was an independent or semi-independent feudal ruler. The possession of Gascony by the Black Prince let loose the Gascons against the French in every direction, and to crown all, the Free Companies carried on wars on their own private account, which were neither more nor less than murder, robbery, and arson on a gigantic scale, and conducted for no other object than that of collecting plunder.

These wars, moreover, were very different from those of later times. A war in the fourteenth century seemed to have meant unlimited license to every one who could raise a small force to fly at the throats of every one else who had anything to lose. We learn from other authorities what were the practical results of wars thus conducted. Great parts of France were reduced to the condition of a desert, which it ceased to be worth while to cultivate. The population took refuge in caves, and endured a degree of misery which has probably been seldom exceeded at any period of history. Such is the picture as drawn by modern historians of the result of the English wars in France, but except by an effort of reflection no one would ever be led to suspect its existence simply by reading Froissart. His history flows on in an interminable stream of narratives of petty contests, the interest of which has long since entirely ceased. Castle after castle is besieged and taken, town after town burnt, skirmish after skirmish won or lost; but it never seems to occur to the chronicler that there is anything shocking in his story, or that any one can recognise in it anything but a delectable record of magnificent exploits.

With Joinville war between Christians at least is a great evil, and the preservation of the lives and property of his subjects is the great duty of a feudal lord—a greater and more pressing duty even than crusading. Comines again is full of moral reflections on the iniquitous and monstrous character of many of the events which he witnessed, but Froissart, 'l'insouciant Froissart,' as M. Michelet calls him, is perfectly at ease in his conscience, and never feels shocked at anything that he has to record.[1]

[1] I. 54.

In Edward III.'s first invasion of Picardy 'A troop of English and Germans came to Origny St Benoit, a tolerably good town but weakly enclosed so that it was soon taken by assault, robbed and pillaged, an abbey of nuns violated, and the whole town burnt. They then marched towards Guise and Ribemont. The King of England came and lodged at Vehories, where he remained a whole day while his people overran all the country thereabouts and laid it waste. The King then took the road to La Flamenque on his way to L'Eschelle in Tierache. The marshals with the Bishop of Lincoln accompanied by upwards of 500 lances crossed the river Trisaque entered the Laonnois near the estate of the Lord of Coney and burnt St. Gouvin and the town of Marle.' Learning the approach of the main French army they lay one night at Var below Laon, and the next day returned to the main army, as they had learnt from some of their prisoners that King Philip of France was come to St. Quentin with 100,000 men and there intended to cross the river Somme.[1] They 'burnt in their retreat a very good town called Crecy sur Selle with a great many others as well as villages in that neighbourhood.' The French, entering Hainault 'came to the town of Haspres which was a large handsome town though not fortified; nor had the inhabitants any fear for they had never the smallest notice of war being declared against the country. The French on entering the town found every one

[1] I. 60.

within doors. Having taken and pillaged what they pleased they burnt the town so completely that nothing but the walls remained.'[1] The French were fired upon from Huesnoy by cannon 'which flung large iron bolts in such a manner as made the French afraid for their horses so they retreated and burnt Grand Warguy and Petit Warguy, Frelaines, Hamary, Maitre Semery, and Oirtre, Jariten, Turques, etc., and the Hainaulters fled from their towns to Valenciennes. The French afterwards encamped their battalions upon the hill of Valenciennes where they lived in a rich and splendid manner.' The Duke of Normandy, who commanded on this occasion, ' gave orders for his army to dislodge and enter Hainault and burn and destroy everything without exception.'

The burning of twenty-four other towns and the devastation of large tracts of country is mentioned in the same chapter. The only observation made is as follows. After staying for a night at Main and Fontenelles 'they burnt Main and Fontenelles and also the convent which belonged to Madame de Valois, sister-german to the King of France. The Duke was much vexed at this and had those who set it on fire hanged. In their retreat they completed the burning of the town of Tire and its castle, the mills were also destroyed.'[2] It would be easy to fill pages with similar extracts,[3]

---

[1] I. 65.   [2] I. 67-69.
[3] See *e.g.* invasion of Normandy, I. 154-158. Treatment of Auvergne by the Black Prince I. 210. A few persons survived the ravages by the assault, I. 248.

but difficult to find a single expression of pity or disapproval unless indeed churches are attacked.

In describing, for instance, the storm of Durham by the Scotch, Froissart says, 'All were put to death without mercy and without distinction of persons or ranks, men, women, children, monks, canons, priests; no one was spared, neither was there house or church left standing. It was pity thus to destroy in Christendom the churches wherein God was served and honoured.'[1]

Froissart draws the line above profanity. An English squire profaned the elements of the sacrament at a village called Roney in order to steal the chalice, and having struck the priest with his gauntlet 'his horse began to caper and to play such violent tricks that no one dared to approach him. After many plunges they both fell to the ground with their necks broken' (it was rather hard upon the horse), 'and were immediately turned into dust and ashes. His companion seeing this made a vow that from henceforward they would never violate the sanctity of any church.'[2]

The places in which he shows genuine pity are very few. I have noted one or two: Limoges, having gone over to the French, was retaken by the Black Prince and was not only sacked and burnt but all the population massacred. Upon this Froissart goes so far as to say, 'It was a most melancholy business for all ranks, ages, and sexes, to cast themselves on their

---

[1] I. 99. The famous story of the sparing of the lives of the men of Calais is perhaps entitled to notice on the same ground. I. 185-186.   [2] I. 262.

knees before the prince begging for mercy, but he was so inflamed with passion and revenge that he listened to none, but all were put to the sword wherever they could be found even those who were not guilty; for I know not why the poor were not spared who could not have had any part in this treason, but they suffered for it and indeed more than those who had been the leaders of the treachery. There was not that day in the city of Limoges any heart so hardened, or that had any sense of religion, who did not deeply bewail the unfortunate events passing before their eyes; for upwards of 3000 men, women, and children were put to death that day. God have mercy on their souls! for they were veritably martyrs.'[1]

He observes too, in reference to the wars between the men of Ghent and the Earl of Flanders, that they were caused by the devil. 'You know wise men think that the devil, who is subtle and full of artifice, labours night and day to cause warfare wherever he finds peace and harmony,' and he accordingly did so in Flanders.[2] 'The devil, who never sleeps, put it in the heads of the people of Bruges to make a canal from the river Leys.' He also contrived quarrels between some of the inhabitants and the Earl of Flanders, and so by trifling events stirred up war between Ghent, Bruges, and the Earl of Flanders. The cause of the war lay a good deal deeper than Froissart supposed, but it is something that he admits that war is in any case a work of the devil.

[1] I. 453, 454. [2] I. 575.

Repulsive as this way of regarding war is to our modern view, it must be owned that there are many passages in Froissart, which enable us to understand the view which he took of war, and to appreciate its attractive and romantic as well as its brutal side. The actual belligerents, the fighting men themselves, treat each other throughout with distinguished courtesy, and much more in the spirit of competitors in a game of skill and strength than in that of real deadly enemies. Great part of the book consists of accounts of tournaments, single combats, captures, rescues, and ransoms, and it is remarkable to observe in how very many cases, the most desperate personal encounters end without loss of life or even without serious wounds.

A single illustration will be enough upon this point. Certain English and Navarrese knights were on their journey to Cherbourg under a passport from the Constable of France. They stopped to dine at Château Josselin. 'When they had dismounted at the inn, like travellers who wished to repose themselves, the knights and squires of the castle came to visit them, as brother soldiers who always see each other with pleasure particularly the French and English.' A French squire, John Boucmel, met an English squire, Nicholas Clifford, and insisted on having three courses with a lance with him, as each had a high reputation as a man-at-arms; Clifford made a variety of excuses, but Boucmel insisted on tilting, and at last the constable, who was at the castle, the inn being in the town below, insisted on keeping them there all night that they might fight in the morning. They fought accordingly, and at the first course 'Clifford struck with his spear John Boucmel on the upper part of his heart, but the point slipped off the steel breastplate and pierced the hood which was of good mail and entering the neck cut the jugular vein and passed quite through.' Boucmel of course was killed on the spot. Clifford 'was exceedingly vexed for having by ill-fortune slain a valiant and good man-at-arms.' The constable, however, remarked that 'such things were to be expected in similar combats.' He then said to the English 'Come, come to dinner, for it is ready.' Clifford, being deeply distressed, refused to go, but the constable fetched him almost by force.[1]

The whole book, as most people know, is full of such traits, but it may be doubted whether the true inference is as generally drawn as it ought to be. People in those days were not more romantic, certainly not more humane than they are at present; but the gentry of all countries formed a class with common feelings, habits, and sentiments, whose only chance of rising in the world, and in particular of making fortunes, was by distinctions in war. A battle comprised the attractions of a prize-fight and a lottery. To take a valuable prisoner was a piece of good luck which might and often did make a man's fortune; and there were besides the prospects of unlimited pillage amongst the townspeople and peasants who felt the whole edge of the war.

[1] I. 634-636.

Many passages, especially in the latter part of Froissart (which is also much the best part of the book), set this in a striking light. He continually observes upon the extreme fondness of the English for war, and it is plain from various passages near the end of the book that the unpopularity of Richard II. arose to a very great extent from his wish to produce if possible a durable treaty between France and England.

The following passages illustrate this. 'Many persons will not readily believe what I am about to say though it is strictly true, that the English are fonder of war than of peace. During the reign of King Edward of happy memory, and in the lifetime of his son the Prince of Wales, they made such grand conquests in France and by their victories, and ransoms of towns, castles, and men, gained such wealth that the poorest knights became rich, and those who were not gentlemen by birth, by gallantly hazarding themselves in these wars were ennobled for their valour and wealth.' Richard II. did all in his power to make a durable peace, but 'the majority of the commons were desirous of war; and two-thirds of the young knights and squires knew not how to employ themselves—they had learnt idleness and looked to war as the means of support.'

So eager were they for war that they were rather pleased than otherwise at the prospect of an invasion which was threatened in 1386. Froissart says, 'The great lords such as prelates, abbots, and rich citizens were panic-struck, but the commonalty and poorer sort held it very cheap. Such knights and squires as were not rich, but eager for renown, were delighted and said to each other: "Lord, what fine times are coming, the King of France intends to visit us! He is a valiant king and of great enterprise, there has not been such a one in France these three hundred years. He will make his people good men-at-arms, and blessed may he be for thinking to invade us, for certainly we shall be all slain or made powerfully rich; one or the other must happen."[1]

The pleasant side of the sort of life which was led by the feudal aristocracy in Froissart's days, is best shown by the accounts which he gives of some of his acquaintances at the court of the Count of Foix, his account of his residence at which is one of the most interesting parts of the whole book.[2] He visited the Count at his capital, Orthes in Béarn, in 1388. His journey thither was made in the company of a knight of Foix called Sir Espaign, who told him histories all the way about the different skirmishes which had occurred in the places by which they passed. The stories are all of the same kind, about sieges, stratagems, and battles. One of the most curious relates how a certain knight called the Bourg d'Espaigne once carried a donkey with a load of wood on his back up twenty-four steps, and threw the donkey

[1] II. 196.
[2] Vol. ii. All the early part of vol. ii. is occupied by Froissart's tour to Foix.

and the wood all in a heap on the fireplace of the hearth.[1]

On his arrival Froissart found Count Gaston de Foix the handsomest, the most prudent, and yet the most splendid prince he had ever seen. His accounts of his habits and court are too long to quote, but it is one of the most interesting passages in Froissart.

The following is a summary of the principal points in it. 'In short, everything considered, though I had before been in several courts of kings, dukes, princes, counts, and noble ladies, I was never at one which pleased me more, nor was I ever more delighted with feats of arms than at this of the Count of Foix.

[1] 'Three years ago I saw him play a ridiculous trick which I will relate to you. On Christmas Day when the Count de Foix was celebrating the feast with numbers of the knights and squires, as is customary, the weather was piercing cold, and the Count had dined with many lords in the hall, which has a large staircase of twenty-four steps. This gallery is heated by a fire when the Count inhabits it, otherwise not, and the fire is never great, for he does not like it. It is not for want of blocks of wood, for Béarn is covered with wood, plenty to warm him if he had chosen; but he accustomed himself to a small fire. When in the gallery he thought the fire too small, for it was freezing and the weather very sharp, and he said to the knights around him, "Here is but a small fire for this weather." Ernauton d'Espaigne instantly ran downstairs, for from the windows of the gallery he had seen a number of asses laden with billets of wood for the use of the house, and seizing the largest of these asses with his load, threw him over his shoulders and carried him upstairs, pushing through the knights and squires who were round the chimney, and flung ass and load, with his feet upwards, on the dogs of the hearth, to the delight and astonishment of all at the strength of the squire who had carried with such ease so great a load up so many steps' (ii. 87).

There were knights and squires to be seen in every chamber, hall, and court, going backwards and forwards, and conversing on arms and amours. All intelligence from distant countries was there to be learnt; for the gallantry of the court had brought visitors from all parts of the world. It was there I was informed of the greater part of those events which had happened in Spain, Portugal, Arragon, Navarre, England, Scotland, and on the borders of Lanquedoc, for I saw during my residence knights and squires arrive from every nation.'

Froissart passed a considerable time in this feudal paradise enjoying himself in every way to perfection, but especially in acquiring information. One of his pieces of good fortune in this respect, was the opportunity which he enjoyed of hearing the history of a certain Gascon squire called 'le bastol de Mauleon,' who may be taken as a typical example of the military adventurers of that age.

He was about fifty when Froissart knew him, and 'arrived at the Hotel of the Moon, where I lodged, in grand array, having led horses with him, like a great baron, and he and his attendants were served on plate of gold and silver.' . . . 'One night as we were sitting round the fire chatting and waiting for midnight, which was the hour the Count supped,' Mauleon's cousin asked him to tell his adventures, which he did accordingly. Mauleon first served at Poitiers under the Captal de Buch, where he made three prisoners, who paid him 4000 francs. He then went to Prussia under the

Captal de Buch. Next he was employed in putting down the Jacquerie. Afterwards he served under the Count of Foix in Picardy, and the King of England against the French, 'and gained very large sums of money.'

After the peace between England and France he became a free companion, and at the battle of Brejnais overpowered the Constable of France, where he and his friends 'enriched themselves by good prisoners and by the towns and castles which they took in the Archbishopric of Lyons.' He then formed part of a body hired by the Pope at Avignon for 60,000 francs. Part of them went into Italy, but others, of whom Mauleon was one, stayed in France, where they had possession of many towns and castles, and ransomed the whole country, and they could 'only be freed from us by well paying.' They were nominally in the service of the King of Navarre, but in reality were carrying on war on their own account. Mauleon at this time held, with forty lances, a castle called Le Bec d'Allier, 'where I made great profit.' He was on one occasion taken prisoner by a cousin, who ransomed him on the field for 1000 francs, and gave him a passport home to the Bec d'Allier.

He went on a raid with an English knight, Sir John Aymery, but fell into an ambush and was again taken prisoner. He was set free, and went to Brittany, where 'I made such good prisoners they paid me 2000 francs.' Thence he went into Spain with Sir Hugh Calverley, then back again into Gascony, where he fought for the Black Prince. Most of his companions were killed in the course of time, but 'I have guarded the frontiers and supported the King of England, for my estate is in the Bordelois; and I have been at times so miserably poor that I had not a horse to mount; at other times rich enough, just as good fortune befell me.' He held various castles, one in particular, 'which has been worth to me, as well by compositions as by good luck, 100,000 francs.' This valuable castle he took by disguising himself and some of his companions as women who had gone out to draw water. As there was no guard at the gate but a cobbler mending shoes, they easily took possession. At the time of telling his story he was, he said, doubtful how to act. 'I am in treaty with the Count d'Armagnac and the Dauphin d'Auvergne, who have been expressly commissioned by the King of France to buy all towns and castles from the captains of the free companies. Several have sold their forts and gone away. I am doubtful whether I shall sell mine' (ii. 101-107).

There is not a word in Froissart's account of Mauleon's adventures which indicates that he thought them in the least degree disreputable or worthy of blame. On the contrary, he displays throughout the most lively satisfaction in his society, and appears to have regarded with respect, not to say admiration, a man who, according to our modern standard, was simply a robber on a large scale.

The following soliloquy, which he puts into the

mouth of one Aymerigon Marcel, is a good description of the pleasures of such a life. 'There is no pleasure nor glory in this world like what men-at-arms such as ourselves enjoyed. How happy were we when riding out in search of adventures, we met a rich abbot, a merchant, or a string of mules well laden with draperies, furs, or spices from Montpellier, Beciers, or other places; all was our own, or at least ransomed according to our will. Every day we gained money. The peasants of Auvergne and Limousin loved us, and provided our castle with corn, oats, hay, good wine, fat hens, sheep, and all sorts of poultry; we lived like kings, and when we went abroad the country trembled; everything was ours both in going and returning. How did I and the Bourg de Copaire take Carlat? and how did I and Perrot le Bearnois win Chalnet? How did we—you and I—without other assistance, scale the strong castle of Marquel that belongs to the Count Dauphin? I only kept it five days, and was paid down on a table 5000 francs for it, of which I gave back 1000 from love to the Count's children. By my troth this was a profitable and pleasant life, and I feel myself much reduced by selling Alosse, which was strong enough to resist any force that could be brought against it, and was besides, at the time of my surrendering, so plentifully stored with provisions and other necessaries that it would not have needed anything for seven years' (ii. 450).

Froissart does afterwards speak of these people as 'robbers,' but though one or two such expressions occur in his pages, and though there may perhaps be some degree of conscious irony in Marcel's soliloquy, such feelings are altogether exceptional in him. On the whole he is perfectly satisfied with the age in which he lives, the notion of reform or even of reproof hardly presents itself seriously to his mind.

He gives, for instance, without observation of any sort, as the last words of Geoffrey Teate, captain of the Castle of Ventadour[1] the following among other observations: 'I beg you' (his followers) 'will tell me if you have taken any steps, or have thought of electing any one able to govern and lead you as men-at-arms ought to be governed and led, for such has been my manner of carrying on war, and in truth I cared not against whom. I did indeed make it under shadow of the king of England's name in preference to any other, but I have always looked for gain and conquest wherever they may be had, and such should ever be the conduct of adventurous companions who are for deeds of arms and to advance themselves.'

One of the most striking illustrations of the perfect ease and satisfaction with which Froissart regarded the existing state of things is to be found in his account of the various outbreaks which took place in his time on the part of the peasantry against the nobility. He describes the *jacquerie* simply as a

---

[1] II. 387. The whole history of Ventadour, its importance, its stories, the organisation of the garrison, and the manner in which it was captured, is highly illustrative of the fourteenth century, but *est modus in rebus*, see II. 9, 314, 387, 428, and I. 568.

modern writer would describe any ordinary crime, without a word of explanation even of the causes of the revolt, or of pity for the fearful (though not undeserved) punishment which it met with. His account of Wat Tyler's insurrection goes rather more into detail, and is curious on several accounts and especially on account of its callousness, and the utter ignorance which it shows of principles which in our days are universally familiar.

After describing Ball's sermons at some length he concludes with the following observation. 'In order that gentlemen and others may take example and correct wicked rebels, I will most amply detail how this business was conducted.'[1] Farther on he tells, without the smallest mark of disapprobation, the manner in which Richard II. got out of his difficulties for the moment, by promising the insurgents general enfranchisement, and giving them letters under his seal granting it,[2] and how he afterwards got the letters back and tore them up,[3] and hanged or beheaded upwards of 1500 persons in various parts of the country for having obtained them.

Such being the general style and tone of Froissart's work, it is natural to ask what can be collected from his book as to his opinions and those of his age on

[1] I. 654, 666, 667.   [2] I. 666, 667.
[3] 667. This was one of the earliest instances of the much contested power of martial law. See charge of C.-J. Cockburn in the cases of Nelson and Brand. Several passages in Froissart illustrate this subject, but he is so loose a writer and knew so little of law, that what he says is not worth quoting.

great subjects? Froissart was a priest, and for this as for other reasons, it is natural to look first at the light which his book throws on the religious condition of the age which he described. The result is curious.

Every page of Joinville is stamped deep with the impress of religion. Comines never misses an opportunity of dwelling after his manner on the providential government of the world, but M. Michelet's strange remark that the word God is not to be found in Shakespeare would be far less unjust if applied to Froissart. It is not so much the word as the thought that is wanting, and that not only in Froissart himself, but in the persons about whom he writes and the general nature of the events which he has to relate. His book suggests that religion, and morals too, were in his time under an almost total eclipse, and that the only substitute for them, such as it was, which his writings show to have existed was polished manners, as between gentlemen. The only observation which I have noticed of what may be called a pious character in the whole book occurs in the description of the sudden attack of madness which came upon Charles VI. when in his march against Brittany. 'It was manifestly the work of God, whose punishments are severe, to make his creatures tremble.'

Here follows a reference to Nebuchadnezzar, and then Froissart observes, 'To speak truly, God the Father, the Son, and the Holy Ghost, three in name but one in substance, was, is, and ever will be of as sufficient power to declare his works as from the beginning, and one ought not therefore to be surprised at whatever wonderful things happen.'

There is a little, but not very much more, trace of ecclesiastical as distinguished from religious feeling in Froissart. He refers several times to the great schism between the Urbanists and the Clementists, which lasted through nearly the whole of the period of which he writes. His tone upon the subject is that of a sensible man of the world who hated to see his profession lowered in influence and public estimation by the disputes of its members. As to the dissensions between the clergy and the nobles, he says, 'To satisfy the people and excuse the great barons, I may say, that as there cannot be a yolk of an egg without its white, nor a white without the yolk, so neither the clergy nor the lords can exist independently of each other, for the lords, not being ruled by the clergy, would degenerate into beasts' (ii. 145).

The secret contempt of the priest for the noble, which peeps out at the end of this passage, is all the more remarkable because it is so seldom and so shortly expressed. The tacit assumption in the last sentence that the clergy could not possibly dispense with the support of the nobility and that the Church was essentially an aristocratic institution is also notable.

These observations are contained in an account of one Friar John de la Roche-Tailtade, who enforced the doctrine that it was necessary for the clergy to bear their honours meekly, by a parable showing how a certain bird, 'a prodigiously handsome bird,' was born without feathers, and was on account of his beauty supplied with feathers by others. Becoming proud, those who had lent their feathers reclaimed them, whereupon the bird begged for mercy and 'promised henceforward never to risk by pride or presumption the loss of his feathers.' His friends agreed to his conditions. 'We will gladly see thee fly among us so long as thou shalt bear thyself meekly, for so it becometh thee, but if ever thou shalt act arrogantly we will pluck thee bare and leave thee in the naked state we found thee.'

The fortunes of John de la Roche-Tailtade are worth notice. He gave the obvious interpretation of the parable, and the cardinals 'would willingly have put him to death but they could not find any just cause for it. They suffered him to live, but confined him a close prisoner, for he proposed such deep questions and examined so closely the Scriptures that he might perhaps, had he been at liberty, have led the world astray.'[1]

The view which is disclosed by this story of the relation between the Church and the nobles, and of the necessity of the feathers to the prodigiously handsome bird, is delightfully simple and natural. So, too, is the fate of poor John de la Roche-Tailtade. Elsewhere [2] Froissart describes him as a prophet who 'made many books full of much science and learning,' and foretold many events 'which he never could have foretold as a prophet but by means of the ancient Scriptures and the Holy Spirit.' Froissart

[1] II. 145, 146.   [2] I. 280.

obviously regarded him as on the whole a dangerous character.

Small as is the part allotted to religious feeling or reflections in Froissart's pages, there is a fair share of superstition and plenty of ignorance. Several instances of this occur in the account which he gives of the siege of the French and English jointly, during one of their truces, of the town of Africa, a fortress in Morocco.

The Saracens sent to ask the Christians why they attacked people who had never offended them? Hereupon 'twelve of the greatest barons in the army assembled in the Duke of Bourbon's tent, and the messenger and interpreter being called in, the last was ordered to tell him from the lords present "that in consequence of their ancestors having crucified and put to death the Son of God called Jesus Christ, a true prophet, without any cause or just reason, they were come to retaliate on them for this infamous and unjust judgment. Secondly, they were unbaptized and infidels in the faith to the holy Virgin Mother of Jesus Christ, and had no Creed of their own. For those and other causes they held the Saracens and their whole sect as enemies, and were come to revenge the injuries they had done to their God and Faith."' Upon this 'the Saracen laughed heartily and said they made assertions without proof, for it was the Jews who had crucified Jesus Christ and not they.'[1]

Various miracles occurred at the siege. The

[1] II. 471.

Genoese had a dog which belonged to no one in particular, and always barked when the Saracens came out, whence he was called the dog of our Lady.

'Through the grace of God and the Virgin Mary a remedy was found for a swarm of flies in the shape of a thunderstorm. The Virgin herself and a company of ladies dressed in white appeared to and frightened the Saracens.[1] Probably this was because the business was in the nature of a Crusade, but there are some though not many miracles reported on other occasions. The oddest story by far in the whole book relates to a rapping spirit, who appears to have behaved himself in a castle in the Pyrenees, in the fourteenth century, in the very same way in which Wesley's Ghost behaved at Epworth, in the eighteenth, and the ghosts of our own time in Europe and America. He was, however, a very superior sort of ghost, as, unlike his successors, he had something to say for himself, and anticipated the electric telegraph. The story is this :—

Raymond of Corasse, a Baron of Foix, had a suit about tithes against a priest of Catalonia, to whom he refused to do justice though the priest got judgment. The priest said he would send a champion whom the baron should fear, and took his departure. Three months after, while the baron and his wife were in bed, 'There came invisible messengers who made such a noise, knocking about everything they met with in the castle, as if they were determined to destroy all within

---

[1] II. 472, 473.

it, and they gave such loud raps at the door of the chamber of the knight that the lady was exceedingly frightened. On the following night the noises and rioting were renewed, but much louder than before, and there were such blows struck against the door and windows of the chamber of the knight that it seemed they would break them down.' The knight got up and asked who was there. The ghost (who was able, it seems, to talk) said his name was Orthon and he was sent by the priest. The knight said, 'Serving a clerk will not be of much advantage to thee, I beg thou wilt therefore leave him and serve me.' Orthon, who 'had taken a liking to the knight' said, 'Do you wish it?'—'Yes,' replied the knight, 'but no harm must be done to any one within these walls.'—'Oh no,' answered Orthon, 'I have no power to harm any one, only to awaken thee and disturb thy rest or that of other persons.' At last it was settled that Orthon was to serve the knight, and he accordingly called frequently, and told him news from all parts of the world for five years. 'Two or three times every week he visited the knight and told him all the news of the countries he had frequented, which the knight wrote immediately to the Count of Foix, who was much delighted therewith, as there is not a lord in the world more eager for news from foreign parts than he is.' Being pressed to appear to the knight, Orthon did so, first in the shape of two straws and then in the shape of a 'sharp pointed lean sow.' Unluckily the knight set his dogs at the sow and so affronted Orthon and broke off the connection. The story is introduced to explain the alleged fact that the Count of Foix knew of the battle of Algerbarola in Portugal, in which the French and Béarnese were defeated with great loss by the Portuguese and English, the day after it was fought,[1] though the news did not arrive by the ordinary route for ten days. The story was told with much mystery. 'He drew me aside to a corner of the vault of the Chapel of Athes and thus began his tale.'

One of the most interesting of the matters to be collected from Froissart is his estimate of the character of the different nations which he had occasion to describe, and his accounts of their manners and customs. His observations on national character are mere passing remarks. The notion of set dissertations on such a topic had not occurred to him. Indeed the limits of race and nation were then but ill fixed. Froissart constantly speaks of people becoming Englishmen and Frenchmen; in the sense of taking the side of the French or the English. He constantly speaks of Gascons as Englishmen, and on the other hand remarks that in England he thought a Hainaulter was called a Frenchman 'for all who speak the *langue d'oil* are by English considered as Frenchmen, whatever country they come from.'[2] He makes hardly any general observations on the French character, but a good many on that of the English. It is pleasant even at this distance of time to read his

[1] August 1385.   [2] II. 5, 69.

laudatory observations on the warlike qualities of our ancestors (who however continually met their match). For instance, in speaking of the battle of Otterbourne, he says,[1] 'Of all the battles that have been described in this history great and small, this was the best fought and the most severe; for there was not a man, knight, or squire who did not acquit himself gallantly hand to hand with his enemy. It resembled somewhat that of Cockerel[2] which was as long and hardily disputed.' 'The English and Scotch are excellent men-at-arms, and whenever they meet in battle they do not spare each other; nor is there any check to their courage as long as their weapons endure.'

So in speaking of the army which the Black Prince took into Spain, he says, 'The prince had with him the flower of chivalry, and there were under him the most renowned combatants in the whole world.' Otherwise, however, he had not a very good opinion of the English. He says, 'Consider how serious a thing it is when the people rise up in arms against their sovereign, more especially such a people as the English. In such a case there is no remedy, for they are the worst people in the world, the most obstinate and presumptuous, and of all England the Londoners are the leaders, for to say the truth they are very powerful in men and in wealth.

---

[1] II. 368.
[2] I. 319, 22, fought on the 24th May 1364. The French under Du Guesclin defeated the English and Navarrese under the Captal de Buch.

In the city and neighbourhood there are 24,000 men completely armed from head to foot and full 30,000 archers. This is a great force, and they are bold and courageous, and the more blood is spilt the greater is their courage.'[1]

He speaks too of their 'hot and impatient temper,'[2] and describes their behaviour to the Gascons very unfavourably. 'I was at Bordeaux when the Prince of Wales marched to Spain, and witnessed the great haughtiness of the English, who are affable to no other nation than their own; nor could any of the gentlemen of Gascony or Aquitaine, though they had ruined themselves by their wars, obtain office or employment in their own country, for the English said they were neither on a level with them nor worthy of their society, which made the Gascons very indignant.' He says, indeed, in describing his visit to England, 'that the English are courteous to strangers;' but it is easy to recognise in these remarks the stubborn courage and intense self-reliance, of which we are accustomed to boast, in connection with that unsympathetic harshness of character, which we have had such bitter cause to regret. A characteristic little touch is introduced in[3] the description of the feelings with which the English received the news of the French victory over the Flemings at Roserque. We can, as it were, hear the voice of John Bull growling to us his descendants over an interval of five hundred years. When the English knights conversed together

[1] II. 694.   [2] I. 548.   [3] I. p. 756.

on the subject they said, 'Ha, by Holy Mary, how proud will the French be now for the heap of peasants they have slain! I wish to God Philip van Artevelde had had 2000 of our lances and 6000 archers, not one Frenchman would have escaped death or imprisonment; by God they shall not long keep this honour,' etc. etc. Might not this have been said in any club in London *apropos* of the news of Magenta or Solferino?

The Scotch came off even worse than the English at Froissart's hands. 'The Scots,' he says, 'are a wicked race, and pay not any regard to times or respites but as it suits their own convenience.'[1] Elsewhere he observes that a horse was missed, 'for a Scotsman (they are all thieves) had stolen him.'[2] There are two passages which give a very clear notion of the state of Scotland, but they are too long to quote. One is an elaborate account[3] of the Scotch manner of making war, the other an account[4] of the quarrels between the Scotch, and the French who came to help them against the English, and were all but starved to death by their allies.

Froissart was never himself in Ireland, but one of the best passages[5] in the book is the account which he gives, on the relation of a squire called Henry Castide, of their manners. Castide had been taken prisoner by an Irish chief and lived with him seven years, during which time he married his daughter.

[1] II. 567.   [2] II. 363.
[3] I. 18, 20, 23, 24.   [4] II. 55.   [5] II. 575-578.

From his connection with Ireland he was appointed to take charge of four petty kings, who had sworn obedience to the English government, and to give them an English education. He describes their savage habits (*e.g.* 'They had another custom I knew to be common in the country which was the not wearing breeches'), and how he gradually accustomed them to civilisation, as then understood. Nothing can be more thoroughly kind, judicious, and gentleman-like than his whole account of his treatment, or than the treatment itself. He describes the Irish as mere savages: 'The inland natives are unacquainted with commerce, nor do not wish to know anything of it, but simply to live like wild beasts.'[1]

I may say in conclusion a word or two as to the literary merits of Froissart. His power of narrative has never probably been exceeded, and the force and beauty of particular passages of his book are too well known to require illustration. The only misfortune is that they are imbedded in such a mass of matter which has lost whatever interest it once possessed. As instances I may refer to the exquisite story of Edward III. and the Countess of Salisbury, the account of the battle of Otterbourne, the account of the death of Queen Philippa. It may perhaps interest some readers, who may not have read it, to see the story told in the words of Lord Berners—the spelling only being altered.

'There fell in England a heavy case and a common,

[1] I. 427.

howbeit it was right piteous for the king, his children, and all his realm, for the good Queen of England that so many good deeds had done in her time, and so many knights succoured, and ladies and damsels comforted, and had so largely departed of her goods to her people, and naturally loved always the nation of Hainault, the country where she was born. She fell sick in the castle of Windsor, the which sickness continued on her so long that there was no remedy but death; and the good lady whenever she knew and perceived that there was no remedy but death, she put out of her bed her right hand, and took the king by his right hand, who was right sorrowful at his heart. Then she said: "Sir, we have lived in peace, love, and great prosperity, and all our time together. Sir, now I pray you at our departing that you will grant me three desires." The king right sorrowfully weeping, said: "Madam, desire what you will, I grant it."—"Sir," said she, "I require you first of all to all manner of people such as I have dealt with in their merchandise on this side the sea and beyond, that it may please you to pay everything that I owe to them or to any other; and, secondly, Sir, all such ordinances and promises as I have made to the churches, as well of this country as beyond the seas, where I have had my devotions that it may please you to accomplish and fulfil the same. Thirdly, Sir, I require you, that it may please you to take none other sepulture whensoever it shall please God to call you out of this transitory life, but beside me in West-

minster." **The King** all weeping said: "Madam, I **grant all** your desire." Then the good lady and queen made her the sign of the cross, and commended her husband to God, and her youngest born prince who was then beside her.'

III

PHILIPPE DE COMINES[1]

THE memoirs of Comines probably contain a larger amount of matter of general and permanent interest than any other book of the fifteenth century. In general vigour of mind, in shrewdness of observation, in all that we mean by mother-wit, their author was a man of the very highest class. He had, moreover, a turn for generalising and moralising upon the events which came under his notice, which gives his memoirs a kind and degree of interest quite peculiar to themselves. His reflections show us, with the utmost possible distinctness, what was the tone of thought current in his day amongst the most vigorous men of the age,—men who took their views from the facts which they saw around them, and who had not been affected in any appreciable degree by the revival of learning, which was then in its infancy.

Comines was just twenty years older than Erasmus

[1] *Mémoires de Philippe de Comines*, par Mlle. Dupont, 1840.

(born 1466), and he died thirty years before Luther (1546). The whole furniture of his mind, all his principles of thought and action, were derived from intimate intercourse with the men of action of his day —Louis XI., Charles the Bold, and their various generals and ministers, the last kings and nobles of the Middle Ages. No writer, accordingly, sets in so strong and definite a light, or illustrates in such a variety of ways, the spirit by which that age was informed or the general principles which its leading men believed and acted upon. As, however, his reflections are inextricably mixed up with the facts to which they refer, and as the outline of these facts is less familiar to ordinary readers than their general purport and bearing, it is necessary to give some short account of the connection and sequence of the events in order to make the observations themselves intelligible.

Louis XI. succeeded to the crown on the death of his father Charles VII., which took place on the 22d July 1461. Politically, his position was most unfavourable and precarious. In fact he was rather the head of a confederacy than an actual sovereign.

The Dukes of Burgundy ruled almost as independent princes over a heterogenous mass of provinces which included Belgium, Picardy and the north-eastern side of France, as far south almost as the borders of Switzerland. Brittany was independent, or nearly so, under its dukes. Navarre and Foix were independent in the south. The Count of St. Pol held an important district between the territories of the King of France and the Duke of Burgundy, including the frontier towns on the Somme—Amiens, Abbeville, and St. Quentin, which stood pledged to the Duke of Burgundy for 400,000 crowns, and opened to him, and therefore to his English allies, a road by which invaders could advance straight upon Paris at their pleasure.

Besides these real feudatories, who were more or less in the position of independent sovereigns, there were a host of nobles who aspired with hopes of success to gaining for themselves a similar position. Within less than four years after Louis's accession (December 1464) they formed for this purpose the association called the Ligue du Bien Publique, the principal members of which were the Duke of Berry, the King's younger brother, the titular King of Sicily, and his son the Duke of Calabria, the Count of Armagnac, the Duke of Orleans, and his brother the Duke of Angoulême, the Duke of Bourbon, and the Counts of Nevers, St. Pol, Tancarville, and Penthievre.[1] The head of the conspiracy was Charles the Bold, then Count of Charolais. Their object in general terms was to compel Louis to parcel out France into appanages, over which they were to have rule.

With this view their armies, headed respectively by Charles the Bold, the Duke of Brittany, and the Duke of Bourbon, took the field against Louis in the spring of 1465. Louis marched against the latter and speedily compelled him to sign an armistice.

[1] Réne, the King of Sicily, ruled in Provence.

He then returned towards Paris, and at Mont-l'Héry encountered the army of Charles the Bold advancing from the north. An indecisive action between them took place on the 16th July 1465, in which one wing of each army defeated the wing of the enemy's army which was opposed to it. After the battle Louis continued his march to Paris, whither, after some delay, he was followed by Charles the Bold. After some indecisive attempts at a siege the war was ended by the treaty of Conflans (29th October 1465), by which Louis made enormous concessions to the different princes, giving in particular the Duchy of Normandy to his brother the Duke of Berry, and returning to Charles the Bold the towns on the Somme which about two years before (September 1463) he had redeemed from Duke Philip.

So far the princes had triumphed. The rest of the reign of Louis was occupied principally by the successful efforts which he made to reduce them to the position of subjects. The principal thing which enabled him to do so was the excessive rashness and presumption of his rival Charles the Bold, of which, however, Louis took advantage in most cases with consummate skill, though at least on one memorable occasion his over-cunning nearly ruined him.

Liège, and the towns on the Meuse, especially Dinant, had always been favourable to France and ill-affected to the Dukes of Burgundy. Charles the Bold marched against them in November 1465 as soon as the treaty of Conflans was concluded. By

January 1466 he had extorted great concessions from Liège, and in the following August he utterly destroyed Dinant and inflicted further humiliations on Liège, which tried to help it. Louis took the opportunity of stirring up a quarrel between his brother and the Duke of Brittany, under the cover of which he dispossessed his brother of Normandy with very little resistance (January 1466). On the 15th June 1467 Duke Philip of Burgundy died, and was succeeded by his son, who soon after his succession fell into new and still more serious quarrels than before with Liège, which was again encouraged to revolt by the agents of Louis. On the 12th November Charles entered the town by a breach in the wall, executed many of the citizens, and suppressed the franchises of the town. Louis took the opportunity of attacking the Duke of Alençon and deposing him from his duchy. He further fortified his position by domestic measures. He put into the hands of Tristan l'Hermite, the provost-marshal, a summary power of jurisdiction exactly corresponding to what has been so much discussed in our own times under the name of martial law. He assembled the states-general at Tours, which sat only for eight days, but made unbounded professions of obedience, and he encouraged up to a certain point the formation of militia amongst the great towns, and in particular at Paris. These measures at once proved and extended his popularity with the mass of the population who, on the whole, rather admired the 'bonne et roide justice' of Tristan, and were willing to support Louis to any extent against the princes. He accordingly assumed the offensive, and marched forces into Brittany, which compelled the Duke of Brittany and the Duke of Berry to sign a treaty at Ancenis (10th September 1468), by which they gave up their alliance with the Duke of Burgundy, the Duke of Berry renouncing his pretensions to Normandy, and contenting himself with a pension instead of an appanage.

Louis was now in a position to attack the Duke of Burgundy openly, but he was too jealous of his generals to give any one of them so important a task. He preferred to try the effect of a personal interview with the Duke, and went for that purpose to Peronne on the 9th October 1468. Whilst he was there in the power of his rival the news arrived of a fresh outbreak at Liège, which had been excited by Louis's manœuvres. In order to save his life Louis was compelled to join Charles in an attack upon Liège, and to give a new appanage to his brother the Duke of Berry. He accordingly assisted in the storm of Liège (31st October), at which the town was burnt and the people massacred, and gave his brother the Duchy of Guienne instead of Champagne and Brie, which he had promised to give him. The object of giving the larger and more important province was to separate him as far as possible from the Duke of Burgundy.

About this time Louis began to try to injure Charles by intrigues with England. About eighteen years had passed since the final expulsion of the

English from France (1450), but Charles the Bold had preserved and extended his father's relations with the English. He had married Margaret the sister of Edward IV., and there was much commercial intercourse between England and the Low Countries. Louis XI. accordingly favoured the Lancastrians, and having entered into relations with Warwick, then in disgrace in his government of Calais, did all in his power to favour his descent into England (September 1470), which led to the expulsion of Edward IV. Edward, however, returned in the following spring, and re-established himself by the victories of Barnet and Tewksbury (14th April, 4th May, 1471). This policy naturally irritated Edward on the one hand and Charles on the other, but its failure was almost recompensed by the birth of a Dauphin, afterwards Charles VIII., on the 30th June 1470, and the death of the Duke of Guienne, the king's brother, on the 24th May 1472. Charles accused Louis of having poisoned his brother, and marched an army into France, which failed before Beauvais. On this occasion St. Pol, in his capacity of Constable, acted the part of a double traitor, doing his best to betray Beauvais to Charles; but failing to join him openly or effectually, Charles retired from France, and proceeded to negotiate with the Emperor of Germany, Frederic III., the erection of his states into a kingdom (September 1473). Louis upon this made a more serious attack than before on the remaining princes of the Ligue du Bien Publique.

The Count of Armagnac's capital, Lectoure, was taken, he was killed, his wife poisoned, and the town destroyed. The Duke of Alençon was taken prisoner, was condemned to death, but kept in prison. The Duke of Lorraine died (August 1473), it was said, of poison. The Count of Maine died April 1473. The house of Bourbon was represented by daughters, and, in a word, the coalition of the princes of the blood was at an end. In eight years from the battle of Mont-l'Héry the only enemies whom Louis had left were the Duke of Burgundy, the Duke of Brittany, and the Count of St. Pol. Death and his own use of his opportunities had freed him of the rest. His enemies, however, were as bitter as ever. The Duke of Burgundy concluded a treaty with Edward IV. in July 1474, which led to an invasion from Calais in May 1475. The consequences of this might have been almost fatal to Louis if the Duke of Burgundy had not chosen to spend the winter of 1474-75 in besieging Neuss in the Bishopric of Cologne, by way of carrying out designs into which he had entered, of extending and consolidating the scattered parts of his dominions and revenging himself on the Emperor for refusing to make him a king. The siege of Neuss did not succeed, and prevented Charles from assisting Edward, who was induced by all sorts of wily flatteries on the part of Louis to sign with him the treaty of Pequigny (29th August 1475), which provided for seven years' truce between England and France, and ridded France for the time of the presence of the invaders. The Duke of Burgundy, not discouraged by his check before Neuss, formed a scheme for the conquest of Lorraine and Alsace, and set out to besiege Nancy. Before he did so he made a separate truce with Louis, one article of which bound him to give up St. Pol, who, having been driven by the king from St. Quentin, had taken refuge at Mons in the Duke's dominions (26th August). St. Pol was accordingly given up on the 24th November, and was tried, condemned, and (19th December 1475) executed as a traitor at Paris.

Louis and Charles were now left face to face, but the rashness of the latter soon delivered his rival from all danger. Charles employed the period of peace on which he had entered in invading Switzerland. The Swiss called upon Louis for help, according to former promises, but he left them to themselves. They soon showed that they wanted no help. Charles's army was routed at Granson, 3d March 1476.

He underwent a murderous defeat at Morat on the 22d June. These reverses encouraged René, the son of the titular King of Sicily, to make an attack upon Lorraine, which Charles had conquered, and he accordingly possessed himself of the Duchy and of its capital Nancy, which was besieged by Charles in the latter part of October. René with 8000 Swiss marched to raise the siege, and Charles was defeated and killed in the neighbourhood of the town on the 5th January 1477.

Without the loss of a moment Louis proceeded to

take possession of the greater part of the states of Mary of Burgundy, the heir and daughter of Charles, on the ground that she was his ward in chivalry, and not contenting himself with this he raised an insurrection against her and her principal counsellors in the Flemish towns. She sent an embassy to him from the states of Ghent to treat of peace, instructed amongst other things to say that she would be guided in all respects by the advice of the states. He gave the ambassadors a letter written in part in her own hand, in which she said she would be guided by three of her father's ministers, of whom the Chancellor Hugonet and Humbercourt were two. This so enraged the people of Ghent that Hugonet and Humbercourt were put to death. Louis, however, did not succeed altogether in detaching the Flemings from the Duchess. Indeed, in betraying her confidence he overreached himself, for he prevented her from marrying the Dauphin, which, notwithstanding their difference of age (she was twenty and he eight), she was not indisposed to do. To secure herself a protector she married Maximilian of Austria (19th April 1477), through whom began the long connection of the Low Countries with the Empire. He was at first vigorously supported by the Flemings, but was obliged to give up the Duchy of Burgundy to Louis (August 1480).

In the spring of 1480 the King's health began to fail. He had an illness from which he never fully recovered. His fortunes, however, culminated in the most extraordinary manner. René, the titular King of Sicily, died 10th July 1480, and Louis united Provence to France; Mary of Burgundy died 27th March 1482, and the states of Burgundy, who were disgusted with Maximilian, made a treaty with Louis at Arras (23d December 1482) by which they agreed that her daughter Margaret of Austria, a child of two years of age, should be delivered over to Louis to be educated by him till she was old enough to be married to the Dauphin; and in the meantime he received possession of the county of Burgundy, Charolais, and Artois as her dowry. Finally, Edward IV. died 9th April 1483, leaving England under the government of his unfortunate infant son, and in a condition in which Louis had nothing to fear from it. Louis was thus triumphant at home and abroad. The Duke of Brittany was the only one of his vassals who still retained any independence. He was the unquestioned and substantial ruler of the rest of France, interpreting that word in a wider sense than had ever belonged to it before. He did not live, however, to enjoy his triumph. He died on the 30th August 1483.

Such is a very short outline of the principal events which Comines witnessed, and in one of which he played a part by no means unimportant. Let us now turn to his own observations upon them. The principal dates in his own career are as follows:—

.. He was born at Commynes on the Lys in 1447. He entered the service of Charles the Bold (then Comte de Charolais) in 1464. He passed to the service of Louis XI. (8th August 1472), receiving from him grants, and especially a grant of the principality of Talmont, which were afterwards the cause of litigations which embittered his later life. He served Louis XI. till his death in August 1483. He passed several years in litigation with the La Tremoille family, who contested the grant of Talmont, and was finally imprisoned in 1487 for two years and banished from court till 1492. He was again taken into favour by Charles VIII., accompanied him in his Italian expedition in 1493-95, remained with him till his death in April 1498, and then retired into private life till his own death on the 18th October 1511 at the age of sixty-four.

He begins his work with a prologue[1] addressed to the Archbishop of Vienne, a statesman, a scholar, a physician, and more or less an astrologer, for it is said that he predicted to Charles the Bold some of the principal events of his life. His object, says Comines, is principally to commemorate Louis XI.

The King was not perfect certainly—'Perfection belongs to God alone; but when in a prince virtue and good qualities are more prominent than vice, he is worthy of great honour and praise,' inasmuch as princes have greater temptations than other men. Upon the whole Comines 'never knew a prince who had fewer vices than Louis,' though he had known many. The book, he adds, is written at the archbishop's request, —'a gentleman of excellent conditions'—and he, the author, hopes that the archbishop means to use it as materials for a book upon the subject to be written

[1] I. 1-4.

in Latin. It is obvious that Comines himself knew no Latin, and did not think much of French.

The first book of the memoirs[1] contains an account of the war of the public good, and in particular of the battle of Mont-l'Héry (27th July 1465), a clumsy, indecisive scuffle,. not quite unlike the battle of Sheriffmuir, in which each army beat half the other. Comines's description of it is full of curious reflections, the effect of which is heightened by the way in which he passes from shrewd practical[2] observations to the most refined speculation. Many of the Burgundian nobility, he says, fought on foot, 'for amongst the Burgundians at that time those who dismounted with the archers were held in most honour, and a great number of the gentry always did so, that the common people might be more encouraged and might fight better; this they learned of the English whom Duke Philip had served in France in his youth.' The English were good soldiers, and 'tres grans cappitaines.' However, 'when God was tired of doing them good, they fell into trouble, and the House of York usurped the realm, or had it by a good title, I can't say which, for of such things heaven disposes.'

Comines adds farther on, 'Archers are the best of troops, but they ought to be in thousands, and ill mounted so that they may not be afraid of losing their horses,—indeed they need not have any. Moreover, those who have never seen anything are better

[1] I. 5, 113.   [2] 3, 33.

in this business for a single day than those who have much experience. This is also the opinion of the English who are the flower of the archers of the world.' The superiority of soldiers who do not know their danger to those who do is not a very uncommon remark in our own days, but the observant and rather cynical vein which tends to it is relieved in the case of Comines by one of quite a different order. The horse, he says, did not wait for the foot at Mont-l'Héry according to the orders given. 'And in this God showed that battles are in his hand, and that he disposes of victory at his pleasure. And I do not believe that the human mind can sustain and set in order so great a number of people, nor that matters pass in the field as they are planned in the chamber; and any one who believed in himself to the point of thinking so would be mistaken towards God if he had natural reason.'

I suppose Comines means that men ought to act for the best, and recollect that God overrules their conduct, and that this is one of the ways in which the works which he has commenced are accomplished. 'However, every man ought to do what he can and what he ought, and to admit that it is one of the ways of accomplishing the works which God has sometimes commenced by small movements and occasions, and by giving the victory sometimes to one sometimes to another, and this is so great a mystery that kingdoms and great lordships sometimes are desolated by it, and others increase and begin to reign.'

He goes on to describe the extreme confusion of the battle. The Burgundian men-at-arms charged their own archers and rode over them. On account of the long peace hardly 50 out of 1200 'knew how to put a lance in rest,' none of the servants were armed and there were no regular troops. They thus broke themselves. However, 'God who orders such mysteries' determined that the right wing of the Count of Charolais should win, which it accordingly did. 'I was with him that day and was less frightened than I ever was afterwards, because I was young (he was eighteen) and knew nothing of danger; but I was surprised that any one should dare to defend himself against such a prince as my master, for I thought he was the greatest of all.'[1] What with the dust, the high corn, the inexperience and absolute want of discipline of the troops, everything fell into the wildest confusion, and Comines had occasion to make many shrewd observations. Louis and Charles, he said, ought to have thought highly of those who stood by them so well on this occasion, 'but they behaved like men not like angels. Men lost their estates and offices for having run away, and they were given to others who had run ten leagues farther. One man on our side lost credit and was banished from his master's presence, and a month afterwards he had more credit than before.'[2] Charles stayed on the field, considering that he had won the day, and certainly he was a remarkable man. 'Great princes ought

[1] 39.   [2] 47.

to know that favour and good fortune comes from God. I will say two things of him, one is, I think no man ever worked harder in all opportunities for bodily labour. The other is, I never knew a hardier man. I never heard him say he was tired or saw him appear to be frightened, and I was seven years in the wars with him, always in the summer, and sometimes winter and summer too.'

The interval between the battle and the treaty of Conflans is made by Comines the occasion of several curious observations and reflections. Whilst the Burgundian army was lying at Estampes before it marched to Paris, the Duke of Berry, Louis XI.'s brother, who, by the final treaty became Duke of Normandy, was talking about the battle. 'He was very young and had never seen such actions, and it seemed by his words that he was pained by them, for he spoke of the great number wounded whom he had seen on the side of the Count of Charolais, and showed by his words that he should have wished that this enterprise had never been undertaken than to see so many evils happen by him and in his cause.' Charles the Bold was disgusted at this weakness and observed, 'Did you hear what that man said? He is overcome by seeing 700 or 800 wounded men going about the town who are nothing to him, and whom he does not know. He would soon be overcome if the matter in any way affected him himself, and would be just the man to make terms readily and leave us in the mud; and on account of the old wars which have formerly happened between his father and mine, both parties' (*i.e.* Louis XI. and the French princes) 'would readily join to turn upon us, so it is necessary to look out for friends.' This 'imagination,' and nothing else, says Comines, caused Charles the Bold to send an embassy to England to make an alliance with Edward IV., 'and many such works are done in this world by imagination, especially amongst great princes, who are much more suspicious than other people by reason of the doubts and warnings suggested to them very often on account of flattery and without any need.'[1]

In speaking of the Burgundian party in Paris, Comines says that they hoped to get offices or places 'which are more desired in this city than in any other in the world, for those who have them get out of them what they can and not what they ought; and there are unpaid offices which are sold for more than fifteen years' purchase of their fees.' This introduces a chapter[2] headed 'Digressions on state offices and ambition from the example of the English.' The Duke of Bedford, when Regent of France and living at Paris, had never less than 20,000 crowns a month;[3] and when he and others returned to England they did not choose to diminish their state, whence arose civil war which led ultimately to the establishment on the throne of Henry VII. 'Thus it is not at Paris or in France only that people fight for the worldly goods and honours, and princes and great

---

[1] I. 56-58.   [2] Bk. I. ch. vii. 1-66.   [3] I. 67.

lords ought to fear greatly to allow parties to arise in their households, for from thence the fire runs over the provinces, but I think this happens only by divine disposition; for when princes and realms have been very prosperous and rich and do not acknowledge the source whence such graces proceed, God raises up enemies male or female against them, whom no one could expect, as you may see by the kings mentioned in the Bible.'[1]

Paris, however, suggests more practical observations to Comines. The following little bit of description is very picturesque. 'I must say that this town of Paris is well situated in the Isle of France, to be able to supply two such strong armies, for we were never in want of provisions, and inside Paris they hardly perceived our being there. Nothing rose in price except bread, and that rose one denier only; for we did not hold the upper rivers which are three, namely, Marne, Youne, and Seine, and other small ones which fall into them. Taken altogether I never saw a city surrounded by better or more fruitful country, and the quantity of goods arriving there is almost incredible. Since that time I have been at Paris with King Louis half a year without stirring, lodged at the Tourelles and eating and sleeping with him as a rule, and since his death for twenty months against my will, kept a prisoner in his palace, where I saw from my windows whatever came up the Seine from Normandy. Incomparably more

[1] I. 70.

came than I should ever have believed had I not seen it.'

The description of Paris introduces a further digression on some vices and virtues of Louis XI. It is introduced by a remark on the necessity of keeping your party out of the way of people who can seduce them, especially of a 'prince who wishes to gain people, which is a great grace which God gives to princes who know how to do it, and is a sign that he is not stained by that foolish vice and sin of pride which procures hatred towards all persons' (who are proud). 'For which reason when people come to such negotiations as treaties of peace, they should be made by the most trustworthy servants whom princes have and men of middle ages so that their weakness may not lead them to make a dishonourable bargain, or to frighten their master on their return more than necessary.' It is in illustration of this that Comines describes Louis XI. 'I have entered on this matter because I have seen much cheating in this world, and in that on the part of many servants towards their masters, and they cheat princes and lords who are proud and will not hear people speak more often than the humble who listen to them willingly. Of all that ever I knew the wisest in getting out of scrapes in time of adversity was King Louis XI. our master; and the most humble in words and in dress, and the one who worked hardest to gain a man who could serve him or hurt him, and he did not give up on being once refused by a man whom he was trying to gain, but continued making large promises and actually giving money and estate to one whom he knew to please him. And those whom he had turned out of their places in time of peace and prosperity he bought back very dear when he needed them, and used them and bore no grudge against them for the past. He was naturally a friend to people of middling condition, and the enemy of the great, who could do without him. No man ever listened so much to people or inquired into so many things as he did or wished to know so many people; for to say the truth he knew all people of authority and worth who were in England, Spain, Portugal, the Lordships of the Dukes of Burgundy, and in Brittany, as well as his own subjects, and these habits and manners of his saved his crown, if we consider the enemies whom he had made on his accession to the realm. But, above all, his great liberality served him, for as he was wise in adversity; so on the contrary, as soon as he thought he was in security or even in a truce, he set himself to discontent people by small means which were of little use to him, and he could hardly bear to be at peace. He spoke of people highly, and as readily in their presence as in their absence, except those whom he feared, who were many, for he was a sufficiently timid character. When his talk had done him some harm, or when he suspected that it had, and wished to set it to rights, he spoke thus to the person in question. I know my tongue has done me much harm; also at times it has given me great pleasure.

It is at all events right that I should make amends. He never used these private speeches without doing some benefit to the person to whom he spoke, and he never did small ones.'[1]

Comines concludes this character of his hero by dwelling on the advantage of his early adversities and contrasting him with the common run of the French nobility. 'Their education has no other end but to make them fools as to dress and as to words. They know nothing of literature. Not a single man of sense is put about them. They have governors to whom people speak of their affairs, but to themselves nothing; the governors do their business, and I know lords who have not thirteen livres' rent in money who are proud of saying "Speak to my people," thinking by such expressions to imitate the very great. So I have often seen their servants make a profit of them, making them well understand that they were fools.'

Besides the interest which attaches to the description of Louis XI. contained in this passage, it deserves notice as being one of many illustrations afforded by Comines's memoirs of the contempt which he felt for the average princes of his day, and of the degree in which his admiration of Louis XI. was due to the fact that he considered him superior to the natural weaknesses of his class. Comines hated and despised crowned heads as a rule, and his book is full of cynical maxims and reflections about them. Upon the treaty of Conflans he observes, 'Thus you may

[1] I. 84, 85.

see that it is almost impossible that two great Courts should agree on account of the reports and suspicion which they continually feel. Two great princes who wished to love each other well ought never to see each other, but to send good and sensible men to each other who might discourse with them and make up quarrels.'

This amiable sentiment is by way of commentary on the affair of Peronne, repeated more fully in another part of the book. If two princes meet it is probable that they will hate each other. 'It is great folly for two great princes, who are, as it were, equal in power, to see each other unless they are very young, which is the time when they think of nothing but their pleasures; but as soon as they have been seized with the desire of increasing at each other's expense, even if there were no danger to their person (which is almost impossible), still their ill-will and envy increase.'[1]

At all events, their servants are sure to quarrel; 'the servants cannot but talk of past times, and one side or the other will take offence. The team of one must be better equipped than that of the other, whence mockeries, which marvellously displease those who are mocked; and when they are of different nations their language and dress are different, and what pleases the one displeases the other. Of the two princes, it generally happens that one is handsomer and more agreeable than the other, of which he is vain and for which he likes to be praised, and this cannot be done

[1] I. 163.

without blaming the other. The first days after they have gone good stories are put about, and afterwards by habit, by carelessness, by way of continuation they are told at dinner or supper, and then on each side they are reported.'[1]

Nothing can exceed Comines's hatred for princes. He gravely compares the relative demerits of the fools and the rogues, under which heads most of his many royal acquaintances appear to have come. Farther on[2] he says, 'I have known two kinds of princes, some so subtle and suspicious that one could not know how to live with them, and they always thought that they were being deceived. The others trusted their servants sufficiently, but they were so heavy and understood their business so ill that they could not know whether they were treated well or ill. The latter are easily turned from hatred to love and love to hatred, and though there are very few good ones of either sort, either of those with whom there is no great business, or of those with whom there is no security, still I should prefer to live under the wise rather than the foolish, for there are more ways of escaping from them and propitiating their favour; for with the ignorant it is impossible to find any expedient, for business must be done, not with them, but with their servants, of whom many often deceive them. However, every one must serve and obey them in their own territories as a matter both of duty and force. All well considered, our only hope must be in God;

[1] I. 170.   [2] I. 112.

for in him lies all our strength and all our goodness which can be found in nothing in this world; but this we all find out late and after we have had need of it. However, better late than never.'[1] There is a sort of cumbrous resignation in the very run of these sentences, which shows how completely Comines had brought himself to regard princes as inevitable evils, against which there was no refuge except in God.

Various other passages are scattered through the book which show his opinion of princes very plainly. I will refer to a few of them. 'It is a great advantage to princes,' he observes, 'to have read histories in their youth, in which may be seen in plenty the meetings, the great frauds, cheats, and perjuries, which some of the ancients committed towards each other, taking and killing those who had put trust in their assurances. I do not say that all did so, but the example of one is enough to make many others wise and put them on their guard.' 'I cannot help blaming ignorant princes. Almost all lords are surrounded by clerks and men of the long robe (as is natural), and they are useful if they are good and very dangerous if they are bad. They always have in their mouths some law or history, and the best which can be found may easily be ill applied, but wise men who had read would not be abused, nor would their people be so bold as to tell them lies. Do not think that God has established the office of king or

[1] 163, 192, 156.

prince to be exercised by fools or by those who, from vainglory, say "I am no clerk, I leave matters to my council. I trust to them." And then without giving any other reason, go and amuse themselves.'[1] This is followed by a curious practical application from the case of Louis XI., which shows amongst other things that Comines recognised the distinction between reading and mother-wit. He (Louis) was well read enough.

'He liked to ask and hear about all sorts of things. His natural sense was fearfully good, which takes precedence of all the other sciences which can be learnt in this world, and all the books which are written would be useless if they did not bring to memory past events, and if it were not that you see more in one book in three months than twenty men in a row, living one after the other, could with their eyes see and learn by experience.'

The conception of history, as a vast Newgate calendar, which is shown by the first part of this passage, and the glimpse which the end of it gives of the nature of purely personal governments administered by ignorant and idle boys, are both characteristic. Boys or men, however, it is all the same. The only effect of maturity is a development of the power of lying. 'Here you may see,' says Comines, after describing some of the intrigues between Louis and Charles, 'the miserable condition of princes who cannot by any means take security against each other. These two had made a final peace not fifteen days

[1] I. 157.

before, and solemnly sworn to keep it honourably; still confidence could not be found by any means whatever.'

After describing the transactions which ended in the treaty of Conflans, Comines proceeds to relate his experiences of the wars between Charles the Bold and Liège and the destruction of, Dinant. Dinant, he observes, had been separated from Liège. 'It is the true sign of the destruction of a country when those who ought to hold together separate and abandon each other. This I say as well of princes and lords in alliance as of towns and communities; but as every one, I suppose, has heard and read examples of this I say only that King Louis, our master, better understood this art of separating people than any other prince I have ever seen or ever known.' He goes on to describe how Dinant was taken and the prisoners drowned before Bouvines. ('I do not know whether God allows it on account of their great wickedness, but the vengeance was cruel for them.')[1] And he proceeds to describe the peace made between the Duke and Liège, and the manner in which the people of Liège broke the treaty and were attacked a second time by the Duke for not fulfilling it. Before making the attack a consultation was held as to what was to be done with the hostages given by the town for the fulfilment of the original treaty. Comines's account of it is very curious. 'A little before he set out he had had the question debated

[1] I. 115-117.

whether he should put his hostages to death, or what he should do with them. Some thought he ought to put them all to death, and amongst others the Lord de Contay (of whom I have often spoken) was of this opinion; and I never heard him speak so ill or so cruelly as this time. The wisest are sometimes mistaken, very often either from being passionate about the matter of discussion, or from love, or from hatred, or from wishing to contradict each other, and sometimes on account of the state of their persons, for what is done after dinner ought not to be regarded as a council. Some may say that people who commit any of these faults ought not to be a prince's council. To which I answer that we are all men, and if you want people who never talk foolishly, and are never more moved at one time than at another, you must look for them in heaven, for you cannot find them amongst men. On the other hand, you will always find at council people who will speak very well and wisely, though they are not generally in the habit of doing so, and thus one corrects another.'[1]

Returning to the particular council, Comines goes on to state the opinion of Humbercourt (afterwards executed by the people of Ghent), 'one of the wisest and best-instructed knights I ever knew, which was, that in order to put God on his side in every respect, and to show all the world that he was not cruel or vindictive,' Charles ought to return the three hostages. His advice was taken, and it is fair to say that De

[1] I. 123-125.

Contay's opinion appears to have been regarded as monstrous. 'After the said Lord de Contay had given this cruel sentence against those poor hostages, part of whom had become hostages from mere goodness, one of the persons present whispered to me, "Look well at that man; though he is very old he is in very good health, but I would bet heavily that he will not be alive in a year from this day, which I say on account of the terrible opinion he has expressed." And so it happened, for he did not live long; but before he died he served his master well one day in battle.'[1]

The history of the operations before Liège contains some curious remarks. The Liègeois attacked Duke Charles (his father had died some time before) in order to make him raise the siege of St. Tron and were defeated.[2] 'They lost 6000 men, which seems a great deal to every one who does not care to lie; in my time I have seen in many places that where one man was killed people speak of a hundred, because they think it will give pleasure, and with such lies the masters are often deceived.' The people of Liège were thoroughly beaten. Two days after the battle 'the pride of this foolish people thoroughly changed and for slight loss.' Comines moralises on this. 'If the wrong party were wise he would risk nothing with those who have run away, but would be on his guard and try to find something to conquer to put them in heart and take away their fear. In every

[1] I. 124-126.   [2] 131, 132.

way lost battles have long tails and are bad for the losers.' He proceeds to describe very pithily the way in which victory gives confidence and defeat produces discouragement, and ends with his usual remark—'On this I speak from what I have seen, and such grace comes from God alone.'

This indeed is Comines's invariable result. In speaking of the success which Charles had in his campaign of 1467 against Liège, he says:[1] 'And thus I conclude that he won great honour and glory in this campaign, and it came to him solely by the grace of God against all reason, and he would not have dared to ask for what he got; and according to human judgment he received all these honours and advantages on account of the grace and goodness he had shown to the hostages as before mentioned. I am glad to say this because princes and others at times complain as if they were discomfited when they have pleased or benefited, saying that this is unfortunate for them, and that for the future they will not pardon so lightly, or be liberal, or show favour, all of which appertains to their office. I think of such language as this and that those who act so show a cowardly heart; for a prince or any one else who never was deceived should be a mere fool not knowing good or evil or the difference between them.'

Comines follows at considerable length the course of events which ended in the storm of Liège by the united forces of Louis and Charles. His principal

[1] I. 139, 140.

observation upon them is the one which I have already quoted about the importance of keeping princes apart if they are to be on good terms. The story is in every way degrading.[1] Comines despised but pitied them. In describing the Duke's entry into Liège he says: 'The people is a poor thing, unless it is led by some chief whom they fear and reverence, but there are hours and times when their fury is much to be feared.'[2] Few were killed when the town was taken, not more, Comines thinks, than about two hundred. He himself saw only four dead bodies, three men and a woman, but the misery endured was very great. 'I return to speak a little of the poor people who fled from the city. These poor wretches fled over the Ardennes with their wives and children.' Many were killed. A knight of the country routed a great band, and by exaggerating the number of killed—and there were in reality plenty[3]—made his grace with Charles.

Others died of cold and hunger, and no wonder for the whole country was laid waste by the Burgundians, who divided their army into two bands the better to destroy the country;' and the frost was so intense that 'for three days the wine was served out in lumps cut with hatchets, for it was frozen in the barrels,[4] and the ice had to be broken up into pieces, which people carried away in their hats or baskets.' Having

[1] See also this brought out in Michelet, Bk. xv., etc.
[2] I. 194.   [3] I. 197.   [4] I. 203.

described the fall of Liège, Comines proceeds to give an account of the various intrigues which were carried on between the King, his brother, the Duke of Guienne, and the Duke of Burgundy, showing how by degrees Louis contrived to remedy the effects of his false step in putting himself in the power of the Duke at Peronne, and to get rid of the treaty which he had signed as the price of his liberation. His chief methods being to separate his enemies by setting them against each other, and the great means which he used for that purpose being bribery, as regarded his brother and the Constable of St. Pol, and the Duke of Burgundy's overreaching pride and ambition, which gave him the opportunity of setting the others against him. The most characteristic passage in this part of the book is Comines's reflection on the Duke of Burgundy, whom few men knew so well. After saying that the Duke could not make up his mind to marry his daughter to the Duke of Guienne, he proceeds: 'I think that he would not have liked to have a son, and that he would never have married his daughter as long as he lived, but would always have kept her by him to keep people waiting on him who might serve and help him, for he aimed at so many great objects that his life was not long enough to accomplish them: and they were things almost impossible, for half Europe would not have contented him. He was bold enough for any undertaking. His person could endure the necessary labour. He was powerful enough in men and money;

but he had not enough sense or shrewdness[1] to manage his undertakings. For other things being favourable to making conquests, everything comes to nothing unless very strong sense is present, and this, I think, must come from God. If any one could have taken some of the qualities of the King, and some of his qualities, he might have made a perfect prince. No doubt, in point of sense the King overmatched him; in the end he showed it by what he did.'

The intrigues which took place between Louis and Charles, Warwick and Edward IV., furnish Comines with the occasion of making some observations upon English affairs which have great interest for us. Referring shortly to the wars of the Roses, he says :' There had been in England seven or eight pitched battles,[2]

---

[1] 'Malice.' The word as used by Comines contains exactly the same implied compliment to the intellectual merits of wickedness as our own 'shrewd.'

[2] His editor observes that there were twelve between 1455 and 1471, viz.—

1. St. Albans	...	...	...	1455
2. Bloreheath	...	...	...	1459
3. Northampton	...	...	...	1460
4. Wakefield	...	...	...	1460
5. Mortimer's Cross		...	...	1461
6. St. Albans	...	...	...	1461
7. Towton ...	...	...	...	1461
8. Hexham ...	...	...	...	1463
9. Banbury ...	...	...	...	1470
10. Stamford ...	...	...	...	1470
11. Barnet ...	...	...	...	1471
12. Tewksbury	...	...	...	1471

and eighty lords and princes of royal houses died cruelly, as I have already said; and those who were not dead were refugees in the house of the Duke of Burgundy. They were all young lords, for their relations were dead in England; and the Duke of Burgundy had received them into his house as his relations on the side of Lancaster before his marriage. I saw them in such great poverty that beggars are not so poor. I saw a Duke of Exeter walking barefoot after the Duke's train, begging his bread from house to house without naming himself. He was the nearest of the line of Lancaster and had married the sister of King Edward. He was afterwards recognised and had a little pension to live upon. The Somersets and others were there. They have all been bribed since into these battles. Their fathers and relations had pillaged and destroyed the kingdom of France, and possessed most of it for many years. Those who lived in England and their children ended as you see, and then people say God does not punish people any more as he used in the days of the children of Israel; he endures bad princes and bad people? It is very true, indeed, that he no longer speaks to men as he used, for he has left examples enough in this world to be believed; but you may see when you read this, in addition to what you know besides, that none or few of these bad princes and others having authority in this world, who use it cruelly and tyrannically, remain unpunished; but it does not always come at a given day or at the time which those who suffer desire.'¹

After some account of the expedition of Warwick, the expulsion of Edward IV., and his return and re-establishment by the battle of Barnet,² Comines makes a curious observation on English battles.³ 'Their custom in England is that when they have gained a battle they kill no one, especially not the common people (the common people know that every one tries to please them because they are the strongest), nor do they fine any one.⁴ For which reason when the king had gone no harm was done to his party. Moreover, King Edward had told me that in all the battles which he gained, as soon as he got the upper hand he mounted on horseback and cried out that the people were to be spared and the lords killed, and of the lords none or very few escaped.'

Comines, of course, moralises over Edward. He despises him for being expelled from England so easily.⁵ 'What excuse could he allege for having made such a loss and all by his own fault, except by saying "I never thought it would happen"? Well ought a prince to blush if he is a grown-up man at having to make such an excuse; for it cannot be allowed. This is a good example for princes who never doubt or fear

---

¹ 231, 232.   ² Sept. 1470; 14th April 1471.   ³ 245.
⁴ I cannot understand this; the law of forfeiture was then in full force. Perhaps Comines may have heard an indistinct report of the effect of the device of uses which was principally intended to defeat the law of forfeiture, and which the statute of uses was intended to defeat.   ⁵ 247.

their enemies, and should put them to shame.' Their servants may flatter them and call it courage, but the wise will be of a different opinion. 'It is very honourable to fear what one ought to fear and to provide against it.'[1]

Comines himself was a good deal employed by the Duke of Burgundy in negotiating with the English, in particular at Calais. It was the first time I ever knew 'that the affairs of this world are unstable.'[2] He had, however, learnt some other things. Being at Calais, which was held for Warwick and Edward IV. during Edward's expedition, he was asked for news: 'I answered on every occasion that King Edward was dead, and that I was well assured of it, although I well knew the contrary.' There is some humour in the contrast between the coolness of this statement and the moralising vein of the whole book. He makes a curious observation on the battle of Barnet, and one much opposed to our common conception of the king-maker.[3] 'Warwick never would fight on foot, but when he had set his people to work his custom was to mount on horseback. If matters went well for him he was in the melly.[4] If they went ill he took himself off early. This time he was forced by his brother, the Marquis of Montague, a very valiant knight, to dismount and send away the horses.' Edward put many people to death after this, for 'he had conceived great hatred against the people

[1] 254.   [2] 254.   [3] 260.
[4] Mr. Kinglake has authorised the use of this word.

of England' on account of their love for Warwick. In leaving the subject Comines remarks, 'Of all the people in the world the English were most inclined to these (pitched) battles.'[1]

I may here refer to several observations on the English character which occur in different parts of Comines, and which are slightly connected with the main stream of his narrative. The English, he says, are very civil[2] ('tres honorables'), but they are very stupid. 'Never was there a treaty between the English and the French in which the sense and cleverness of the French did not show itself superior to those of the English. It is indeed a common saying with the English, which I have heard in treating with them, that they always or generally have got the best of their battles with the French, but loss and damage in the treaties they have had with them.' Elsewhere he observes : 'Without doubt the English are not so subtle in treaties as the French, and whatever people may say they are clumsy in business, but you must have a little patience and not debate with them angrily.[3] This clumsiness applied to war as well as to peace. Speaking of the Duke of Burgundy's plan of getting helped by the English, he says, 'If he had wanted their help he would have had to keep them in sight for a whole season to help them to provide for and lodge themselves, and to teach them

[1] 262.
[2] 252, 'Le sens des Francois et leur habillete ne se moustrant par dehors celle des Anglois,' 267; and see I. 337.
[3] 368.

things necessary to be known in our continental wars; for nothing can be more stupid and clumsy than they when they first crossed the straits, but in a very little time they became excellent soldiers, wise and hardy.'[1]

The merits of the English government, however, struck him quite as much as the roughness of the nation.[2] Edward IV. could not help Charles the Bold without the consent of Parliament. 'The King cannot undertake such a business without assembling his Parliament, which is a great and holy thing; and the kings are stronger and better served when they do so, in such matters. When the estates are assembled the King declares his intention, and asks aid of his subjects, for no aids are raised in England unless it is to pass into France or to go to Scotland, or other such expenses; they give then very liberally and willingly, especially to pass into France.'[3] In another famous passage, he says: 'In my opinion, of all the countries in the world that I know England is the one in which the public interests are best treated, where there is least violence done to the people, and where no buildings are broken down or destroyed in war, but the grief and loss falls on those who make the war.'[4]

Comines's account of the various intrigues between

[1] 337.
[2] 'En Angleterre les choses y sont longues car le Roy ne peult entreprendre une telle œuvre sans apeller son parlement (que vault autant a dire comme les trois Estats) qui est chose tres juste et saincte et en sont les rangs plus fort et mieux.'
[3] 314.   [4] II. 142.

Louis XI. and Charles the Bold, which at last resulted in the sacrifice by Charles of the Constable of St. Pol, are interesting principally on account of a few incidental observations which he makes upon their general character. The picture of Louis flattering the English, deceiving St. Pol, and overreaching Charles the Bold, partly by treaty and partly by deceit, is too intricate to be reproduced in miniature. Very shortly their purport was as follows: St. Pol had betrayed in turn Louis XI., Charles the Bold, and his nephew by marriage, Edward IV.; although Louis had paid him enormously in land and power to secure his fidelity, and though he had been one of the principal agents in inviting Edward into France to help Charles. He was no doubt one of the very worst and most deceitful of the men of that age. By various artful devices Louis bought off Charles on the one hand, and Edward on the other, and made them aware of the character of St. Pol. To illustrate the general effect of the story I will quote three passages which show in general terms how matters stood between Louis and Charles, Louis and St. Pol, and Charles and St. Pol.

'It may appear hereafter,' says Comines, 'to those who read this, that there was no great good faith in these two princes' (Louis and Charles), 'or that I speak ill of them. I should be sorry to speak ill of either. Every one knows that I am obliged to the King, but to continue what you, my Lord Archbishop of Vienne, have required of me, I must tell part of what I know, however it may have happened. But, if you think of other princes, you will consider these great noble and notable and our King very wise; for he left his kingdom increased and at peace with all his enemies.' He then says that he will consider which of the two wished to cheat the other, in order that any young prince who happened to read the book might be on his guard. And he adds:[1] 'To tell my opinion I think it clear that each prince meant to cheat the other, and that their objects were very similar.'

As between Louis and St. Pol matters were still worse. The King very much wished to see St. Pol and offered him terms to come.[2] 'The Constable was very willing to come, provided that the King would swear by the Cross of St. Lou d'Angers,[3] to do no harm to his person, and not to consent to any one else doing it; and he said that he might just as well make this oath to him as to the Seigneur de Lesent which he had formerly done. The King replied that he would not take that oath to any one, but that he was content to take any other oath that the Constable chose to ask for. You can well understand that the King and also the Constable were in great trouble of mind ('grant travail d'esprit'), for not a single day passed for a period of time without messengers about this oath going from one to the other. And for one who would well consider it, this is a miserable life of ours to take so much time and trouble

---

[1] 278, 279.   [2] I. 341.
[3] A bit of the true Cross kept at the Church of St. Lou at Angers.

in wasting life, in saying and writing so many things nearly opposite to our thoughts.'

To make the combinations complete I must give an instance of the relations which Louis managed to establish between St. Pol and Charles the Bold. St. Pol sent an ambassador, Louis de Creville, to Louis, who arrived at the same time as an ambassador from Charles. Louis put Charles's ambassador together with Comines behind a curtain, and led on De Creville to talk of the Duke of Burgundy and his indignation at the moment against the English. 'And in saying this, Louis de Creville, thinking to please the king, began to mimic the Duke, and to stamp on the ground, and swear by St. George and call the King of England Blancborgne (Blackburn), the son of an archer of that name, and every sort of mockery which could possibly be used about a man. The King laughed greatly and told him to speak out, and said that he began to be a little deaf and that he must say it again. The other began again with right good will. M. de Contay, who was with me behind the curtain, was greatly astonished and never could have believed whatever had been said to him the words he heard.'[1]

The result of a long train of ingenious devices and negotiations of which these stories show the character, was, as I have already said, that St. Pol was sacrificed by the Duke of Burgundy and executed by Louis (19th Dec. 1475). The

[1] 357, 358.

observations of Comines on the folly of St. Pol on the one hand, and the mixture of vice and folly on the part of the Duke of Burgundy on the other, are very characteristic. As St. Pol, after enumerating his resources and referring to his connection with Edward IV. who had married his niece, and to the advantage which he might easily have made of the enmity between the King and the Duke, who never agreed in anything in all their lives but in this'—*i.e.* attacking him—Comines continues,[1] 'We must see that the deceiver Fortune had looked on him with an evil eye, or rather we must answer that these great mysteries do not come from fortune, and that fortune is nothing but a poetical fiction, and that God must have abandoned him, when we look at the matters above mentioned, and at others which I have not referred to, and if it appertained to a man to judge (which it does not, especially not to me), I should say that what reasonably must have been the cause of his punishment, was that he had always laboured with all his power to keep up the war between the King and the Duke of Burgundy, for on that was founded his great authority and great estate.' . . . 'It is probable and certain that he was removed from the grace of God, in having made himself the enemy of these three princes, and in not having a single friend who dared to lodge him for one night; no other fortune put her hand to it.'[2] As for the Duke of Burgundy, he says that he behaved very ill to the

[1] 395, 396.   [2] 395, 396.

Constable, and that he soon 'received damage and thus to see the things which God has done in our time and does every day, it seems that he will leave nothing unpunished; and one can evidently see that these strange works come from him, for they are beyond the course of nature, and are sudden punishments, especially against those who are violent and cruel, who in general cannot be small personages, but very great, either lords or of princely authority.'

The principal reason which induced Charles to deliver St. Pol to Louis was his anxiety to get possession of Nancy, which he was besieging when St. Pol was given up.[1] He took it a few days afterwards, and made it the point of various ambitious schemes for extending still further the limits of his heterogeneous empire.

In the following spring he invaded Switzerland, and suffered the defeats of Granson (3d March) and Morat (22d June). Nancy in the meantime was retaken by René, the nephew of the old King of Provence (19th October), and in the winter was besieged by Charles, who was killed in front of it (6th January 1476). Comines gives a full account of these transactions.

I will refer only to a few characteristic remarks on the principal actors in them. As to Louis, he observes that after the battle of Granson he 'had very great joy, and was displeased only at

---

[1] St. Pol was executed at Paris, 19th December 1475. Nancy was taken 30th November 1475.

the small number of men killed.' After Morat, his sister, the Duchess of Savoy, appealed to him for protection against Charles, who had entered Savoy after the battle, and had put her under a sort of guard near Dijon. She was very much afraid of her brother, but she found means to join him, and what was still better, to leave him safely. 'They were very glad to part from each other, and remained ever afterwards a good brother and sister till death.'[1]

As to the Duke of Burgundy, 'his grief at the loss of the battle of Granson was so great, and so troubled his spirits that he fell very ill. He was so ill that whereas his natural heat was such that he never drank wine, but generally drank tisanne and ate preserved roses to cool himself, his grief affected his constitution, so that he was obliged to drink strong wine without water; and to draw the blood from his heart they put lighted tow to his blisters and thus applied heat to the region of the heart.[2] About this, my lord, you know more than I, having helped to treat him in this illness, and having made him shave his beard, which he allowed to grow; and I think he never was so wise as before after this illness, but that his sense was much diminished.'

'Such are the passions of those who never suffered adversity, and can find no remedy for it, and in particular proud princes; for in these and similar cases

---

[1] II. 37-39.
[2] II. 39. Mettoient des estouppes ardentes dedans des ventouses.

the first refuge is to return to God, and consider whether we have in any way offended him, and to humble ourselves before him, and confess our misdeeds; for he it is who determines such cases, nor can any one find any error in his judgments.

'Next to this it does great good to talk to one friend if possible, and boldly to lament one's faults to him, and not to be ashamed to show our grief before that special friend, for that lightens and comforts the heart.'[1] The Duke, however, was too proud for this, and determined to try to retake Nancy. 'It would have been better for him not to be so obstinate, but God prepares these extraordinary resolutions for princes when it pleases him to change their fortune.'[2]

The siege of Nancy began in the winter of 1475-76. A gentleman of Provence, Seffron by name, tried to enter the town to join the Duke of Lorraine, who commanded there.

He was taken prisoner. 'The Duke of Burgundy commanded him to be immediately hanged, saying that when a prince has opened a siege and made his artillery fire upon a place, those who try to enter it are worthy of death by the laws of war. However, this is not the practice in our wars, which are more cruel than the wars of Italy and Spain where this custom prevails.[3] Seffron begged for his life, saying that he had a secret of importance to tell the Duke, which was the treason of Campo Basso his

[1] II. 40.   [2] II. 46.   [3] II. 48.

general. He was, however, executed. 'It would have been better for the Duke not to be so cruel, and to have heard him humanely.' He might then have escaped, and his house might have stood and been increased; 'but probably God had otherwise arranged since the dishonourable trick which the Duke had played upon the Count of St. Pol.'[1]

A little farther on Comines go so far as to say, 'You have heard how God made the Count of Campo Basso commissary to execute vengeance for the business of the Constable at the proper place, in the proper manner, and far more cruelly,' *i.e.* than Charles had treated St. Pol. Comines preaches a striking little funeral sermon on Charles the Bold. It is an excellent specimen both of his manner and of the habitual cast of his thoughts. It begins with a story, glides off into a character, and is full of reflections.[2] 'I have since seen a seal at Milan which I have often seen hanging to his doublet. It was a ring, and had a gem[3] engraved on a cameo with his arms, which was sold at Milan for two ducats. The person who took it from him was a bad servant of his bedchamber. I have often seen him dressed and undressed in great reverence, and by great personages, and at this last hour his honours had left him, and he and his house perished, as I have said, at the place where he consented from avarice to give up the Constable; and soon afterwards, God pardon his sins, I saw him a great and honourable prince, as

---

[1] II. 52.   [2] II. 65.
[3] One of the emblems of the Golden Fleece.

much esteemed and in request amongst his neighbours at one time as any prince who ever was in Christendom, and perhaps more.

'I saw no reason why he should incur the wrath of God sooner than others, except that he considered all the graces and honours which he had received in this world as proceeding from his own sense and virtue without, as he ought, attributing them to God; for in truth he had good and virtuous qualities. No prince ever excelled him in the desire to support the great and keep them in good order. His favours were not very great, because he wished every one to feel them. No one gave audience more liberally to his servants and subjects. When I knew him he was not cruel, but he became so before his death, which looked as if he would not last long. He was very magnificent in dress and other things, indeed rather too much. He highly honoured ambassadors and strangers; they were very well treated and received by him. He desired great glory, which was what caused more of his wars than any other thing, and he would willingly have resembled those ancient princes of whom so much has been said after their death; as bold as any man who reigned in his day. Well, all these thoughts are finished, and everything has turned to his shame and prejudice, for those who win always have the honour.'[1]

He then goes on to describe the sufferings produced by the death of Charles in his various dominions, of

[1] II. 65-67.

which he observes: 'I have never known any lordship or country, size for size, or even of much larger extent, so abundant in riches, in furniture, and in buildings, and also in all sorts of prodigality, expense, feasting, and cheer as his territories were when I knew him; and if those who were not there at the time I refer to think that I say too much of them, others who were there like me will perhaps say that I say too little.'

After describing the death of the Duke of Burgundy, Comines goes on to describe the manner in which Louis XI. received the intelligence.[1]

He got the news by means of the post which he had established, and 'was so overjoyed at the news that he hardly knew how to behave,' although the first letter did not mention the Duke's death.

He behaved in a very characteristic manner to his own nobility on the occasion.[2] 'He sent into the town of Tours for all the captains and other great personages and showed them these letters. They all testified great joy, and it seemed to those who looked into matters very close that many of them forced themselves to do so, and that, notwithstanding their behaviour, they would have preferred the Duke's fate to be different. The cause might be that the King was greatly feared, and they doubted whether, if he found himself freed from his enemies, he would not wish to make many alterations, especially in estates and offices; for there were many in the company who had been opposed to him in the matter of the Public

[1] II. 70.   [2] II. 73.

Good, and some in the matter of his brother the Duke of Guienne.

After having talked with them for a time, he heard the Mass, and then had the table laid in his chamber, and other members of his council were there. As he dined he talked over these matters; and I know well that I and others noticed how those who were at table would dine, and with what appetite; but, to tell the truth (whether from joy or sorrow, I do not know), not one seemed to me to eat half his fill. They were not ashamed to eat before the King, for every one there had often eaten with him before.'[1]

Louis lost no time after the death of Charles in taking possession of his dominions. I have already sketched very shortly the steps by which this was effected. Comines's account of the matter enters a good deal into details, which have lost much of their interest, but they suggest to him reflections which form far the most interesting part of his work. Indeed the last three chapters of the fifth book[2] would give any one who does not care to read the whole work a very good notion of the general view of thought by which it is pervaded. They are introduced by the following remark upon the town of Ghent, suggested by the narrative which he had just given of the troubles caused there by the breach of confidence of Louis towards Mary of Burgundy, which ended in the execution of Humbercourt and Hugo-

---

[1] II. 73.   [2] 132, 164; xviii., xix., xx.; II. 117-153.

net (?)[1] 'I cannot think why God has so preserved this town of Ghent, from which so much mischief has come, and which is of so little use to the territory in which it is situated, and of much less to the prince, and is not like Bruges, which is a great depot for merchandise, and a great place of meeting for foreign countries, and in which, perhaps, more merchandise is sold than in any other town in Europe, and its destruction would cause irreparable damage.' The answer to the difficulty is that the case of Ghent is merely an illustration of the working of a general law.[2] 'I think that God has created nothing in this world—man or beast—without making something contrary to it to keep it in fear and humility.' The turbulence of Ghent is thus intended as a reproof to the love of pleasure, which specially distinguished the Low Countries. And this is not the only nation to which God has given a string, 'for he has given the English as a check to the French, the Scotch to the English, Portugal to the Spaniards. I don't mention Granada, because the Moors are enemies to the Christian faith, still Granada has been a great trouble to Castille' (the tacit assumption that the divine government extends only to Christian countries is very characteristic). 'To the princes of Italy (most of whom hold their territories without any title, unless it is given to them by heaven, and of that we can only guess), who rule cruelly and violently over their people in the matter of taxation, God has

[1] II. 131.   [2] II. 132.

given as a check the republics of Italy, such as Venice, Florence, Genoa, sometimes Bologna, Sienna, Lucca, and others which in many things are opposed to the nobility and the nobility to them. Each, too, has an eye on its fellows, to prevent their increase.'

After giving a good many other examples of this perpetual opposition, by which every prince and nation is punished for its faults, Comines diverges with a long and not very systematic discourse about the faults which require all this punishment. The principal cause, he says, of the evils of life is the stupidity ('bestialité') of the princes, and the wickedness of others who are better informed. Knowledge, he says, makes the good better and the bad worse, but, on the whole, it is a good thing, partly because it makes people ashamed of their own vices, partly because it makes them 'fear the punishment of God, of which they have more knowledge than the ignorant, who have neither reading nor experience. Ill-informed princes do not know how far the power and superiority which God has given them over their subjects extends.'

Upon the whole, however, he thinks that 'we must conclude that neither natural reason, nor our own sense, not the fear of God, nor the love of our neighbours prevent us from being violent towards each other or from keeping each other's property or taking it away from each other by every means in our power.' Hence, 'God is probably almost forced and constrained or summoned to display various signs, and to beat us with many rods by our stupidity, or, as I rather think. our wickedness; but the stupidity and ignorance of princes is very dangerous, and much to be feared, because upon them depends the prosperity or adversity of their territories.'[1]

This reflection leads Comines to discuss at length the political evils of his time, and in particular to give an elaborate account of the condition of France and the French government which is full of interest.[2] He introduces it by observing that soldiers ought to be regularly paid, and that when their pay falls into arrear they grievously oppress the population. He then goes on thus. 'Is there in the world a king or lord who has power beyond his own demesne to lay taxes on his subjects without the consent of those who are to pay, unless by tyranny and violence?

'It may be said that there are occasions when the assembly of the states cannot be waited for, and that to assemble the states would put off the commencement and undertaking of the war too long. Do not be in such a hurry. There is time enough; and I tell you that kings and princes are much stronger when they take their subjects' advice and are feared for it by their enemies. When you have to defend yourself you see the cloud come from a distance, especially when they are foreigners, and in such a case good subjects should refuse nothing and make no complaints.' After some further observations in the same strain he adds: 'Of all the lordships in the world[3] that I know, England is the one where

[1] II. 136, 137. [2] Ch. xix., II. 141, 153. [3] II. 143.

the public interests are best cared for, where the least violence is done to the people, and where no buildings are destroyed or knocked down in war, and the bad luck and misery falls upon those who make the war.'[1]

This favourable view of England leads him to say that the natural disposition of the French is such as to make inexcusable in their kings to tyrannise over them. The people, he says, are naturally loyal.[2] 'Our king is of all lords in the world the one who has least cause to say, "It is my privilege to levy what I please on my subjects." Neither he nor any one else has that privilege, and those who say he has to raise his reputation for greatness do him no honour, but cause him to be hated and feared by his neighbours, who for no consideration would be under his rule, and indeed some of his subjects would be glad to be out of it. If our king or those who wish to praise and honour him said, "I have such good and loyal subjects that they refuse me nothing that I ask of them; and I am more feared, obeyed, and served by my subjects than any other prince who lives in the world, and they endure more patiently all evils and hardships and less remember past evils" —I think that would be a great credit to him.' He goes on to prove his point by reference to the proceedings of the States-General of Tours held in 1483. After a good many discursive observations and illustrations upon various points he works round

[1] II. 142.   [2] II. 142, 143.

again to his favourite reflections upon the divine government.[1] 'The greatest evils come from the strongest, for the weak seek only patience. It is by the care of the great that we know the power and justice of God. As for misfortunes that happen to one poor man or to a hundred no one notices them; everything is ascribed to his poverty or folly, or if he gets drowned or breaks his neck, inasmuch as he is alone, people hardly care to hear about it. If a misfortune falls upon a great city people do not speak of it so much as of the misfortunes of princes.

'We must say then why the power of God shows itself rather against the great than against the small' (the preceding observations seem to imply that the difference is only that in the case of the poor it is not noticed, but this want of system is very characteristic of Comines). 'It is because there are plenty of people to punish the little and the poor when they give cause; indeed, they are often punished enough without giving any cause, either as an example to others or to get their goods, or perhaps by the fault of the judge, and sometimes they do deserve it well and justice must be done'—but who is to punish the great and how come they to want punishing? 'I say it is for want of faith, and in the case of the ignorant for want both of faith and of sense, but principally for want of faith, from which I think proceed all the evils in the world, and in particular the evils of those who complain of being oppressed

[1] II. 146.

by others and by superior force. For if a poor man who had true and good faith, be he who he might, believed firmly that the pains of hell are such as they really are, and also believed that he had wrongfully taken the property of another, or that his father or grandfather had taken it and that he held it (whether duchies, counties, towns, or castles, furniture, a meadow, a pond, a mill, each according to his condition), and firmly believed as we ought to believe, "I shall never enter Paradise unless I make satisfaction and return what I wrongfully possess," is it credible that any prince or princess in the world would keep anything from his subject or his neighbour, or put any one to death wrongfully, or keep him in prison, or take from one to enrich another (which is the most cruel of their trades), or make base designs against their relations or servants for their pleasure as in the case of women or the like? On my faith, no. It is not credible. If then they had firm faith, and believed what God and the Church order as under pain of damnation, knowing their days to be so short, and the pains of hell so horrible and without any end, or remission for the damned, would they act as they do? We must conclude that they would not, and that all evils arise from want of faith.'

He then enters at length into the history of the enormous ransom which King John paid to get out of the hands of the English, whereas the worst which Edward III. could have done to him was not 'one hundredth thousandth part as bad as the least pain of hell;' and concludes thus —'There are no princes or but few who if they hold a town of their neighbour's will choose to give it up upon any remonstrance, or for fear of God, or to avail the pains of hell. Yet King John gave all that merely to deliver his person from prison; I say then that it is want of faith, which causes all our evils.'

Comines need not by the way have gone so far for his illustration. The tenacity with which he himself clung to property which he had derived from a most unjust grant of Louis XI., proved clearly enough that all the terrors of another world were overbalanced in his own estimation by present wealth.

Having concluded his reflections, Comines returns to his history and describes at length the various intrigues which were connected with the attainment of Louis XI.'s great object,—the appropriation of the dominions of Charles the Bold, and Comines's own embassy to Florence. This part of the memoirs contains little that is of special interest till we come to the death of Louis XI.

Comines returned from Italy a little before the battle of Guinegate (7th August 1479), in which the Flemings fought, on behalf of the Archduke Maximilian, a drawn battle with the French army. Louis was much vexed at the news, but determined to make peace if possible with the archduke, and to attend, as we should say, to internal reforms. 'He desired with all his heart to be able to make great reforms in his kingdom, and in particular to shorten trials, and thereby to reform the procedure of the Parliament not to diminish their number or authority,[1] but he had several things on his mind for which he disliked them. Moreover, he much desired that the whole realm should use one customary law, and one set of weights and measures, and that all the customs should be written in French in a fair book to avoid the chicanery and plunder of the advocates, which is greater in this realm than anywhere else in the world.'

These plans, however, were cut short by a fit from which he never quite recovered.[2] He was aware of his danger and was greatly alarmed at it, and took the most extraordinary measures to prolong his life.[3] He sent for a kind of saint from Calabria—a hermit who 'at twelve years of age settled in a cave where he lived till the age of forty-three, when the king sent one of his household to fetch him.[4] When the hermit came Louis fell on his knees before him,[5] 'that it might please him to prolong his life.' Comines obviously believes in the hermit, and says that he 'seemed inspired by God' in what he said, and displayed supernatural knowledge, but he did his employer no particular good. Louis, however, tried other expedients. He determined, in the first place, to conceal his condition from his subjects. 'He inflicted severe punishments to be feared, and for fear of losing his authority, for so

---

[1] II. 209.   [2] I. 2211-14.   [3] II. 228, 231.
[4] II. 229.   [5] 231.

he told me. He changed offices and dismissed soldiers, diminished or took away pensions in all directions, and told me a few days before his death that he passed his time in making and unmaking people; and he made himself more talked of through the kingdom than he had ever done, and this he did for fear he should be supposed to be dead, as I have said few people saw him, and when they heard of the things which he did every one doubted and could hardly believe that he was ill.'[1]

He undertook new schemes, he made expensive purchases, 'he bought a good horse whatever he cost, or a fine mule in countries where he wished to be thought well, for he did not do so in this kingdom. He sent to buy dogs everywhere. In Spain he bought allans.[2] In Brittany little greyhound bitches, greyhounds, and spaniels, for which he paid a high price; at Valence little hardy dogs which he paid for at a higher price than their owners asked for them; he sent to Sicily to buy a particular mule from an officer of the country, and he paid twice its value; at Naples he bought horses. He bought curious beasts on all sides. In Barbary he bought a sort of little lions, not larger than small foxes, which they call aditz. He sent to Denmark and Sweden for two kinds of beasts, one called elks, which have bodies like stags, are as big as buffaloes, and have thick and short horns; the others called

---

[1] II. 232.
[2] Especes de chiens grand, fort, et courageux.

reindeer, which are in body and colour like bucks, except that their horns are larger, for I have seen a reindeer with fifty-four points. For six of each of these beasts he paid to merchants 4500 German florins. When these creatures were brought to him he took no notice of them, and generally did not speak to those who brought them. In fact he did so many things of this sort that he was more feared by his neighbours and subjects than he had ever been; this was his object and he acted thus with this view.'

'He continued and even pressed on all the negotiations in which he was engaged, and extended his influence over Flanders, Brittany, Spain, Italy, and Switzerland. The kings of Scotland, the kings of Portugal, and his allies, and part of Navarre did as he pleased. His subjects trembled before him. What he commanded was instantly accomplished without difficulty or excuse.' He did not, however, neglect the spiritual arm. 'Touching the things which were thought necessary for his health, they were sent to him from all parts of the world. The last Pope Sixtus' (Sixtus IV.) 'being informed of his illness, and hearing that as a matter of devotion the King wished for the altar-cloth on which my lord St. Peter sang mass, sent it him at once with several other relics which were returned. The holy jar which is near Rheims, which had never been removed from its place, was brought to him in his chamber at Plessis, and was on the sideboard when he died. He intended to be anointed from it as he had been at his coronation, and many people thought that he wished to anoint his whole body, which is not likely, for the said holy jar is very small and there is not much in it. I saw it at the time I speak of, and also when the King was buried at Nostre Dame de Clery.

'The present Sultan' (Bagazet II.) 'sent him an ambassador who came as far as Riez in Provence, but the King would not hear him nor allow him to come further. This ambassador brought him a great roll of relics which are still at Constantinople in the possession of the Sultan. He offered them to the King with a large sum of money, if the King would be good enough to keep in prison the Sultan's brother who was in France, under the protection of the knights of Rhodes, and is now at Rome under the protection of the Pope.' The only effect of all this devotion was that 'one favour God gave him.' He lived longer than the other princes of his day 'but not much.' 'All had their good and bad points, for all were men; but without flattery he had more royal and princely qualities than any of them. I have seen them all and know their powers.'[1]

His fear of death was almost entirely moral. He retained all his faculties. 'Never in all his illness did he complain, as all kinds of people do when they are ill. At least I do, and I have seen others do so, and they say that to complain eases one's sufferings.'[2] His illness lasted from Monday till Saturday night. 'Here,' says Comines,

[1] 252.   [2] 256.

'I would compare the evils and pains which he caused to others with those which he suffered himself before he died; for I hope they will have taken him to heaven, and that this caused part of his purgatory. If they were neither so great nor so long as those which he caused to others, he bore a different and higher office in the world than they; besides he had never suffered personally, but was so much obeyed that it seemed almost as if all Europe was made only to obey him, whereby the little that he suffered against his nature and habit was harder for him to endure.'

Nothing can be more curious than the mixed feelings with which Comines regards his hero's sufferings. He looks on them as expiations for the faults which had disfigured a great and good career; but he constantly keeps in view the faults of which they were the expiation. He goes into this, after his fashion, at great length, and in a wandering, gossipy manner, which nevertheless is highly characteristic.

Certain persons, whom Comines does not name, 'whom he had elevated too suddenly and without occasion, one being his physician, took upon themselves without fear to say things to so great a prince which did not become them, and they did not observe the reverence and humility which belonged to the occasion, as those who were brought up in his court, or those who had been a short time before driven away by his fancies, would have done: not just as two great personages whom he had put to death in his time had had their death signified to them by commissaries appointed for the purpose, who declared their sentence to them in few words. So did the three persons aforesaid signify to our King his death in words short and rude, saying, "Sir, we must do our duty, hope no more in this holy man or in other things, for assuredly it is all over with you, therefore think of your conscience, for there is no remedy." . . . What pain it was to him to hear the news. Never man feared death so much, or did so many things to avoid it. Throughout his life he had begged his servants and me, like the rest, if we saw him under the necessity of dying, to say nothing to him except "speak little," and that we were only to move him to confess himself without pronouncing that cruel word death, for he thought he should never have the heart to hear such a cruel sentence. However, he bore it bravely, and everything else besides even to death itself, better than any man whom I ever saw die.'[1]

The mixture of sympathy and respect for the king, with a recognition of the retributive justice of his sentence which appears in these words is still more strikingly displayed in what follows. 'His illness lasted, as I have said, from the Monday to the Saturday evening, and I will compare the misfortunes and sufferings which he caused others to suffer, with those which he suffered before he died, because I hope they will have got him into heaven, and that this was in part the cause of

[1] 260.

his purgatory' (*i.e.* here on earth). 'If his sufferings were not so great or long as those which he inflicted on others, he had a different and a higher place in the world from theirs, and he had never suffered in his own person but had been so much obeyed, that it seemed as if nearly all Europe had been made to obey him, so that the little that he suffered against his nature and custom was harder for him to bear. The principal sufferings, however, which he underwent were moral. For five or six months before his death he suspected every one, and in particular all those who were deserving of authority.' . . . 'If he had made many people live in fear and suspicion under him he was well paid for it; whom could he trust when he suspected his son, his daughter, and his son-in-law?'[1]

His physician was an additional punishment. He was so very 'rude that one would not say to a lacquey the rude and outrageous things which he said to the King, and the King feared him so that he dare not send him away.' The physician had told him that he would not live eight days after dismissing him. 'This so frightened him that ever afterwards he flattered and paid him, which was a great purgatory for him in this world, considering the great obedience which he had had from so many honourable and great personages.'[2]

It is true, says Comines, that he had made cruel prisons, such as iron cages, which 'many have since

[1] 262, 263. [2] 264.

suffered, I amongst the rest, who tasted of them under the present King for eight months;' but in his last days he made a larger and stricter prison for himself, 'which, I think, was a great grace for him and part of his purgatory, and I say so to show that there is no man, of whatever dignity, who does not suffer either secretly or in public, and in particular those who have made others suffer.' This larger and stricter prison was the palace of Plessis, which, says Comines, he 'caused to be enclosed with great iron bars in the form of huge grates, and at the four corners of the house four turrets of iron, good, large, and thick.' He surrounded the castle with guards, and the strictest rules were laid down as to admission to it. Is it possible to keep a king 'who is to be honourably guarded in a closer prison than that in which he kept himself? The cages in which he kept others were eight feet square, and he who was so great a King had but a small court in the castle to walk in; he hardly ever came there, too, for he stayed in the gallery, except when he went to mass through the rooms without passing through the court. Can it be said that this King did not suffer as well as others when he thus shut himself up and had himself guarded, and was so much afraid of his children and near relations, and changed and moved every day his servants and the companions of his meals, who were dependent upon him for their property and honour, and dared not trust any of them, and thus chained himself with a strange chain and restraint? If the place was larger than a common prison, he was greater than common prisoners.'¹

Louis, Comines adds, had very little pleasure in life. For the latter part of his life he was faithful to his Queen, which, as Comines oddly observes, was no doubt right; but was a great thing to do, considering how many other ladies were 'at his orders,' and that the Queen 'n'etoit point de celles ou on devoit prendre grant plaisir mais au demeurant fort bonne dame.'

He was very fond of hunting, but in that 'he had almost as much fatigue as pleasure.' He got up early and hunted late, and often came home very tired and generally out of temper with some one.' He was constantly engaged in war, but that was very laborious. 'Whilst he was resting, his mind was at work, for he had business in many places, and took part in his neighbours' affairs as readily as in his own'; when he was at war he desired peace or truce; when he had it he could scarcely endure it. He mixed himself up in many small matters in his kingdom, many of which he might have avoided; but such was his constitution, and so he lived. His memory, too, was so good that he remembered everything and knew everybody in every country near him. He seemed, indeed, fitter to govern a world than to govern a kingdom.'²

After running through the chief events of his life, Comines remarks upon it, 'At what time, then, can one say that he enjoyed himself in all these affairs?

---

¹ 267-269.   ² 273.

I think that from his infancy and innocence he had nothing but suffering and labour till his death; and that if all the good days, which he had in his life in which he had more joy and pleasure than labour and fatigue, were well counted, few would be found. I think that there would be twenty days of labour and sorrow for one of pleasure and ease.'

As his manner is, this leads Comines to make similar remarks on others. Charles the Bold was no happier.[1] 'What ease had he? Always labour of body and mind without pleasure. And what did he get by his labour? What need had he of it? He who was such a rich lord and had so many towns and lordships under his orders, where he might have been so happy if he had pleased.'

He makes similar remarks about Edward IV. and Mahomet II., and at last concludes with the following passage—the most characteristic, perhaps, in the whole book.[2] 'Look, then, at the death of so many great men in such a short time, who laboured so hard to increase themselves and to get glory, and have suffered for it so much in passions and in troubles, and shortened their lives, and perhaps their souls may suffer for it. In this I do not refer to the aforesaid Turk, for I consider this point settled, and that he is lodged with his predecessors. Of our King I have hope (as I said) that our Lord will have mercy on him and also on the others, if he pleases. But to speak naturally, as a man who has no great

[1] 277.   [2] 279.

natural or acquired sense but some little experience, would it not have been better for him and all other princes and men of middling estate who have lived under the great, and will live under those who rule, to choose a middle course in these things? That is to say, to be less careful, and to work less, and to undertake fewer things, to have more fear of offending God and oppressing the people and their neighbours in the many cruel ways which I have sufficiently described already, but to take harmless ease and pleasure. Their lives would be the longer for it, illnesses would come later, and their deaths would be more regretted, and by more people, and would be less desired, and they would fear death less. Can we see better examples to show that man is but a poor creature, and that this life is miserable and short, and that great and small come to nothing when they are dead? for to every one their bodies are an object of horror and detestation, and the soul when it leaves the body must go to receive judgment, and their sentence is given according to the works and deserts of the body.'[1]

Such is the picture drawn by Comines of the great men with whom the most stirring part of his life was passed. I have tried to reproduce it as fully as is consistent with great condensation, because it appears to me to show with unrivalled clearness how in the fifteenth century the most unhesitating religious belief might be entertained by what we should call a bad

[1] 289.

man, and how if this happened to be the case his mind would be affected by it.

It is perfectly clear from Comines that both Louis XI. and Comines himself believed with an absolute conviction of its truth in the current creed of the day. They had, in the fullest measure, that certainty which in these days so many people long for with a passionate longing, and are willing to buy at any price whatever. No one can deny that it had a great effect upon them. It is hardly too much to say that Comines's whole mind was haunted at all times and at every point by a belief in an invisible and immensely powerful and artful man whom he called God, and whom he believed to be continually engaged in devising all sorts of plans by which the visible rulers of the earth might be outwitted and controlled, in order that effect might be given to a set of general rules, constituting, according to Comines's view, a code of supernatural criminal law.

It was hopeless, no doubt, to try to outwit God, but it was by no means impossible to effect bargains and compromises with him, and by different ways and means known to, and at the disposal of, the priesthood to escape from the penalties which he would otherwise have inflicted.

The moral effect of this belief is fully displayed by every step in the history of Louis XI. It did not make him a good man. It had not, so far as we can judge, the very smallest tendency in that direction. It did, however, beyond all doubt, impose a very strong check on his conduct. It drove him into odd round-about ways of doing outrageous things, and seems to have made him feel when he was winning, much as a boy feels when he does something which he particularly wishes to do, taking his chance of being punished if he is found out.

Christianity, regarded as a system by the operation of which he might very probably be punished, had thus a considerable and a rather wholesome, though a distorted and on the whole ignoble effect on Louis XI. As a system by which his heart could be touched, by which the aims of his life could be regulated and his feelings purified, it would seem hardly to have affected him at all. His biographer displays perhaps even more fully the same state of mind. He does not disapprove of his hero, or even like him much the less, on account of his admitted iniquities. Comines appears to regard his sins as matters, so to speak, between him and his Maker, which, if he chose to run the necessary amount of risk, he was justified in committing as far as his fellow-creatures were concerned.

Another matter upon which every page of Comines throws a broad light is the extreme ignorance of the times in which he lived. The complete absence of any sort of literary or scientific training amongst the aristocracy of his day is proved by half the passages which I have extracted above; and the general tone of the whole book shows how the absence of such training lowered the most conspicuous natural gifts into something little better than cunning and violence. It is melancholy to see how men like Louis XI. and Charles the Bold, whose natural gifts were on a level with those of the greatest modern statesmen, looked upon politics as a mere field for personal ambition. When either of them by any accident gets a glimmering notion of the importance of promoting the general good of the state and improving its institutions, Comines looks upon their virtue and wisdom as something prodigious. The utmost that he appears practically to expect of any one is that he will be rather moderate, and not inhumanly cruel or treacherous in the pursuit of his personal objects.

IV

MONTAIGNE'S ESSAYS[1]

MONTAIGNE (1533-1592), says Mr. Hallam, is the first French classic—the first writer of whose works an educated man is ashamed to be entirely ignorant. It is scarcely necessary to give any minute account of a book which is so familiar to almost every reader as Montaigne's Essays. Most people have dipped into it more or less extensively; though it may be doubted whether any one, in the absence of some special motive or special sympathy with the author, ever read it through.

Its proper use is to be treated as its author treated other books. 'Je ne cherche aux livres,' he says, 'qu'à m'y donner du plaisir par un honneste amusement.' 'Si ce livre me fasche, j'en prends un autre, et ne m'y addonne qu'aux heures où l'ennuy de rien faire commence à me saisir.' The Essays are just the sort of book which may be taken up at odd times, opened anywhere, and laid aside at any moment; and this, no doubt, is the manner in

[1] Essais de Michel de Montaigne.

which they are, and ought to be generally read. For, after all that has been said in their praise, it must be owned that they are long-winded to a degree, full of repetitions of the same thought under a variety of very similar forms, and as garrulous, vain, and egotistical as the letters of a newspaper correspondent in the middle of the long vacation.

Montaigne's delight in spilling himself over reams of paper was a peculiarity in his own day, and the undeniable vein of genius which runs through his writings combined with the novelty of the process to give it extraordinary interest. Since his time we have been deluged with confessions and self-revelations. Novelists and journalists have vied with each other in beating out their own and their neighbours' experiences, feelings, and loose thoughts upon things in general into sheets of literary tinfoil; and Montaigne stands at the head of an immensely large and by no means respectable literary family. It would, however, be foolish to allow this to blind us either to Montaigne's real merits, or to the peculiar position which he undoubtedly fills in literary history.

Times have changed since he wrote, and his critics ought to remember that Bohemianism, as we call it, was far more excusable in his day than in our own. Irregularity, unsystematic shrewdness, gay audacity in speculation have their place and their use as well as more solemn qualities; and if ever there was an age in which an emphatic expression of such a turn of mind was needed, it was the age of fierce war and passionate controversy in which Montaigne lived.

It ought also to be said of Montaigne that his eternal babble and wandering were unaffected. He was not himself a penny-a-liner, though he was the father of the whole brood. He actually was what the modern gossip wishes to be, and he lived at a time when intelligent gossip was greatly required as a counterpoise to fierce, ignorant, and overbearing dogmatism.

The babble of the present day is bad because it indisposes people to serious thought on serious subjects, on which materials for serious thought are available in any quantity. We live in an age of real science, authentic history, and fruitful inquiry, upon which men both can and ought to exercise their faculties steadily and in earnest. Hence the levity of style which so many modern writers choose to assume in discussion and description is for the most part mere idleness and self-indulgence; for it is seldom graceful enough to have an independent artistic value. In Montaigne's time it was nearly the only available weapon of offence against a harsh tyranny which had so darkened counsel by words without knowledge, that the first and most pressing of all intellectual necessities was to get rid of the burdens which it had laid on the minds of men.

The best thing to be said of Montaigne is that his essays are a protest on behalf of human nature and common sense against mock science, and that in his days there was hardly any true knowledge to be disrespectful to. 'Science,' he says, 'treats matters too finely, in an artificial way, different from that which is common and natural. My page makes love and understands it. Read him Leon the Jew or Ficinus; it is about him, his thoughts and his actions, yet he understands nothing. I do not know my own common movements when I read about them in Aristotle. They have been covered and dressed up in different clothes to suit the schools, God prosper them! If I was in the trade I would naturalise art as they artificialise nature.' ('Je naturaliserois l'art autant comme ils artialisent la nature.') This appears to us to be the true view, and the justification of his scepticism, which, in our own days, would no doubt have been far less thoroughgoing than he makes it.

It is difficult to choose particular specimens as illustrations of Montaigne's way of thinking, because characteristic sentences and illustrative points occur in every part of the essays in a manner which baffles all calculation, and without any apparent connection with the matter ostensibly in hand. To take one illustration amongst a thousand. Near the end of the book (Book iii. chap. vi.), Montaigne gives a striking sketch of the magnificence and luxury of the old Roman spectacles, and, passing from it, repeats the reflection which every one makes, but which can never be worn out, as to the indefinitely small proportion which our knowledge of past times bears to our ignorance of them.

He justifies his general tone by the example of the English. He says: 'Depuis que je suis nay, j'ay veu trois et quatre fois rechanger celles des Anglois, nos voisins; non seulement en subject politique qui est celuy qu'on veult dispenser de constance, mais au plus important subject que puisse estre, a sçavoir de la religion, de quoy j'ay honte et despit, d'autant plus que c'est une nation à laquelle ceulx de mon quartier ont eut aultresfois une si privée accointance qu'il reste encores en ma maison aulcunes traces de notre ancien cousinage, et chez nous icy j'ay veu telle chose qui nous estoit capitale, devenir légitime; et nous, qui en tenant d'aultres, sommes à mesme, selon l'incertitude de la fortune guerrière, d'estre un jour criminels de lèze majesté humaine et divine, nostre justice tumbant à la mercy de l'injustice et en l'espace de peu d'années de possession prenant une essence contraire. Comment pouvait ce dieu ancien plus clairement accuser en l'humaine cognoissance l'ignorance de l'estre divin, et apprendre aux hommes que leur religion n'estoit qu'une pièce de leur invention propre à lier leur société.'

Thence he diverges into a really beautiful set of reflections on the discovery of America, full of that delicate sense of humour which has become rare amongst French writers.

'Our world has just found another (and who can say whether it is the last of the family, since the dæmons, the sibyls, and we were ignorant of this one till the other day?), as large, as full, and as well limbed (*membru*) as itself, and yet so new and so childish that we are still teaching it its a b c. It is not yet fifty years since it was ignorant of letters, weights and measures, dress, corn, and vines; it was still naked, and lived only on the supplies of its nursing mother. . . . It was a baby world; we have not whipped it and forced it into our manners by our valour and natural force, nor have we won it by our justice and goodness, nor subdued it by our magnanimity.'

He goes on to show how great were the natural gifts of the Mexicans and other natives of America, and how little they had got except injury from the superior knowledge of their conquerors. After several pages about Cortes, Pizarro, and Montezuma, he finishes the digression by returning to the subject of the essay in which it occurs.

What was that subject?—Coaches. The connection is as follows: the essay begins about sea-sickness, to which Montaigne says he was very subject, though he thought it was not caused, as Plutarch supposed, by fear. He adds, that he hated travelling by coach, litter, or boat, or in any other way than on horseback. This reminds him that Mark Antony was the first person who had a coach at Rome, that Heliogabalus had his coach drawn by tigers, stags, dogs, etc., and that Firmus preferred ostriches. 'The strangeness of these inventions puts into my head the fancy that it is a sort of pusillanimity in monarchs, and a proof that they do not sufficiently understand their position, when they labour to set themselves off and make a show by excessive expenses.' This introduces the question, what expenses are excessive? This brings up the Roman shows. They introduce the passage which we have already referred to, and after many pages of that comes the conclusion: ' "Retumbons a nos coches"; instead of them, and of any other sort of carriage, they' (the Peruvians) 'were carried on the shoulders of men, and the last King of Peru, on the day when he was taken, was carried thus on a golden frame sitting in a chair of gold, in the midst of his troops.' As his bearers were killed, others took their places till the King himself was killed. With this the essay abruptly concludes. This essay is as good a specimen of the way in which Montaigne put down upon paper whatever came into his head as any one of scores of others which might be chosen instead of it.

There is indeed one essay, and only one, which is rather more systematic, and which may be considered as the nearest approach to be found in Montaigne's writings to a definite exposition of his views on the subjects to which he attached real interest and importance. It is the Apology of Raymond of Sebonde. It fills 112 octavo pages, very closely printed in small type, and sets forth—not, it is true, systematically nor even consecutively, but at all events fully—the views which have specially associated with the author's name the reputation of universal scepticism.

We will try to give a concise account of it. It begins

by saying that Pierre Bunel, 'a man of much reputation for knowledge in history,' after staying at Montaigne with the essayist's father, gave him, on leaving, a book called *Theologia Naturalis sive Liber Creaturarum, Magistri Raimondi de Sebonde*. It was written in bad Spanish with Latin terminations, and Bunel thought it would be very useful and appropriate to the time, 'for it was then that the novelties of Luther began to come into credit, and to shake our ancient faith in many places; in which he was quite right, foreseeing well, by the principles of reason, that this malady would rapidly degenerate into an execrable atheism.'

Old Montaigne laid the book aside, but a few days before his death told his son to translate it into French, which he accordingly did :—

'I thought the imagination of this author beautiful, the frame of his work well arranged, and his design full of piety. As many people amuse themselves by reading it, and especially the ladies, to whom we all owe service, I have often been able to help them in freeing the book from two principal objections which are made to it. Its object is bold and courageous. The author undertakes by human and natural reasons to establish and verify against atheists all the articles of the Christian religion; in which, to tell the truth, I find him so firm and so happy that I do not think it possible to argue that case more powerfully.'

Of the author himself Montaigne says he knows nothing except that he was a Spanish physician at Toulouse who lived about two hundred years before his own age—*i.e.* in the fourteenth century; and that 'Adrianus Turnebus, who knew everything, told me that he thought the book must be some quintessence taken from Thomas Aquinas, for that that genius alone, full as it was of infinite erudition and wonderful subtlety, was capable of such thoughts.'

The 'two principal objections' which Montaigne undertakes to answer in his apology are, first, that Christians are wrong in wishing to support their faith by human arguments, as it is to be conceived only by faith, and by a particular inspiration of divine grace; and secondly, that the arguments of Raymond are weak and inconclusive. His answer to the first objection appears to be that the behaviour of Christians in general shows that they are Christians only by accident, and have little or no supernatural faith :—

'We find ourselves in a country where Christianity is professed; or we think of its antiquity, or the authority of those who have maintained it, or we fear its threats to unbelievers, or follow its promises. These considerations ought indeed to be employed upon our faith, but only as makeweights; a different religion, other witnesses, promises and threats of another kind, might impress on us in the same manner a different belief. We are Christians by the same title as we are natives of Perigord or Germany.'

Hence we need all the arguments we can get, and may be prepared by a writer like Raymond to receive a supernatural faith. The answer to the second objection is, apparently, that Raymond's arguments are no weaker than any others, that we know nothing, or hardly anything, upon any subject, and that we are too poor creatures to have a right to doubt the truth of Christianity :—

'The method that I take to beat down this frenzy, and which appears to me the most proper, is to crush and tread under foot human pride and boldness; to make them feel the inanity, vanity, and nothingness of man; to snatch from their hands the weak arms of their reason, to make them bow the head and bite the earth under the authority and reverence of the divine majesty. . . . Down with Think ('abattons ce cuider') the foundation-stone of the tyranny of the evil spirit.'

The rest of his apology is an outpouring of scepticism which fits as awkwardly as possible to the highly orthodox preface by which it is introduced. Indeed, Montaigne's answers to the two objections with which he has to deal, appear to prove, when put together, that it is right to argue on religious matters, but wrong to require good arguments. We ought to be content with feeble and inconclusive ones, and to look only at those which are used on the orthodox side. To the ordinary human mind this method would probably appear to involve a good deal of waste of time. An argument is simply worthless unless it establishes what it asserts. Whatever may be the imperfections of arithmetic, it is difficult to imagine a greater waste of time than working sums wrong.

Having speedily got through the argumentative

part of his undertaking, Montaigne proceeds to heap up, at an extraordinary and indeed tiresome length, illustrations of the sceptical view of things. He begins with a long sermon on the text that 'presumption is our natural and original malady,' in support of which he gives all sorts of instances of the superiority of beasts to men. Taken as a whole, it is tedious and commonplace, but it is full of shrewdness. It contains, for instance, the assertion which has been so often repeated and argued upon (by Coleridge amongst others) in later times, that when a dog comes to four cross roads he smells at two and runs down the third without smelling, arguing that as his master was not in road A up which he came, nor in B or C at which he smelt, he must have gone down D. Hence the dog is acquainted with what in these days is called the third law of thought—the law of the excluded middle. The difficulty is as to the fact. Beasts, he says, may speak, for all we can tell, for we can say what we have to say by signs :—

'Quoi des mains? nous requerons, nous promettons, appellons, congedions, menaceons, prions, supplions, nions, refusons, interrogeons, admirons, nombrons, confessons, repentons, craignons, vergoignons, doubtons, instruisons, commandons, absolvons, injurions, mesprisons, desfions, despitons, flattons, applaudissons, benissons, humilions, mocquons, reconcilions, recommendons, festoyons, rejouissons, complaignons, attristons, descomfortons, desesperons, estonnons, escrions, taisons, et quoi non?'

And he goes on to tell the story of Agis, who, when asked by an ambassador after a long speech what answer he was to carry home, said, 'That I have let you speak as much and as long as you liked without saying a single word.' 'Voilà pas,' says Montaigne, in French which it would be a shame to try to translate, 'un taire parlier et bien intelligible?' In his comparison between men and beasts, Montaigne shows perhaps rather too little than too much scepticism, for he receives as perfectly authentic the most wonderful fables about animals — as, for instance, that 'in Thrace above Amphipolis' the hunters and the wild hawks go halves in their prey, and that on the Palus Mœotis the wolves go and tear up the fishermen's nets unless they honestly leave them half the fish. He says, too, that 'storks give themselves clysters with salt water.'

It is characteristic of Montaigne that his scepticism never extends to matters of fact. He says, for instance, that sportsmen say that if you want to find out which is the best worth keeping of a litter of puppies, the way is to carry them away from the kennel and keep the one which the mother first brings back. It never occurs to him to ask how, when all the rest are drowned, you can possibly tell that the one so chosen was the best.

After running on at immense length about the inferiority of men to beasts, he gives several pages to a declamation about the advantage of ignorance, the whole of which merely shows that particular cases may be put in which particular pieces of knowledge have been injurious to particular persons. Ignorance in regard to religion, and above all in regard to the nature and attributes of God, is specifically praised as being the right and inevitable condition of man; such ignorance he regards as another form of faith, or at least as closely connected with it.

How the consciousness of hopeless ignorance can produce any other result than that of diverting the thoughts from the object of which we so know ourselves to be ignorant, he does not think of explaining. This, however, introduces the main subject of the whole apology:—

'If at last I am to inquire if it is in the power of man to find what he seeks, and if this search, on which he has been employed for so many centuries, has enriched him with any new force or solid truth; I think he will confess, if he speaks according to his conscience, that all that he has got by this long pursuit is to have learnt to know his weakness.'

This is the text of an elaborate attack on the philosophy of his age, the effect of which is to assert that it was mostly a matter of chopping logic, and contained nothing solid. He begins with the natural theology of the ancient philosophers, by contrasting whose systems he is of course able to produce any amount of evidence of the interminable nature of the disputes which divided them, and of the slightness of the grounds on which their theories were built. Here and there striking passages occur. The following, for instance, is a neat expression of what may be described as the fundamental position of orthodox scepticism :—

'Pythagoras made a nearer guess at the truth in thinking that the knowledge of this first cause and being of beings must be indefinite, imprescriptible, and incapable of being declared ; that it was nothing else than an extreme effort of our imagination towards perfection, each man amplifying the idea according to his capacity; that if Numa tried to model the devotion of his people on this plan, and to attach it to a purely mental religion, without any definite object and without any mixture of matter, he undertook what could not be done ; the human mind cannot sustain itself floating about in this infinity of vague thoughts; it is obliged to confine them in some sort of image fitted to its capacity. The divine majesty has thus, for our sakes, after a fashion, allowed itself to be circumscribed within bodily limits ; its supernatural and celestial sacraments bear signs of our earthly condition ; it is worshipped by outward signs and ceremonies ; for it is man who believes and prays.'

Here, again, is a pointed statement of a thought which has been systematically worked out by others, and especially by Hobbes[1] :—

[1] See the chapter on Speech in the *Leviathan* (Works, iii. 25, pt. 1, ch. IV.)—'The errors of definitions multiply themselves according as the reckoning proceeds, and lead men into absurdities which at last they see, but cannot avoid without reckoning anew from the beginning in which is the foundation

'Our language has its weaknesses and faults like the rest. Most of the occasions of the troubles of the world are grammatical. Our lawsuits arise out of debates on the interpretation of the laws; and most of our wars from the difficulty of clearly expressing the treaties and conventions between princes. How many and what important quarrels have been produced in the world by doubts as to the meaning of the one syllable *Hoc*' (*i.e.* 'hoc est corpus meum').

Another celebrated passage which occurs a little farther on is the one to which Bossuet alludes when he says that it is a pleasure to hear Montaigne make his goose talk.

'Why should not a goose say, Every part of the universe is made for me; the earth is for me to walk upon, the sun lights me, the stars shed their influences on me; I find such conveniences in the wind, such others in the water; the vault of heaven regards nothing so favourably as me. I am the darling of nature. Does not man keep me, lodge me, serve me; does not he sow and grind for me? And if he eats

of their errors. From whence it happens that they which trust to books do as they that cast up many little sums into a greater, without considering whether those little sums were rightly cast up or not,—and at last finding the error visible, and not mistrusting their first grounds, know not which way to clear themselves, but spend time in fluttering over their books; as birds that, entering by the chimney, and finding themselves enclosed in a chamber, flutter at the false light of a glass window for want of wit to consider which way they came in;' and see the whole chapter.

me, he eats his fellow-men as well, and I eat the worms which kill and eat him.'

It was probably also in Pope's mind when he wrote his lines in the first book of the *Essay on Man*—

> Ask for what end the heavenly bodies shine?
> Earth for whose use?   Pride answers, ' 'Tis for mine.'

This attack on morals and natural theology is followed by an equally vehement attack on physical philosophy as understood in Montaigne's days, after which he sums up by telling his readers that they must maintain Raymond's arguments by all ordinary means in the first instance, and resort to the argument from general scepticism only in case of extreme necessity. 'This last fencing trick must be employed only as an extreme remedy; it is a desperate stroke in which you must throw away your own arms to make your adversary abandon his, and a secret thrust which you must use seldom and with reserve.'

As for himself, the general result is that he adheres to his own religion because it is his:—

'As I am incapable of choosing, I let others choose for me' (as if this was not the idlest of all ways of choosing), 'and keep myself in the position in which God has placed me; otherwise I should be continually rolling. Thus have I by the grace of God preserved entire, without agitation or trouble of conscience, the ancient doctrines of our religion, in spite of all the sects and divisions which our age has produced.'

There is a good deal more to the same purpose, but this is the essence of Montaigne's most elaborate discourse. The best answer to it, if it much requires one, is to be found in the immense steps made since his time in every kind of solid knowledge. Science has, in the course of the last three centuries, attained a position which makes general scepticism in good faith hardly possible.

It has taught us, no doubt, that our ignorance is unspeakably great, and that the languages in which we have to express ourselves are very imperfect instruments for describing the world in which we live; but it has also taught us, in a manner which cannot be gainsaid, that there is a fixed order in the world, and in our own thoughts, which we can contemplate, and to a considerable extent describe correctly in words.

To Montaigne's perpetual *Que Scais-Je?* it would be easy in these days to give a definite, though it would be a lengthy answer, which would consist of an enumeration of all the branches of science which since his time have been put on a sound basis, which have been proved, that is by reference to the testimony of the senses duly checked and corrected by repeated observation.

As for the religious application of his argument, it is enough to say that it makes as much against every form of belief as for it. It may, in fact, be reduced to this, that all religions being equally false, or at least equally uncertain, there is no reason for changing the one in which we happen to be brought up; and even this is incorrect, for the religion in which a man is brought up may be exceedingly inconvenient and irksome, though not more false than any other. If an enlightened sceptic had been brought up a worshipper of Bhówani it would be wise in him to consider whether Christianity was not at all events a more convenient creed, even if it were not more true.

Montaigne was, like Bayle, a good deal less sceptical in practice than in theory. Indeed, it is pretty obvious that his scepticism was only a convenient mask beneath which he concealed a condemnation of all existing forms of philosophy and religion. His book is full of positive assertions of his own, especially upon moral subjects. The first chapter of the third book 'De l'utile et de l'honneste' abounds in instances of this. He says, for example:—

'There are false and effeminate rules in philosophy. You have been taken by robbers who have released you, having taken your oath for the payment of a certain sum. It is wrong to say that an honourable man will be released from his word, and need not pay when he is at liberty. It is not so. What fear has once made me will, I am bound to continue to will without fear; and if it has forced my tongue only without my will, I am still bound to make my words good.'

Perhaps the most engaging quality in Montaigne, at least to many readers, is his extreme humanity. It is a good deal like the humanity of Comines. Thus, for instance, in continuation of the passage just quoted, he enters into an elaborate panegyric upon

Epaminondas praising in particular his humanity. He observes: 'Let us not fear upon the authority of so great a master to believe that some things are unlawful, even against enemies, that the common interest does not oblige us all to everything against private interest nor are all things permissible to a man of honour for the service of his king or of the common cause of the laws' (p. 508).

He seems to have been revolted at the harshness which prevailed in his generation, and he never misses an opportunity of protesting against it. The following passages are pleasing illustrations of this:—

'I think ill of the custom of forbidding children to call their father, father, and of making them give him a strange name as being more reverential, when nature has provided sufficiently for this authority. We call God Almighty, Father, and do not allow our children to call us so. I have set this to rights in my family. If I could not make myself feared I would rather be loved; there are so many defects in old age, so much weakness, it is so open to contempt, that the best gain that old men can have is the affection and love of their family. Command and fear are their arms no longer.'

These are fair illustrations of a tone which runs through the whole of the essay.

A point which ought not to be omitted in a notice of Montaigne, though it is not easy to examine it fully, is his indecency. He is undoubtedly an indecent author, and his indecency is much more than mere plainness of speech. He constantly goes out of his way, if he can be said to have any way to go out of, to bring in indecent stories. It is, however, difficult not to admit that his demerits in this particular are closely connected with the naturalism which is the main characteristic of all that he writes. His one rule of composition seems to have been to put down whatever came into his head, clean or unclean; and to have suppressed anything which he was minded to tell, from a sense of modesty, would have been opposed to his whole scheme. After all, there is more grotesqueness and humour than prurience in Montaigne's indecencies. He has none of the nastiness of Rabelais or Swift, and none of the brutal half-mad vanity of Rousseau.

Upon the whole, it may be said of him that no one ever succeeded so perfectly in the enterprise which many people have undertaken of painting a perfectly honest and complete portrait of oneself; but his success was rather a warning than an example. It was due to the fact that the age in which he lived was one in which a protest against bigotry and science, falsely so called, and an honest confession of ignorance, had accidental and exceptional importance.

His garrulity, personal vanity, and affectation of general scepticism were the arms by the use of which he was able to protest at once effectively and safely against the besetting sins of his generation. In a more humane and better instructed age such arts are not required, and if they are employed, not for the legitimate purpose for which Montaigne employed them, but because they suit the real taste of the author, they are generally contemptible and sometimes disgusting.

Except by way of protest against the temper of the sixteenth century, it would not have been worth while to make so much of the fact that Michel de Montaigne, who lived in an unfortified house with a gallery here and a study there, who liked Plutarch, who had an 'esprit prime saultier,' and had an attack of stone which he particularly disliked, who never pursued a subject which he found difficult, and who did, thought, and felt a thousand trivial things, did not know what to make of the world in which they happened. The really important point was, that his neighbours were quite as ignorant as himself, not nearly so honest or so kind, and quite ignorant of their own ignorance; and this Montaigne's peculiar style enabled him to assert very effectively.

V

HOOKER'S 'ECCLESIASTICAL POLITY'[1]

IF the value of Hooker's *Ecclesiastical Polity* be considered in relation to the age and the state of thought prevalent at the time of its appearance, it will perhaps be considered one of the most remarkable books in English literature. It may, indeed, be said to have contained in itself the germ from which several characteristically English schools of thought ultimately grew.

It may be convenient just to mention that Hooker was born in 1553 at Exeter, and died at his living of Borne, three miles from Canterbury, in the year 1600, and probably in the month of November. His lifetime thus coincided very nearly with the reign of Queen Elizabeth (1556-1603), and with the second great outburst of Protestantism, which began after the Diet of Augsburg in 1555, and was thrown back in the later part of the century, by the efforts of the Jesuits, aided by the great Roman Catholic sovereigns, and especially by Philip II.

[1] *Eight Books of the Law of Ecclesiastical Polity*, by Richard Hooker.

Hooker's earlier impressions must thus have been those of hope and victory. He belonged to the party of progress in the greatest crisis which the world had seen for many centuries—a greater crisis in some respects than any which has followed it. In his later years, on the other hand, he must to some extent have felt himself more or less upon the defensive, though the firmness with which Protestantism was settled in England, and the slightness of the communication with foreign countries which existed in those days, in comparison with what exists at present, may have prevented him from perceiving the full force of the turn in the tide.

The *Ecclesiastical Polity* has, so to speak, a triple aspect. It is at once a philosophical, a theological, and a political treatise; and in order to do justice to the importance of this, we ought to remember how vast a change had, at that time, come over the literature of all Europe, and especially over that of England. It was the age of the great revival of letters; and books were just beginning to be published which were constructed on the classical, rather than on the scholastic model. All that we now understand by moral science—metaphysics, logic, theology, law in all its various applications—had for centuries been treated as so many branches of theology, and had been investigated, if at all, by the scholastic methods. Hooker was the first great English writer who broke through these fetters, except for exclusively controversial purposes; and although he had in other parts of Europe a few predecessors — as, for instance, Machiavel (1469-1527) — and a few contemporaries, as Bodin (1530-96) and Montaigne (1532-92), he is undoubtedly entitled to a leading place in the class of literature to which he belonged.

Nor must it be forgotten that there were peculiarities in his situation as an Englishman, which gave a degree of practical importance to his writings that belonged to those of no other man till we come to Grotius, in the next generation. The Church of England, the theory of which he did so much to form and to enunciate, was an almost unique institution. It was the most important of the Protestant bodies. Its constitution had more comprehensive aims, and was constructed on more statesmanlike principles, than that of any other church, and it was much more closely connected than any other with the active political life of a great nation.

Our own experience has shown us in many different ways how all English speculation is affected by the closeness of its relation to practice. This gives it on the one side great vigour and originality, and, on the other, a fondness for details, and an adaptation to immediate results, which more or less hampers and narrows it. This peculiarity is to be traced more or less in all our great writers, and we know of no one in whom it is more conspicuous than in Hooker. Sometimes we find him discoursing about the essence of law and the broadest principles of morals; and then again, we fall upon endless discussions with Cartwright as to the pettiest of petty matters—the turn of some particular phrase, or the propriety of some small ceremony in the Prayer Book.

Of all the limitations which his character as an Englishman imposed upon him, as on other English theological writers, none probably has detracted more from the permanent value of Hooker's writings, and from those of others like him, than the necessity of writing controversy. Most of our great theological books are more or less controversial, and though this occasionally gives them surprising spirit and precision, it certainly impedes the flow and development of their authors' thoughts, and encumbers their books with a great deal of matter, the interest of which, such as it was, has entirely died away. Most readers of Hooker must have got very much tired of Cartwright and his errors, but it is fair to say that few, if any, controversial books are so little disfigured with the polemical spirit as the *Ecclesiastical Polity*.

Upon the whole, it may be viewed as the first great effort made in modern times to give the full theory of a great institution, to show the ideal principles upon which it was founded, and to indicate its substantial agreement with that ideal. The number of books even now which can claim such a character is by no means great, and in that day it stood almost alone.

Taking this view in general of the character and position of the *Ecclesiastical Polity*, we will now attempt to give some sort of sketch of what we have called its triple aspect—its aspect, namely, towards philosophy, towards theology, and towards politics, and to show how the principles which its author inculcated, have been represented in the subsequent history of the Church and State of England. The work falls naturally into three great divisions. The first contains the first and second books, though perhaps the second book might with more propriety be put in the second division. The second contains the third, fourth, fifth, sixth, and seventh books; and the third the eighth. These divisions may not unfairly be taken to represent the three aspects of which we have already spoken—the philosophical, the theological, and the political respectively—though the seventh book is closely connected with the eighth.

The first book of Hooker is well known to every one who has anything like a competent acquaintance with English literature. Perhaps its most remarkable quality is its extraordinary poetical power. The magnificent sentences with which it ends, sum up its doctrine with such an incomparable majesty and nobility of phrase that we shall be pardoned for repeating them, familiar as they are:—

'Wherefore that here we may briefly end: of law there can be no less acknowledged than that her seat is the bosom of God, her voice the harmony of the world; all things in heaven and earth do her homage, the very least as feeling her care, and the greatest are not exempted from her power; both angels and men and creatures of what condition soever, though each in different sort and manner, yet all with uniform consent, admiring her as the mother of their peace and joy.'

This, it is hardly necessary to say, is the keynote of Hooker. The Law of Nature is his name for that majestic order which he believed to reign over all things, divine and human, and to conform to which is the great object of human life :—

'All things do work, after a sort, according to law; all other things according to law whereof some superior unto whom they are subject is the author; only the works and operations of God have been both for their worker, and for the law whereby they are wrought. The being of God is a kind of law to his working, for that perfection which God is, giveth perfection to that he doth.'

After much of this somewhat mystical but marvellously eloquent extolling of the ultimate principles of morals, as being, so to speak, identified with the Divine existence—in which both the style and the thought often recall Bossuet—Hooker goes on to show how, in all created and imperfect beings, there is 'an appetite or desire whereby they incline to something which they may be, which as yet they are not in act.' They are thus moved to seek their law or the rule of their conduct, for 'that which doth assign unto each thing the kind, that which doth moderate the force and power, that which doth appoint the form and measure of working, the same we term a law.' Reason enables them to do so, and therefore 'the sentence that reason giveth concerning the goodness of those things that they are to do' is 'the rule of voluntary agents upon earth.' Its main principles are self-evident, and the rest are to be discovered by deduction from them. This natural or rational law is, according to Hooker, the very foundation of all consistent conduct, and is, as a matter of fact, universal with but few, and those insignificant exceptions; and the highest of all the laws which reason discovers is the love of God. 'Something there must be desired for itself simply, and for no other,' and this must be infinite, otherwise it could not be infinitely desired. 'No good is infinite but only God, therefore he is our felicity and bliss.' The Scriptures are a supernatural law forming a complement to the law of nature, and resting on and guaranteed by it.

The second book is an argument to refute the Puritanical view of the Bible as being a cyclopædia of all knowledge and all truth, so that nothing could be affirmed to be right, or to be a duty, which could not be expressly proved to be such out of the Bible. Few passages in the whole work are more interesting or vigorous than that in which this opinion is denounced:—

'Admit this, and mark, I beseech you, what would follow. God, in delivering Scripture to His church, should clean have abrogated amongst them the law of nature, which is an infallible knowledge imprinted in the minds of all the children of men, whereby both general principles for directing of human actions are comprehended, and conclusions derived from them; upon which conclusions groweth in particularity the choice of good and evil in the daily affairs of this life. Admit this, and what shall the Scripture be but a snare and a torment to weak consciences, filling them with infinite perplexities, scrupulosities, doubts insoluble, and extreme despairs.'

After denouncing this doctrine, Hooker goes on to describe at length the objects for which, in his opinion, the Bible was written. He views it throughout as being the natural ally of reason, resting itself for its authority on reason, whereby alone its true character could possibly be proved. 'The authority of man, if we mark it, is the key which openeth the door of entrance into the knowledge of the Scripture.'

These, amplified and illustrated in various ways, are the points which form the philosophical introduction to Hooker's great work. Their connection with the rest of the book is not altogether clear, though probably Mr. Hallam was right in thinking that Hooker's object was to lay a foundation for his distinction between laws which are, and laws which are not, of perpetual obligation; and to reach the conclusion which is the fundamental principle of his whole work, that the laws of Church government are mutable and temporary. For it follows, from his view of the case, that those laws only are of perpetual obligation which can be shown to exist by self-evident principles of reason, or which are declared perpetual by express revelation contained in Scripture itself.

Whatever was the connection of the first book of Hooker with the remainder of the work, its connection with the subsequent course of moral and political speculation in England was most important, and is sufficiently manifest in all the great Church of England theologians. The doctrine, thrown into a very few words, is, indeed, nothing else than that the ultimate tests of moral and religious truth are conscience and reason. They are to be applied to all subjects, and especially to all subjects connected with Church government, using for their instruction all other knowledge that may be available, and especially the experience of past times, but using it in the spirit not of servility to a tradition, but of free inquiry applied to a profoundly interesting branch of knowledge, and employed in solving one of the most difficult of all the problems of the art of government. Hooker preaches this doctrine with a degree of unction and enthusiasm which it seldom excites, but which in him was obviously sincere, and quite natural.

The effect of this great example on the subsequent course of speculation in the Church of England has been prodigious. It has supplied the High Church school, from Laud downwards, with those affinities to liberalism of which it has never altogether lost the tradition; and it gave the first example of another kind of religious speculation which has been far more powerful and widely influential. It would be difficult to say whether Laud or Chillingworth had most in common with Hooker, and both Laud and Chillingworth stand at the head of a long line of intellectual and spiritual descendants.

Hooker's liberalism deserves to be fully appreciated, and we will accordingly give a few short passages from his writings which show how strong it was, and how directly it led to the well-known and more systematic liberalism of Chillingworth, to say nothing of that of Locke, whose essay on civil government is almost entirely borrowed from Hooker. Take, for instance, his appreciation of Aristotle:—

'When once (the soul of man) comprehendeth anything above (things of inferior quality), as the differences of time, affirmations, negations, and contradictions in speech, we then count it to have some use of natural reason; whereunto, if afterwards there might be added the right helps of true art and learning, there would undoubtedly be almost as great difference in maturity of judgment between men therewith inured, and that which now men are, as between men that are now and innocents. Which speech if any condemn as being hyperbolical, let them but consider this one thing; no art is at the first finding out so perfect as industry may after make it; yet the very first man that to any purpose knew the way we speak of, and followed it, hath surely performed more in very near all parts of natural knowledge, than sithence in any one part thereof the whole besides hath done.'

Or take these general principles:—

'The mind of man desireth evermore to know the truth according to the most infallible certainty which the nature of things can yield. Where we cannot attain unto this, then what appeareth to be true by strong and invincible demonstration, such as wherein it is not by any way possible to be deceived, thereunto the mind doth necessarily assent, neither is it in the choice thereof to do otherwise. And in case these both do fail, then, which way greatest probability, thither the mind doth evermore incline. Scripture being, with Christian men, received as the Word of God, that for which we have probable, yea that for which we have necessary reason, yea that which we see with our eyes is not thought so sure as that which the Scripture of God teacheth. . . . Now it is not required, nor can be exacted at our hands, that we should yield unto anything our assent than such as doth answer the evidence which is to be had of that we assent unto. For men to be tied and led by authority, as it were, with a kind of captivity of judgment, and though there be reason to the contrary not to listen unto it, but to follow like beasts the first in the herd, they know not nor care not whither, this were brutish. Again, that authority of men should prevail with men either against or above reason is no part of our belief. Companies of learned men, be they never so great and reverend, are to yield unto reason, the weight whereof is no whit prejudiced by the simplicity of the person which doth allege it; but being found to be sound and good, the bare-opinion of men to the contrary must of necessity stoop and give place.'

Much of course might be said against Hooker's theories, if we look at them in a critical spirit. His language is by no means exact, and it is a serious defect in his theory that he does not habitually feel, though he sometimes refers to, the distinction between a law and a moral principle. It is not quite unfair to say of him that it is hard to understand how, according to his principles, there can be such things as bad laws; but there are far more important things in the world than the gift of an accurate use of language; and Hooker ought rather to be valued for the richness and magnanimity of his thoughts than blamed for their occasional vagueness—a vagueness perhaps inseparable from that love of the classics and revolt from scholasticism for which he was so remarkable.

As was natural in a writer of that age, his view of logic was essentially scholastic and imperfect. He supposed that knowledge might be indefinitely increased by arguing from self-evident first principles. 'In all parts of knowledge, rightly so termed, things most general are most strong. Thus it must be, inasmuch as the certainty of our persuasion touching particulars dependeth altogether upon the credit of those generalities out of which they grow.' According to our modern views of the nature of knowledge, this was a mistake; but it was one which in Hooker's age was a mistake on the right side, inasmuch as it tended to strengthen men's belief in the powers of their own minds, in the fixed and immutable character of truth, and in the possibility of attaining to it by the efforts of reason. Hooker affords in this respect a splendid contrast to Montaigne and Pascal, and stands on similar grounds with Bossuet, though his conclusions were sufficiently dissimilar, and in our opinion much more rational and consistent. It may not be generally known that Hooker enunciates in so many words a maxim much and justly quoted in our own times: 'No truth can contradict any other truth.'

The second aspect of Hooker is his theological aspect. We shall say but little of this, although the theological part of the book is much the largest part of it. It fills the third, fourth, fifth, sixth, and perhaps the seventh book (on Episcopacy). The third is by far the most interesting. Its object is to prove that there is no ground for the assumption that Scripture must of necessity prescribe a form of Church government.

The essence of the book is that Church government is a matter of expediency, like the government of the State, that it belongs to that class of laws which are mutable, according to the circumstances to which they apply; and that we are to ascertain, from past history, and from other general considerations, what laws are best suited to the circumstances of particular churches. The following sentences are as emphatic as any in the book :—

'For preservation of Christianity there is not anything more needful than that such as are of the visible church have mutual fellowship and society with each other. . . . The Catholic Church is divided into a number of distinct societies, every one of which is termed a church within itself. . . . A church is a number of men belonging unto some Christian fellowship, the place and limits whereof are certain. . . . The several societies of Christian men, unto every of which the name of a church is given, must be endued with correspondent general properties belonging unto them as they are public Christian societies. And of such properties common with all societies Christian, it may not be denied that one of the very chiefest is ecclesiastical polity.'

After an elaborate refutation of the opinion that a system of Church government must necessarily be revealed in Scripture, there follows an argument to show how laws for the 'regiment' of the Church may be made by the 'advice of men following therein the light of reason;' but that these laws, though entitled to obedience whilst they last, are not unchangeable.

The next four books are devoted to the justification of the laws actually made for the Church of England. The fourth book is a defence of the Church of England ceremonies against the charge of being Popish; and the fifth, which is far the longest of the whole eight, contains an elaborate vindication of the Church of England on all the points attacked by the Puritans. Though considerable parts of this book are of little interest in the present day, it is in some respects the most remarkable part of the whole work, for it includes by a sort of odd accident an elaborate statement of the theology of the Church of England as Hooker understood it.

The book consists of eighty-one chapters, many of which relate to very small matters. The thirty-eighth is 'of Music with psalms.' The sixty-fifth, of the cross in baptism. The seventy-eighth relates to the attire of ministers, etc.; but the chapters from the forty-second to the sixty-second contain a sort of body of theology setting forth at length the doctrines of the Trinity, of Prayer, and the Sacraments. The connection at first sight is not easy to perceive, but when carefully considered it becomes plain. They are a set of vindications of the doctrinal parts of the Prayer Book. Thus, in their zeal for the Bible, the Puritans were anxious to exclude the Athanasian Creed from public worship. Hooker insists on its importance, and is thus led into giving an account of the reasons for its adoption in the first instance, and for its subsequent retention.

They objected to several of the Church prayers, in particular to the prayer against sudden death, the expression 'which for our unworthiness we dare not ask,' the petition to be defended 'from all adversity,' and that God will 'have mercy upon all men.' In answer to this Hooker goes into the whole subject of prayer, and, as a branch of it, into the controversy about the two wills in Christ, which he finds it necessary to discuss in order to ascertain the precise value of Christ's prayers as precedents for human prayers.

In connection with the theory of the sacraments, and in justification of the services appointed by the Church of England, he goes at length into the whole subject of the two natures and personality of Christ, his incarnation, and other cognate topics. The leading topics of theology are thus passed in review in connection with the Prayer Book, which makes the arrangement of the matter very awkward.

As regards the substance of Hooker's doctrines we will confine ourselves to a single observation. They represent completely the characteristic features of Anglicanism, conclusions of the most orthodox and ecclesiastical kind based upon a rationalising foundation. The position of his Puritan antagonists was the converse of this. They, following the example of [1] Calvin, regarded the authority of the Christian Revelation, as contained in the Bible, as a self-evident truth, and though this led them to be even more doctrinal and dogmatic than Hooker and his school, it also led them to disregard and disapprove of creeds, the testimony of antiquity, and the like.

In each case religion was a compound of reason and faith; but Hooker founded faith upon reason, and his disciples and successors by an inevitable consequence came to limit faith by reason. The Puritans, on the other hand, starting with faith, reasoned it out much in the spirit of the old scholastic divines, though by the use of different methods and upon the assumption of the truth of different data. The effects of these opposite methods, not only upon theology but upon the general course of thought in the two countries, would form a curious subject of investigation. The repudiation of formularies in the

---

[1] Institute I. 7, 1, 24.

one case and the habit of regarding them principally, if not entirely, as historical evidence of the truth of the doctrines which they assert in the other, produced by degrees very similar results in the two cases, though by different roads.

The sixth book relates to the Presbyterian 'platform' (Hooker constantly uses this word in what we should now call the American sense) of Church government and to the doctrine and practice of confession and absolution.

The seventh book, about bishops, is much more interesting. Its general effect may be shortly described by saying that Hooker carries the dignity and importance of bishops to the very highest point. He says nothing inconsistent with the belief that their power was of divine institution, and much which rather favours that view; but upon the whole, he rests the case, as against those who attack it, on historical and political grounds. The institution is very old and venerable, perhaps it is of divine origin; at all events 'prelacy must needs be acknowledged exceedingly beneficial in the Church.' Such being the case, bishops are entitled to the highest possible honour; church property is God's property; 'ecclesiastical persons are receivers of God's rents, and the honour of prelates is to be thereof his chief receivers, not without liberty from him granted, of converting the same into their own use even in large manner,' says the marginal note of section twenty-three. It would be sacrilege to divert these endowments from them and their successors, even if they are unworthy.

There is a curious passage at the end of the book which throws some light on the condition of church property in Hooker's time. After speaking of the diminution of ecclesiastical revenues, he says:—

'Doth the residue seem yet excessive? The ways whereby temporal men provide for themselves and their families are foreclosed to us. All that we have to sustain our miserable life with is but a remnant of God's own treasure, so far already diminished and clipped that if there were any sense of common humanity left in this hard-hearted world, the impoverished state of the clergy of God would at the length even of very commiseration be spared. The mean gentleman that hath but a hundred-pound land to live on would not be hasty to change his worldly estate and condition with many of these so over-abounding prelates, a common artisan or tradesman of the city with ordinary pastors of the Church.'

On the whole, Hooker's theological attitude is eminently characteristic. He rests everything ultimately on reason and conscience, informed by history and antiquity; but the verdict which, in his view, is given by history and antiquity is orthodox in the extreme. No one can take more exalted views of the Bible, of the great theological doctrines such as the doctrine of the Trinity, or of the importance of Church government and the dignity of Church officers;

though, when carefully examined, the foundations of his theory appear to be capable of supporting quite a different superstructure.

The last aspect in which Hooker is to be regarded is that of a politician. His eighth book is an explanation and vindication of the doctrine of the Royal Supremacy. What he thought upon this subject is not quite so familiar to the world as it ought to be. He begins by going into the origin of legislative power, as to which he lays down principles of the utmost boldness and vigour. He asserts in express words that the consent of the people at large is the foundation of all lawful authority:—

'Unto me it seemeth almost out of doubt and controversy that every independent multitude before any certain form of regiment established, hath, under God, supreme authority, full dominion over itself, even as a man not tied with the hand of subjection as yet unto any other hath over himself the like power. God creating mankind did endue it naturally with power to guide itself, in what kind of society soever he should choose to live.'

A form of government being established, those who are governors are so by divine right, but they must recollect that 'all kings have not an equal latitude.' Whatever kings by conquest may do 'touching kings which were first instituted by agreement and composition made with them over whom they reign, and how far their power may extend, the articles of compact between them are to show;' nor need this compact be express, or made 'at the first beginning,' for such articles 'are for the most part clean worn out of knowledge or else known to very few.' The articles may be 'by silent allowance famously notified by custom.'

These 'articles,' in the case of English kings, are to be found in our ancient laws. The axioms of our regal government are these: 'Lex facit regem'; the king's grant of any favour made contrary to law is void, 'Rex nihil potest nisi quod jure potest.' After this he goes on to show where, by our English institutions, the power of legislation in all matters temporal and spiritual resides, namely, in Parliament.

The Church and State, he says, are one and the same body regarded from different points of view; and its legislature is as competent to make laws on matters spiritual as on matters temporal :—

'The Parliament of England, together with the convocation annexed thereunto, is that whereupon the very essence of all government within this kingdom doth depend; it consisteth of the King, and of all that within the land are subject unto him. The Parliament is a court, not so merely temporal as if it might meddle with nothing but only leather and wool.'

Bishops and other spiritual persons ought no doubt to be advised with, but nothing but the nation at large can make their resolutions into laws; for this is one of the passages in which Hooker seizes the true distinction between law and counsel :—

'In matters of God, to set down a form of prayer, a solemn confession of the articles of the Christian faith, and ceremonies meet for the exercise of religion, it were unnatural not to think the pastors and bishops of our souls a great deal more fit than men of secular trades and callings; howbeit, when all which the wisdom of all sorts can do is done for the devising of laws in the Church, it is the general consent of all that giveth them the form and vigour of the laws, without which they could be no more to us than the counsel of physicians to the sick. Well might they serve as wholesome admonitions and instructions, but laws could they never be, without the consent of the whole Church to be guided by them; whereunto both nature and practice of the Church of God, set down in Scripture, is found every way so fully consonant that God himself would not impose his own laws upon his people by the hand of Moses without their free and open consent.'

He proceeds to point out that the supremacy of the King himself in the 'case of making laws resteth principally in a negative voice;' and after showing how the existence of a superior legislative power or dignity is quite consistent with respect to the office and functions of the clergy, he concludes, with admirable courage, that the King is not our lawgiver, the clergy are not our lawgivers; the nation itself and it alone has the right of deciding what are God's laws, and of attaching to them a legal sanction :—

'Laws being made amongst us are not by any of

us so taken or interpreted as if they did receive their force from power which the prince doth communicate unto the Parliament, or unto any court under him, but from power which, the whole body of the realm being naturally possessed with, hath, by free and deliberate assent, derived unto him that ruleth over them, so far forth as hath been declared.'

This is a higher strain of thought and feeling than most people would be prepared for under Queen Elizabeth. These are to us most memorable passages. They show what the Reformation really was, and in what sense and to what a very great extent it is true that the English nation, even at that time, was radically free. Nothing since Hooker's time has been written more soberly and wisely on the origin of government and the general theory of legislation than the passages which we have quoted. We have indeed lost something of their significance, and may need before long to relearn part of the truth which they contain. We must not, however, lengthen out, by discussing such a subject, an article which is already too long, and we will, therefore, here close our slight sketch of the first great book in English ecclesiastical literature by saying that, after an interval of 260 years, it still remains very nearly the greatest of them all.

VI

ARCHBISHOP LAUD[1]

LAUD is one of the many persons whose character has never been fairly studied, because his name has been made into a kind of symbol by two parties fiercely opposed to each other.

Lord Macaulay, in his review of Hallam's *Constitutional History*—written, it is true, when he was twenty-seven years of age—breaks out into the following characteristic expressions: 'For Laud we entertain a more unmitigated contempt than for any other character in our history. The fondness with which a portion of our Church regards his memory can be compared only to that perversity of affection which sometimes leads a mother to select the monster or the idiot of the family as the object of her especial affection.' The Parliament should have sent him to Oxford to continue 'that incomparable Diary which we never see without forgetting the vices of his heart in the imbecility of his intellect.' . . . 'Contemptuous mercy was the only vengeance which it

[1] *Works of Archbishop Laud.*

became the Parliament to take on such a ridiculous old bigot.' There is a considerable dash of the Cambridge Union about this; but it seems to have expressed not unfairly the deliberate opinion of Lord Macaulay.

On the other hand, the 'portion of our Church' referred to has been of a diametrically opposite opinion. In his preface to Laud's Diary (which is adorned with pictures of stiff little angels saying their prayers and other quasi-ascetic devices) Dr. Newman draws a picture of Laud which, if quieter and in better taste than Lord Macaulay's—it was written in 1839, when Dr. Newman was nearly forty years old—is quite as strong in the opposite direction.

Laud is described as a Christian of the primitive type, 'cast in a mould of proportions that are much above our own, and of stature akin to the elder days of the Church.' There is some speculation as to whether he was technically a martyr, and the writer inclines to think he was. In short, the 'ridiculous old bigot' towers above the level of common men, and rises into an atmosphere which they cannot affect even to breathe. Such works as this preface hardly affect the character of dispassionate critical inquiry, and they considerably exaggerate the sentiment of the older class of Tories and High Churchmen.

These, however, were sufficiently strong, as may be inferred from the well-known lines in the 'Vanity of Human Wishes':—

> See when the vulgar 'scapes despised or awed,
> Rebellion's vengeful talons seize on Laud;

> Marked out by dangerous parts he meets the shock,
> And fatal learning leads him to the block.
> Around his tomb let Art and Genius weep,
> But hear his fate, ye blockheads, hear, and sleep.

If we want to get some notion of the man as he really was, we must turn from the views of later partisans, and look at the evidence supplied by his own works and by those who knew him.

It is always convenient, even in the case of a man so well known, to have under the eye the leading dates of his life. They were as follows: Laud was born at Reading, 5th October 1573. He was elected Fellow of St. John's College, Oxford, in 1593. After holding different livings, he was elected President of his College in 1611, and was made Chaplain to James I. In 1615 he became Archdeacon of Huntingdon; in 1621 Bishop of St. David's. In 1622 he had his famous controversy with the Jesuit Fisher; and in 1624 he was put into the High Commission Court. In 1626 he was made Bishop of Bath and Wells, in 1628 Bishop of London. In 1630 he became Chancellor of the University of Oxford, and in August 1633 he became Archbishop of Canterbury. From this time till the meeting of the Long Parliament he was nearly in the position of a Prime Minister, and was the chief agent in all the arbitrary acts of the time, such as the High Commission prosecutions, the introduction of the Liturgy into Scotland, the licensing of books, and the like. One of the first acts of the Long Parliament was to send him to the Tower in March 1641. His goods were plundered by various violent proceedings. He was brought to trial in March 1644, for high treason. The proceedings lasted, under one form or another, till January 1645, when he was beheaded, in the seventy-second year of his age.

The great events of Laud's life are too notorious to require, or even to justify, more than this passing reference; but it is worth while to try to get some sort of notion of the man from his writings. They consist of seven sermons; a report of the Conference with Fisher the Jesuit, held for the instruction of the Duke of Buckingham's mother; the Diary, of which Lord Macaulay spoke so contemptuously, and a small volume of private devotions; a variety of official papers connected with his duties as Chancellor of Oxford; reports of several of his speeches, especially of speeches at the Council Board and at the Court of High Commission; a history of his troubles and his trial; and a great mass of correspondence with various persons, of whom Strafford is the most remarkable. The most characteristic of them are his conference with Fisher, his speeches, his Diary and book of devotions, and part of his correspondence. The history of his troubles is an intricate and prolix account of forgotten details; and a large part of his correspondence refers to current matters of business which have ceased to have any sort of importance.

The view of his character which these materials suggest to us is as far from that of Lord Macaulay as it is from that of Dr. Newman. To speak of Laud as a 'ridiculous old bigot,' and to balance the vices of his heart against the imbecility of his intellect, is as unjust as it is altogether unreal and fanciful to idealise him into a saint and martyr.

It is hardly probable that Lord Macaulay had read any part of his works, with the exception of the grotesque bits of his Diary, when he launched his juvenile thunderbolts. It is impossible to read either his conference with Fisher or his speeches at the Council Board and the Court of High Commission without seeing that Laud was a man of great ability and extensive learning. In particular, he had remarkable gifts of style. His sermons are rather good in their way, and are by no means pedantic for the age in which they were written. Concede that a preacher ought to consider his text as a motto for observations more or less appropriate to the special subject of the day, and it will be hard to deny to Laud the praise of making a good many judicious and sensible remarks on the topics which he handled. His writings are clear, lively, and simple. His style has none of the involution and amplitude which was common amongst his contemporaries. It is far simpler, for instance, than the style of Clarendon, and has comparatively little of the pedantry of Williams, or his biographer Hacket. It has much resemblance, not merely in the choice and arrangement of words, but also in substance, to that of Chillingworth, whose discussion with Knott has much in common with Laud's conference with Fisher.

One point, which the common notions of Laud

certainly would not suggest, is the existence of a distinct vein of humour in every part of his writings, especially in his correspondence with Strafford. They are continually joking with each other, especially on the subject of Oxford and Cambridge, on which ancient controversy they never miss a chance of having a little fun.

Here and there this humorous vein takes the savage form, and shows what Clarendon meant by Laud's roughness of manner. Preaching, for instance, about some Dr. Cumming of the seventeenth century, who believed in the restoration of the Jews, he observes: 'I cannot tell here whether it is Balaam that prophesieth, or the beast he rode on.' In a sermon on unity he gives this pithy piece of advice: 'Keep unity then, and be sour—it is honourable justice—upon any that shall endeavour to break it.' In a speech on his trial, in answer to one by Lord Say, he thus remarks on his antagonist's complexion: 'What a happiness hath this lord, that his pale meagreness cannot blush at such a speech as this!' In his speech 'at the censure of Bastwick, Burton, and Pryn,' he observes: 'This is the misery, 'tis superstition nowadays for any man to come with more reverence into a church than a tinker and his bitch come into an ale-house.' 'The comparison,' he adds, 'is too homely, but my just indignation at the profaneness of the times makes me speak it.'

If we turn from the style to the substance, and try to ascertain what Laud's real opinions were on the subjects on which his mind was most exercised, it will be very difficult for any fair critic to speak with contempt of him. The two great subjects on which he thought were religion and politics, which indeed in his age were only two sides of the same subject.

His position in regard to each has, we think, been much misunderstood. How he came to receive the worship of the High Churchmen of our own day, except by the accident of his execution, it is hard to understand. The great characteristic of the Oxford movement was the height to which those who belonged to it carried the ascetic, devotional, unworldly side of religion. They surrounded themselves with an atmosphere of mystery and symbolism. They had a leaning to what the rest of the world described as superstition, and, in general, appeared to find a positive pleasure in believing as much as they could.

To judge from his writings, there was singularly little, though there was just a touch, of this temper in Laud. In one or two of his prayers there is a trace of mysticism, and there are a few points in his conference with Fisher which more or less lead up to it, but the general tone of his writings is quite the other way.

The conference with Fisher, as we have said, strongly resembles Chillingworth's *Religion of Protestants*, though it is not so systematic. The book, indeed, is put into such a form that it is not easy, especially near the beginning, to make out who is speaking, and on what occasion. Fisher had two conferences with Dr. White, and afterwards a third conference (24th May 1622) with Laud. Fisher published in 1623 what his antagonists considered an unfair account of the conferences. White and Laud replied by giving their own account in 1624. In 1626 Fisher published an answer under the initials 'A. C.' In 1639 Laud published his final account in the form in which it now stands in his works, replying upon 'A. C.' Much of it, therefore, falls into the form of 'You say that I said that you said so and so, and that I answered so and so; whereas you say that you said something else, and that my answer is wrong. Now I say that I never said that you said what you say that I said that you said, and my answer to what I said that you said was right.' Moreover, 'A. C.,' 'F.,' 'D. White,' and 'B.' (*i.e.* Bishop Laud) come in, especially near the beginning, in a way which reminds the reader of the letter which old Mr. Weller and his literary friend jointly wrote to inform Sam of his stepmother's death.

As the book goes on, however, Laud expounds his own views more and more fully, and with less and less reference to Fisher, and it can hardly be denied that they are very vigorously conceived and stated. There is, of course, a great deal about the Fathers, and what they did or did not believe, and much collateral skirmishing upon various topics; but the point on which the whole controversy really turns is the question, What is the ultimate test of belief? Fisher argued, as Cardinal Manning argues in the present day, that the Church was the only trustworthy witness for the Bible, and that a belief in Church authority was thus the only foundation upon which Christian faith could rest. Laud's answer to this is substantially the same as Chillingworth's, and, strange as it may appear, his answer will well bear repeating even now. He says with pithy vigour :—

'I did never love too curious a search into that which might put a man into a wheel and circle him so long between proving Scripture by tradition and tradition by Scripture, till the devil find a means to dispute him into infidelity and make him believe neither. I hope this is not your meaning. Yet I doubt this question, How do you know Scripture to be Scripture? will cause more harm than you will ever be able to help by tradition, but I must follow that way which you lead me.'

He then proceeds to discuss four different ways by which Scripture may be shown to bear the character claimed for it, the last of which is the use of natural reason; and this method Laud declares to be the right one, though he adds—and in this he differs, more perhaps in expression than in substance, from Chillingworth—that the conviction produced by natural reason in the first instance may be deepened by prayer, and by acquaintance with the character of the Bible, till it becomes stronger than the mere force of the evidence would have made it. Reason, however, is the ultimate foundation of his whole system, and his style and habits of mind bear all the characteristics of that kind of rationalism.

There is in all his writings a remarkable absence of

the mystical emotional way of looking at religion, and he argues with all the sturdiness and point of a man who is thoroughly determined to know his own meaning, and make other people know theirs. The following sentences are good instances of this:—

'For it may further be asked why we should believe the Church's tradition, and if it be answered we may believe because the Church is infallibly governed by the Holy Ghost, it may yet be demanded of you how that may appear? And if this be demanded, either, you must say you have it by special revelation, which is the private spirit you object to other men, or else you must attempt to prove it by Scripture, as all of you do.'

Which of course would be a *petitio principii*. So, again:—

'Their final answer is, they know it to be so, because the present Roman Church witnesseth it according to tradition, so arguing *primo ad ultimum* from first to last; the present Church of Rome and her followers believe her own doctrine and tradition to be true and Catholic because she professes it to be such.'

These are fair specimens of the terseness and vigour with which the whole book is written, and they certainly do not give the impression of a man of an imbecile mind. Besides this, Clarendon's description of Laud, and Laud's undoubted love for learning and learned men, and his benefactions to learned bodies, show that, whatever else he was, he was by no means a 'ridiculous old bigot.'

The principal evidence to show that he was is supplied by his Diary. It certainly does contain a great many odd notes about dreams. Dr. Newman speaks of these passages, in his preface, as showing 'a religious attention to dreams and possible indications of Providence.' They do not appear to me in that light, nor does Lord Macaulay seem to be quite fair about them. In most cases the dreams are simply mentioned without any religious application at all. '7th July. I dreamed that I had lost two teeth.' '21st Aug. In my sleep it seemed to me that the Duke of Buckingham came into bed to me, where he behaved himself with great kindness towards me,' etc. '4th Sept. Afterwards I dreamed of Sackville Crow, that he was dead of the plague,' etc.

This is rather grotesque and queer than superstitious. There is nothing religious about the entries. Laud does not seem to have drawn any omen from the loss of his teeth or the fate of Sackville Crow. He would appear rather to have had a sort of fancy for putting down dreams in a Diary which contains all sorts of odds and ends—for instance, his getting lamed in one leg 'by the biting of bugs,' his being startled by two robin redbreasts flying into the room where he was writing a sermon, the elm leaves being still upon the trees on the 1st of December, 'which few men have seen,' and scores of other trifles.

The Diary is a very short and slight affair altogether, and contains little that can fairly be considered remarkable. Perhaps the most striking sentence in it occurs in an entry on Strafford's execution. 'His mishaps in this last action were that he groaned under the public envy of the nobles, served a mild and a gracious Prince who knew not how to be, nor to be made, great,' etc. This is a singular, and surely not a very saintly, criticism on Charles's character. It tallies well with Clarendon's constant complaints that Charles was uxorious, and so weak-minded that he always allowed himself to be guided by his inferiors.

To those who take their notions of him from his works it will probably appear that the true bent of Laud's mind was far more towards politics than towards theology. How far he really cared about religion, except as the leading political question of the day, is a matter on which it would be presumptuous to form an opinion. That he was as keen a politician as it was possible for a man to be does not admit of a doubt. His whole heart is in his correspondence with Strafford, and it is obvious enough that they felt for each other that kind of strong personal sympathy and liking, which leads men to careless familiarity. It is sufficiently well known what their plans were, how they meant to carry them out, and what was the result.

Often as the story has been told, there is one point in it, specially connected with Laud, and singularly illustrative of his character and position, which is perhaps less generally known than it might be. This is the nature and practical drift of his views of Church government. We do not think that he was in the least degree disposed to be a Roman Catholic. We believe, on the contrary, that he had a genuine intellectual dislike to the Romish system, and that he had a good deal of sympathy with the incipient liberalism which was so strongly developed in Chillingworth, who wrote under his special patronage and direction, and in Jeremy Taylor, who was his chaplain.

There are many passages in his Conference with Fisher, in his sermons, and in his speeches, which show that he held Hooker's theory of the identity of the Church and State, and that he was quite sufficiently inclined to despise the Puritans as illiberal and narrow-minded, and to entertain, *mutatis mutandis*, similar views of the Roman Catholics.

This being so, it is no doubt odd how his name came to be a proverb for petty, narrow-minded bigotry. The answer is to be found in the theory of Church government which he wished to turn into fact. In common with many statesmen and writers of the day —Charles I., Clarendon, Chillingworth, and Jeremy Taylor, for instance—he believed with all his heart in the divine right of episcopacy; a doctrine, by the way, which has an aspect extremely unfavourable, and even diametrically opposed, to the later forms of Popery.

This doctrine substantially was, that the Christian Church was an aristocracy of which the bishops were the rulers, each bishop having, by God's appointment, certain powers in his own bounds, and the bishops of each nation having also certain powers paramount to all human authority, and closely connected with, and forming the natural support to, the powers of the King, the origin of which was also divine.

Like all aristocratic theories, this had no doubt its liberal and high-minded side. As we have shown on other occasions, it had a strong natural affinity for intellectual liberalism, and for learning of every kind. Moreover, the notion of a national Church, governed by an aristocracy of bishops, closely united with the temporal rulers of the nation, is not only larger-minded than the notion of a conventicle, but is really far more dignified than the notion of an immense spiritual despotism with a Dalai Lama, in the shape of a Pope, at the head of it.

It should never be forgotten that the modern Ultramontane view of the Church is not only irrational in itself, but is a modern innovation, for which the world is obliged to a variety of ingenious authors, and especially to the Jesuits. The earlier view, and especially that of the Gallicans, attributed the greatest importance to the rights of national Churches, and Laud and his party held much the same sort of position, as far as Church government was concerned, as would have been held by the Gallican Church had Louis XIV. gone one step farther than he actually went. Their theology was greatly more liberal.

It is important to recognise the dignified and attractive aspect of the intellectual side of Laud's theory, because the other side of it is better known. It cannot, however, be said that the evils usually ascribed to it are exaggerated. If ever there was a system in this world which deserved to be called a 'tyranny of professors,' it was the one which Laud and Strafford laboured to set up, and we are perhaps tempted rather to underrate than to overrate the danger of it.

In the present day we are inclined to smile when a wrongheaded colonial bishop chooses to play at being a judge, and to try to set up a system of jurisprudence which he can mould at his own pleasure, under the name of the common law of the Church; but this in Laud's time was no laughing matter. There was then a real substantial contest, and a most acrimonious and doubtful one, between the law of the Church and the law of the land. So complete was the victory of the latter that the way in which the battle was fought and won has been almost forgotten.

A few words on the subject may perhaps be interesting to some of our readers. If the controversy between the lawyers and the divines had been clearly worked out, it would have resulted in two counter-propositions. The lawyers' proposition was that the ecclesiastical law of England was nothing else than that part of the law of England which related to ecclesiastical affairs, and that it owed its binding force to the will of the English Legislature. This view is worked out elaborately, and asserted with extreme and almost passionate emphasis, by Coke and Hale.

The proposition of the divines was that the ecclesiastical law of England was the common law of the Christian Church as interpreted by clerical judges. To do full justice to their view of the subject, and especially to Laud's view of it, would no doubt be a matter of some difficulty; but this, in general terms, was its character, and the practical consequence was that, in the court of High Commission and in the Ecclesiastical Courts all over the country, the clergy could make pretty nearly whatever laws they thought proper upon all ecclesiastical and moral subjects.

In Clarendon's significant words Laud was determined 'that the discipline of the Church should be seen and felt as well as talked of,' and the way in which he carried out his resolution is to be traced in all the proceedings of the High Commission Court. The imprisonment of persons of high rank for adultery, simply on the ground that adultery was a spiritual offence—or, in other words, a sin—was a strong illustration of the spirit in which he proceeded; but the general tendency of the system is seen more clearly in its daily application.

This is to be traced in a curious publication of Archdeacon Hale on the records of the different Ecclesiastical Courts from the end of the fifteenth till the middle of the seventeenth century. The practical application of the system is set in the clearest possible light by this remarkable book. It shows that the clergy of the day, and especially the archdeacons, were more like our stipendiary magistrates than anything else. They held courts constantly, as often as twenty times a year, and took cognisance in them of every sort of moral offence—breach of trust, defamation, irregular attendance at church; above all, incontinence in all its forms. The procedure was by the course of the civil law, and the parties (till the lay power interfered to prevent it) were compelled, by what was called the oath *ex officio*, to give evidence against themselves. The consequences to which the parties were liable on conviction were either penance or excommunication, the temporal effects of which were most serious.

The High Commission Court dignified, centralised, and methodised this power; and, if the Court had been able to maintain itself, it would have given the bishops a degree of power which, according to our modern notions, would have been altogether intolerable, and which, even in the seventeenth century, people were thoroughly determined to resist, even at the expense, if necessary, of civil war. To us it is not only easy to understand this feeling, but barely possible to understand how the state of things which called it forth should ever have come into existence.

It ought, however, to be observed, and indeed it is one of the most curious points in the whole matter, that in point of discipline the Presbyterians (as witness the Scotch Kirk Sessions) were more severe than the bishops themselves, though probably they were more on a level with those over whom their power was exercised, and had in every way a greater hold on their sympathies.

It ought also to be observed that the dispute to which the King, the Church, and the two Houses were parties was emphatically a question, not of law or liberty, but of power and sovereignty. In England, as in every other part of Europe, the question, Who was sovereign? had, in the seventeenth century, to be settled by the same means by which the States of the American Union settled the question whether they formed a nation or a confederacy.

Logic might be chopped, and authorities quoted, to any length. The real question was, Whom did the people really wish and intend to obey? They were quite clear that they did not mean to obey the bishops or the clergy, except in a very modified manner indeed. They were divided between the King and the two Houses, though with a considerable majority, as events showed, against the King, and this was caused principally by his adherence to the bishops.

Laud appears to us to have been a rather favourable specimen of the class to which he belonged, but his history leaves no room for doubt as to the reasons of the failure of his schemes. A learned, well-meaning, and, in his way, liberal-minded College Don is perhaps the last person in the world whom the English nation is likely to receive as a ruler and governor in all matters human and divine. We think that those who reviled him as a disguised

Papist, or derided him as a bigot and fool, misunderstood him as much as those who turned him into a glorified saint. We also think that it was very wrong to cut off his head; but, with considerable intellectual merits, he was utterly intolerable as a Prime Minister, and deserved almost anything short of what actually happened to him.

In conclusion we may give the following short extracts, both as remarkable in themselves and in proof of our assertion that there was a side on which Laud's views were directly opposed to bigotry, and were such as to expose him rather to the charge of liberalism. They occur in his speech at the censure of Pryn, Bastwick, and Burton. He had been charged with making innovations of a Popish kind in the Liturgy. The following are two of the charges, with his answers:—

'The third innovation is, that the prayer for seasonable weather was purged out of the last fast-book, which was, say they, the cause of shipwrecks and tempestuous weather.'

'*Ans.* When this last book was set out, the weather was very seasonable. . . . 'Tis most inconsequent to say that the leaving that prayer out of the book of devotions caused the shipwrecks and the tempests which followed; and as bold they are with God Almighty in saying it was the cause, for sure I am God never told them it was the cause, and, if God never revealed it, they cannot come to know it.'

Laud was also charged with having left out of the

Litany a prayer to 'cut off those workers of iniquity whose religion is rebellion.' He justified himself as follows :—

'If you make their religion to be rebellion, then you make their religion and rebellion to be all one, and that is against the ground both of State and law. For when divers Romish priests and Jesuits have deservedly suffered death for treason, is it not the constant and just profession of the State that they never put any man to death for religion, but for rebellion and treason only? Doth not the State truly affirm that there never was any law made against the life of a Papist, *quatenus* Papist only? and is not all this stark false if their very religion be rebellion? For if their religion be rebellion, it is not only false but impossible that the same man should suffer for his rebellion and not for his religion.'

VII

CHILLINGWORTH[1]

If *laudari a laudato* be a safe rule for estimating a writer's merits, the name of Chillingworth ought to stand nearly as high in English ecclesiastical literature as those of Hooker and Butler. His *Religion of Protestants* was dedicated, by permission, to Charles I. It was written under the eye of Laud, and was by Laud's request examined by Dr. Prideaux, afterwards Bishop of Worcester; Dr. Baylie, then Vice-Chancellor of Oxford; and Dr. Samuel Fell, Lady Margaret Professor of Divinity; and it was published with their unanimous approval, expressed on its title-page in the strongest language. 'Nihil reperio doctrinæ vel disciplinæ Ecclesiæ Anglicanæ adversum, sed quamplurima quæ Fidem Orthodoxam egregie illustrant, et adversantium glossemata acute, perspicue, et modeste dissipant'—says Dr. Prideaux; and the others are to the same effect. After the Restoration, similar testimony was borne to it by the licenser of the then Archbishop of Canterbury. Locke repeatedly

[1] *The Works of William Chillingworth*, 3 vols., Oxford, 1838.

recommended it as fitted to 'teach both perspicuity and the way of right reasoning better than any book I know.' Tillotson called the author 'incomparable' and 'the glory of his age and nation.'

This great reputation rests substantially on the only considerable work he ever published, the *Religion of Protestants a Safe Way to Salvation*. Few things throw greater light on the changes of times and opinions than to read this book over again, and to think what its author, were he now living, would say of the state of things around him, and what our champions of orthodoxy would say of him. For many reasons, we cannot go into this inquiry; but we propose to give some account of Chillingworth's principal book, and of its place in the controversy to which it belonged, leaving our readers to draw such inferences as they think fit on the great subject of past and present.

Chillingworth was born in 1602, and was educated at Trinity College, Oxford, of which he became a Fellow in 1628. He became a Roman Catholic some time before 1630, being converted by Fisher the Jesuit (whose real name was Percy) by the argument that there must be some one Church infallible in matters of faith, and that this must be the Church of Rome. He studied for a time in 1631 at Douay, and was reconverted to Protestantism shortly afterwards. He published his great work in the year 1637. He was ordained in 1638, and died of exposure to cold and hardship in the winter campaign of 1643, in which he was present at the sieges of Gloucester and

Arundel, where he was taken prisoner by Waller. He died at Chichester, and was buried in the cathedral.

There is a charming portrait of him in Lord Clarendon's Life. It occurs in what is perhaps the most pleasing passage in all his writings—his account, namely, of what we should now call the 'set' in which his own early manhood was passed, and which consisted (amongst many others) of Lord Falkland, Clarendon himself, Hales, Chillingworth, and other persons united in most cases by the common bond of extreme devotion to the Government, and still stronger devotion to the Church. In each case, however, their devotion was largely qualified by the sort of liberalism to which we have often referred as one of the best-marked and least-understood of the characteristics of the early history of the Church of England. Chillingworth displayed in perfection the intellectual side of this tendency, and his book still enables us to understand perfectly well the general theory on which it rested.

The *Religion of Protestants* is a step in a rather entangled controversy. Its place in the series is what special pleaders call a rejoinder. The earlier steps of the controversy were as follows: In 1630 Knott (his real name was Wilson), a Jesuit, wrote a book called *Charity Mistaken*, to prove that Roman Catholics were not uncharitable in excluding Protestants from the hope of salvation. In 1633 Dr. Potter, then Provost of Queen's College, Oxford, and afterwards one of the bishops who advised Charles I. to give way in the matter of Strafford, wrote a book in answer to this, called *Want of Charity Justly Charged*. In 1634, Knott replied by a book called *Charity Maintained*, and to this he added a preface called a *Direction to N.N.* (*i.e.* Chillingworth), having heard that Chillingworth intended to answer him. The *Religion of Protestants a Safe Way to Salvation* is the rejoinder to this reply.

Amongst the many modern inventions for which we have to be thankful, the art of abbreviating controversy is not the least important. We are content in the present day to take the leading points of an obnoxious book or pamphlet and argue against them, having a well-grounded confidence that, when the foundations are overthrown, the superstructure will fall of itself. Two hundred years ago this was not thought enough. A man was not satisfied until he had knocked down the whole of his antagonist's building, stone by stone. Chillingworth reprints the whole of Knott's book in his own, and at the end of every chapter adds an answer to it paragraph by paragraph, embodying very often in the answer a good deal of the paragraph answered. Indeed, he goes farther, for he answers separately every assertion in every paragraph, and every insinuation implied in each assertion.

This practice, no doubt, has some advantages. It prevents misrepresentation, and even the imputation of it. It enables the reader, if sufficiently patient, to form a real judgment as to the merits of the case, and it makes victory, when gained, crushing. If, indeed, controversy were the great object of the lives even of controversialists, it would be the form into which controversy ought to fall; but, as this is happily not the case, and as the points of essential and permanent interest at issue between controversialists are generally few in number, and capable of being stated by *bonâ fide* disputants shortly and broadly, perhaps the modern practice is really better for all parties, especially as it deprives controversy of much of its personal sting, and greatly conduces to candour.

Men can agree to differ upon general principles, but the question whether A or B has got the best of a particular argument can hardly fail to be irritating, and is often altogether unimportant. It must also be owned that the altercation is in itself exceedingly wearisome. You had said A, to which Dr. Potter answered B. In your reply, you falsely allege that he falsely said B', to which you reply A'. Now he did not say B', though B' would have been quite true, and very important if he had said it, and would not have been answered by A'. What he said was B, which does answer A, and is not affected by A'. All this may be true and relevant, but the human mind is hardly so constituted as to take it in, or to care for it much when it has taken it in, especially two centuries after date. Even when it is quite fresh, the constant backwards and forwards produces on many readers a feeling like moral and intellectual sea-sickness.

Chillingworth's book contains so much of this skirmishing, and so many fierce fights on by-points, that a man must be rather a careful student who would care to read it right through in the present day. He bickers with Knott on every point referred to, even incidentally.

Amongst other topics, for instance, Knott had glanced, perhaps rather disrespectfully, at James I.'s proceedings in the matter of Archbishop Abbot. This brought upon him an argument in the shape of a shower of questions drawn up like interrogatories, which certainly are (if it were worth considering them) of the most damaging nature for Knott, but which at the present day appear like interruptions to a very impressive argument. Hundreds of instances of the same kind might be given. It is probably to this that Mr. Hallam referred when he described Chillingworth's style as 'more diffuse' than Knott's. Profusion appears to us the right word. There is too much matter, but the style is severity and precision itself.

Chillingworth's style, indeed, is not only one of the greatest attractions of his book, but is also perhaps the strongest indication which it supplies of the extraordinary qualities of his mind. Its naked severity and nervous simplicity are occasionally dashed by a vein of eloquence which breaks out unexpectedly and with prodigious effect, especially as it depends neither upon a musical ear nor upon pleasure in ornament, but upon the excitement of strong masculine feeling roused by an adequate cause—the feeling, generally speaking, of indignation against oppression, sophistry, and falsehood. An earnest and indeed passionate love of truth was the great characteristic of Chillingworth's mind. He became a Roman Catholic because he thought that in that Church he should find, not peace but truth; and he left it because he found himself cheated with mere pretences to truth, which crumbled away from him when he tried to grasp them.

He was a man of a very different turn from some modern converts to Rome. His object was not to be governed, but to be taught, and when he found that government and not teaching, directions to the mind and not food for it, were what was to be had at Rome, he returned to the Church of England. The following is a good illustration of the fervour with which he expressed himself. It contains, moreover, words which have passed into a proverb :—

'The BIBLE I say, the BIBLE only is the religion of Protestants. . . . I for my part, after a long and (as I verily believe and hope) impartial search of "the true way to eternal happiness," do profess plainly that I cannot find any rest for the sole of my foot but upon this rock only. I see plainly and with mine own eyes, that there are popes against popes, councils against councils, some fathers against others, the same fathers against themselves, a consent of fathers of one age against a consent of fathers of another age, the church of one age against the church of another age. Traditive interpretations of scripture are pretended, but there are few or none to be found; no tradition, but only of scripture, can derive itself from the fountain, but may be plainly proved either to have been brought in, in such an age after Christ, or that in such an age it was not in. In a word, there is no sufficient certainty but of scripture only, for any considering man to build upon. This, therefore, and this only, I have reason to believe; this I will profess, according to this I will live, and for this, if there be occasion, I will not only willingly, but even gladly, lose my life, though I should be sorry that Christians should take it from me.'

The whole of the passage from which this extract is made is eminently characteristic of Chillingworth's occasional fits of eloquence. As instances of his remarkable power of argument, two passages may be referred to. One in the answer to Knott's second chapter (vol. i. pp. 202-212, Oxford edition), in which he retorts Knott's charge that, according to Protestants, nothing more than probability is to be attained in religious belief. He shows what a number of merely probable conclusions as to matters of fact, resting upon hardly any evidence at all, a man must believe before he can be sure that he has received valid absolution—as that the priest who gives it was baptized with due matter, words, and intention; that the bishop who ordained him ordained him with due matter, form, and intention; that the ordaining bishop himself was first a priest and then a bishop; and so on like the house that Jack built. This leads up to the celebrated climax quoted, amongst others, by Lord Macaulay: 'That of ten thousand probables no one should be false; that of ten thousand requisites, whereof any one may fail, not one should be wanting, this is to me extremely improbable, and even cousin-german to impossible.'

A similar instance of his peculiar vein is to be found in vol. ii. pp. 68-70. Knott had charged his antagonist with contradicting himself. The charge was a very obvious quibble, and was merely by the way. Chillingworth retorts by drawing out in form all the contradictions involved in the doctrine of transubstantiation, and asking Knott either to reconcile them or to admit that men might believe contradictions. The retort is out of all proportion to the occasion for it, but it is a model of nervous vigour of expression. The argument concludes with the important and profound remark (re-made long afterwards by Abraham Tucker) that men both may, and constantly do, believe contradictions, when the opposition between the contradictories is not immediately obvious.

I have noticed Chillingworth's style at some length, because the doctrine that the style is the man, has seldom been better illustrated, and also because the style itself is nearly the first specimen, as it is also one of the best of all specimens, of pure, vigorous, modern English, delivered from the trammels of the classics. Like Clarendon and Jeremy Taylor, Chillingworth wants little but a change in punctuation to be a writer of our own day, and a writer as powerful, as expressive, and as idiomatic as any in the whole history of our language. It is remarkable that he uses hardly any obsolete words. In a pretty careful study of his book we have found only the following: 'Disease,' as a verb active for 'inconvenience'; 'Equipage,' for 'equipoise'; 'Crambe,' used as in 'crambe repetita.'

The points in issue between Knott and Chillingworth, when drawn out into a short form and freed from collateral disputes, are neither long nor intricate when they are really understood; but it is easy to misunderstand them and to get a false notion of the whole subject, from the very familiarity of the terms employed. The whole of Chillingworth's book, for instance, is supposed to be summed up in the two propositions that there is a right of private judgment, and that the Bible, and the Bible only, is the religion of Protestants. In order to see precisely what he meant by these doctrines, it is necessary to go a little further into the bearings of his controversy with Knott. The case on the one side and the other stood somewhat as follows:

Both sides agreed that certain doctrines, belief in which was necessary to salvation, had been revealed by God to man.

Both sides also agreed in the absolute truth of the whole Bible, and in the doctrine that the Bible contained a revelation either of all or of some of these doctrines.

Knott affirmed, and Chillingworth denied, that the

Church of Rome was the depositary of unwritten traditions collateral to and of equal authority with the Bible, and that, thereby and otherwise, the Church of Rome was the authorised interpreter both of the Bible and of tradition, and that it was necessary to salvation to believe the whole matter thus put forward.

Chillingworth affirmed, and Knott denied, that the doctrines necessary to be believed were plainly expressed in the Bible, and were contained (with others) in the Apostles' Creed.

Knott concluded that it was necessary to salvation to believe whatever was put forward as an article of faith by the Church of Rome. Chillingworth concluded that whoever believed all matters of faith clearly expressed in the Bible, or, more particularly, whoever believed all the articles of the Apostles' Creed, believed all that was necessary to salvation.

These, as a lawyer would say, were the chief issues between the two disputants. There were, however, several subordinate questions closely connected with these which it is necessary to state shortly in order to give a fair notion of the controversy.

Chillingworth is continually pressed by Knott to give a catalogue of the fundamentals which, as he said, were clearly expressed in the Bible. He admits at last that he cannot give such a list, but he says (which is true) that Knott himself recognises the distinction; and he gives a variety of reasons for the assertion that all fundamentals were contained, along with other things, in the Creed and in each of the four Gospels. Hence he argues that whoever believes either the Creed, or the whole of any one Gospel, may be sure that he believes whatever is necessary to salvation, and something over. He also explains his inability to give a precise list of fundamentals, by alleging the principle that 'fundamental' is a relative term; that what is so to one man is not so to another; that to an infant or lunatic, or a man deaf and dumb, nothing is fundamental; and that the list would vary indefinitely from man to man, according to individual circumstances.

Chillingworth was also pressed by Knott with the difficulty that if men were referred to the Gospels in particular, or the Bible in general, they would err, at all events, in matters not plainly declared. To this Chillingworth replied that a *bonâ fide* student of a matter plainly stated could not err, for that, if he did, the statement would not be plain; that if *bona fides* were wanting, his error was sinful, and that, if plainness in the statement was wanting, his error was innocent. It is by this avenue that Chillingworth introduces reason as the ultimate measure of faith, which is the cardinal feature of his system. Knott's conception of faith was altogether different, and the discussion whether it was right (on which we cannot enter here) is one of the most curious parts of the controversy.

Perhaps the most singular feature in the whole controversy, at least to a modern reader, is that both disputants, but more especially Knott, deal throughout with the whole question as a matter, not of truth, but of expediency or personal danger. Knott's last word and final appeal is to the duty of charity to oneself. He says :—

'In things necessary to salvation no man ought in any case, or in any respect whatsoever, to prefer the spiritual good either of any particular person or of the whole world before his own soul. According to those words of our blessed Saviour, "What doth it avail a man," etc.'

He insists on the arbitrary and technical character of salvation :—

'No ignorance nor impossibility can supply the want of those means which are absolutely necessary to salvation. If an infant die without baptism he cannot be saved.'

Thus—

'If by living out of the Roman Church we put ourselves in hazard to want something necessarily required to salvation, we commit a most grievous sin against the virtue of charity as it respects ourselves, and so cannot hope for salvation without repentance.'

His whole book, indeed, is an expansion of an argument which no dialectical skill can divest of its revolting character :—

'Consider how all Roman Catholics, not one excepted . . . do with unanimous consent believe and profess that Protestancy unrepented destroys salvation and then tell me . . . whether it be not more safe to live and die in that Church which even yourselves are forced to acknowledge not to be cut off from the hope of salvation.'

He works this out systematically in his final chapter. Chillingworth is far bolder and more generous. In reply to Knott's argument, just quoted, he says:—

'In saying this you seem to me to condemn one of the greatest acts of charity of one of the greatest saints that ever was—I mean St. Paul, who, for his brethren, desired to be an anathema from Christ. And as for the text alleged by you in confirmation of your saying, "What doth it avail a man if he gain the whole world and sustain the damage of his own soul?" it is nothing to the purpose; for without all question it is not profitable for a man to do so; but the question is whether it be not lawful for a man to forgo and part with his own particular profit to procure the universal spiritual and eternal benefit of others.'

As to unbaptized infants, he observes:—

'If you may gloss the text so far as that men may be saved by the desire without baptism itself, because they cannot have it, why should you not gloss it a little further, that there may be some hope of the salvation of unbaptized infants?'

This is a very noble passage, and may remind the reader of the utterances of certain well-known contemporary authors on the possibility that a man may think a great deal too much about what one of them calls 'his own dirty soul'; but Chillingworth did not always maintain this tone. He was careful not to be too charitable, for he obviously had a wholesome terror of the practical effect of Knott's argument on those to whom it was addressed. He says repeatedly that ignorance or *bona fides* only can save Roman Catholics, and taunts Knott with admitting as much of Protestants. The only pleasant thing in those mutual threats is to observe how each side devised loopholes to escape from its own doctrines. Both Knott and Chillingworth were better than their theology.

These heads give the main outline of the controversy, but the principle which pervades the whole admits of more consecutive and less controversial statement. It is perfectly true that the assertion of the right of private judgment was the great object of Chillingworth's book; but it is less often observed how emphatic the word 'judgment' was in his system. He used it, not in the loose indefinite sense which is generally attached to it in the phrase in question, but in a more accurate one, which it is not easy to explain in a single phrase.

In order to explain it we must return to the general principles of the controversy, and point out the way in which Knott's claim to infallibility for the Roman Catholic Church arose. It was founded on the principle that there was an original revelation—a certain number of specific propositions announced by God to men, which it was necessary for men to believe; but that, as some of these propositions were unwritten, and as some of the written propositions were ambiguous, the only possible way by which they could be conveyed to men was through an actual living interpreter.

The main stress of Chillingworth's argument, though he does not express it quite in that form, was to show that this, in fact, amounted to a claim for the Church of Rome of supreme judicial and legislative power over all Christians—the legislative power being, in fact, involved in the judicial power as claimed; for it is obvious that a judge who is entrusted with the power of declaring this or that to be a portion of unwritten tradition, and of affixing whatever meaning he pleases to obscure writings, is in reality a legislator, and not merely or principally a judge.

A judge moreover, *ex vi termini*, or nearly so, implies a sheriff. If his decisions are to have the force of law, they must be carried into effect by penalties upon those who disobey them; and thus, as Chillingworth pointed out, the claim to be a guardian and keeper of tradition is in reality a claim to be sovereign of the world, for it is a claim to make laws for the government of men in their highest capacity, and to provide means for putting those laws, when so made, into execution. Such a claim, of course, is in itself perfectly intelligible on the part of any organised body like the Romish clergy; but it is equally obvious that it ought not to be admitted without the clearest evidence.

The great point of Chillingworth's book is, that he brings out both the nature of the claim and the weakness of the evidence on which it rested, with remarkable point and vigour. After showing at length the nature of the claim made by Knott and the consequences to which it would lead, he continually returns to the question of evidence. 'If you really are entitled to this position, show your title. How easy, how simple, and how vitally necessary it must have been to have given you the position which you claim in unambiguous words, if that had been intended?'

It is in answer to this view of Knott's that Chillingworth set up what has since become so hackneyed under the name of the right of private judgment. He did not mean by this at all that religious belief was a matter of indifference. On the contrary, he repudiates the doctrine that men may be saved in any religion as 'most impious and detestable'; and it is clear enough to every reader of his works that he had as positive a creed as Knott himself. That God had given a law to man he strenuously maintained; but, he contended, The law so given purports to be complete, and as you admit it to be absolutely true, you have no right to contradict it. Its admitted obscurity in parts shows that its author regarded diversity of opinion as to those parts as innocent, and indeed necessary. Your argument is, Because it pleased God to give man a vague and incomplete revelation, therefore a body which claims the power of reducing it to a specific form, and of completing its outline, must be divine and infallible. Logic will require the substitution of 'cannot' for 'must.'

In a word, Chillingworth inferred from the absence of any distinct appointment of a permanent judge that every man was meant to apply the law to his own particular case for himself, and at his own risk. This, he says, is necessary at all events for many reasons, two of which will probably never be answered. The first is, that the object to be attained is admitted to be belief, but belief is involuntary and dependent upon reason, and the judge and the sheriff can produce only conformity; or, to use his own expressive words :—

'To force either any man to believe what he believes not, or any honest man to dissemble what he does believe (if God commands him to profess it) or to profess what he does not believe, all the powers in the world are too weak with all the powers in hell to assist them.'

The second is, that at all events every man must judge for himself as to the infallibility of his judge; and as the stream cannot rise above the source, so he can never get beyond his own opinion, mediate or immediate. 'So that, for aught I can see, judges we are and must be of all sides, every one for himself, and God for us all.' It is difficult to exceed the epigrammatic pithiness with which this is maintained and expounded in different places, as thus :—

'The difference between a Papist and a Protestant is this—not that the one judges and the other does not judge, but that the one judges his guide to be infallible, the other his way to be manifest.'

Or again :—

'You that would not have men follow their reason, what would you have them follow? Their passions, or pluck out their eyes and go blindfold? No, you say, but let them follow authority. In God's name let them. . . . But then for the authority you would have them follow, you will let them see reason why they should follow it, and is not this to go a little about? To leave reason for a short turn, and then to come to it again, and to do that which you condemn in others?'

One remarkable point in Chillingworth's book is that he anticipates in order to condemn it, and as a sort of *reductio ad absurdum*, the very doctrine of development which has attracted so much attention in our own time. Knott had spoken of the necessity of a judge to deal with 'new heresies that might arise.' To this Chillingworth answers:—

'To say that new heresies may arise is to say that new articles of faith may arise, and so some great ones among you stick not to profess in plain terms, who yet at the same time are not ashamed to profess that your whole doctrine is Catholic and apostolic.'

Elsewhere he speaks of the 'doctrines which . . . have insinuated themselves into the streams little by little; some in one age, some in another; some more anciently, some more lately; and some yet are embryos, yet hatching, and in the shell, as the Pope's infallibility, the blessed Virgin's Immaculate Conception,' etc.

Such is the general vein of argument which runs through the whole book, and is enforced and repeated in an infinite variety of different ways.

Another runs parallel with it, which is perhaps more interesting in our days. It is in the nature of an answer to Knott's constant demand, 'Where do you get your Bible except from the Church? What is the basis of your whole system?' It is in his answer to this question that Chillingworth displays the greatest amount of boldness. He says that the divine authority of the Bible rests upon general tradition—that is, upon historical evidence; and that it is a conclusion of reason, and that the whole Christian religion rests ultimately upon this foundation.

There is a remarkable passage near the end of the book which sets this in a very clear light:—

'Whatsoever man that is not of a perverse mind shall weigh with serious and mature deliberation those great moments of reason which may incline him to believe the divine authority of Scripture, and compare them with the light objections that in prudence can be made against it, he shall not choose but find sufficient, nay, abundant inducements to yield unto it firm faith and sincere obedience. Let that learned man Hugo Grotius speak for all the rest in his book of the *Truth of the Christian Religion*, which book whosoever attentively peruses shall find that a man may have great reason to be a Christian without dependence on your Church for any part of it.'[1]

---

[1] Modern liberals differ from both Chillingworth and Knott in not regarding the formation of religious opinion as a matter of judgment at all in the sense in which the word was used by Chillingworth.

There are many other curious passages (see especially vol. i. pp. 273-275), to the effect that reason alone can judge in controversies relating to Scripture, which have a direct and important bearing on the great discussions of our own days.

It may naturally be asked how such liberalism as this—for Chillingworth would, in the present day, be described as a Rationalist, and his whole book is directed to prove that a probable opinion is the utmost that can be attained in theological matters—came to be patronised by men like Laud. The answer appears to be, that Laud and Charles were far more disciplinarians than inquisitors. It was less their object to interfere with men's creeds than to regulate their practice. Chillingworth is asked by Knott, how in any case he could blame schism from the Church of England? He replies, in substance, that schism in itself is not a bad thing, but that schism without a reasonable cause is, and that he is willing to show the unreasonableness of the causes alleged by Dissenters for forsaking the ritual established by law.

His position, indeed, was very like that of the Federals as against the Confederates. They admitted that rebellion might be justifiable, but denied that this particular rebellion was justifiable. Most of the Royalist and High Church writers of that generation treat the Puritans, not as heretics, but rather as people of weak scrupulosity, which they ought in common sense to overcome. Laud was no inquisitor. His great offence was his determination to assert, in season and out of season, the right of the public authorities to regulate rituals and observances, and to enforce Church discipline. This, in the particular state of feeling which then prevailed, was consistent with extreme liberalism (not that Laud himself was extremely liberal) in matters of belief.

VIII

'THE LIBERTY OF PROPHESYING'[1]

THOSE who claim for the Church of England one of the highest places amongst Christian bodies for literary eminence, would naturally put forward Jeremy Taylor as one of the leading witnesses in favour of their proposition; and certainly it may be doubted whether any English ecclesiastical writer would be entitled to take precedence of him in a literary point of view, though he has been surpassed again and again by writers on special subjects whose eloquence, versatility, learning, and dexterity were greatly inferior to his.

It may seem a paradox, but it is nevertheless true, that there was a good deal of the journalist in Taylor, as in many of our other great ecclesiastical writers. The change which journalism has produced in the whole organisation of literature in modern times is

[1] *A Discourse of the Liberty of Prophesying, with its Just Limits and Temper, showing the Unreasonableness of Prescribing to other Men's Faith, and the Iniquity of Persecuting Differing Opinions.* By Jeremy Taylor.

very insufficiently understood. Look over the works of most of the great writers whose names are better known than their works, and you will find that a very large proportion of the many volumes which they fill consists of what, in the present day, would be articles in reviews, magazines, or newspapers. If, in the days of Jeremy Taylor and Baxter, or even in those of Swift, Burke, and Johnson, periodicals had been anything like what they are now, the names of these, and of many other great men, would have been far less well known, and their works would have consisted of many fewer volumes.

The system of journalism was very imperfect in Burke's days, but, such as it was, it absorbed much of his literary activity, especially in the earlier part of his career. Taylor had no such resource, but it would be easy to show, from the number and the character, no less than from the style of his minor works, how eminent he would have been as a journalist had journalism existed in his days. His style speaks for itself. It is incomparably eloquent and spirited. It has also the great merit of a singularly rich vein of wit, kept in check by regard to the nature of the subjects discussed, but constantly present; and it is harmonious and musical beyond that of any other English writer. There is in its periods a singular subdued pathos which it is difficult to analyse, but which is indicated with exquisite subtlety and skill by means of the choice and arrangement of very simple words in the midst of long passages.

Taylor has been justly reproached for redundance and prolixity, but in his case, as in Clarendon's, the reproach is often due rather to peculiar punctuation than to laxity of thought. One of the most eloquent passages, for instance, in the *Liberty of Prophesying* contains a sentence of thirty-one long lines.

By substituting full stops for the semicolons, and by avoiding a few Latin constructions which no modern writer would think of using, the passage would become a model of condensed and nervous eloquence. Indeed, the power of condensation was one of Taylor's great gifts. After expatiating over a subject at almost wearisome length, he will sum up the whole argument in a few lines with extraordinary vigour both of thought and expression.

Take, for instance, the following summary of the objections to the arguments in favour of the supremacy of the Pope, founded on the text, 'Thou art Peter.' The objections are the common ones as to the uncertainty of the meaning of the words, and as to the uncertainty of the fact that St. Peter ever was Pope at all, or ever was at Rome: 'A goodly building which relies upon an event that was accidental, whose purpose was but insinuated, the meaning of it but conjectured at, and this conjecture so uncertain that it was an imperfect aim at the purpose of an event which, whether it was true or no, was so uncertain that it is ten to one there was no such matter.' The condensation here is so great that it produces obscurity.

On the whole, Taylor's style comes very near to

modern English. He has almost shaken himself clear of the Latin tradition, but he has still a certain smack of it. Latin words which the language refused to assimilate are to be found here and there in his writings. 'This is a *complexion*'—*i.e.* complication — of several distinct propositions. 'Scripture in its plain *expresses*.' 'We have an *express* out of the same sermon of St. Peter.' 'All the particulars are now united by way of *constipation*'—a word which is now exclusively medical. 'Adiaphorous' for indifferent is common, and so is the word 'consign' in the sense of marking by a sign—'*Consign* that covenant,' 'he did *consign* his love,' etc. The word has now become either mercantile, as when we 'consign' a parcel of goods—or historico-sentimental; some writers would talk of consigning a man's remains to the tomb.

The *Liberty of Prophesying* is one of the most characteristic of its author's works, and though in later life he receded from some of the positions there taken up, it seems probable that it will always be his principal title to fame. It is an extraordinary book, and proves to demonstration the fact that, amongst writers of the very first class, theological liberalism, as we should call it in the present day, had made extraordinary progress in the seventeenth century, though, by a singular combination of circumstances, it was not only not connected with the contemporary movement towards political liberty, but was actually opposed to it.

Clarendon, Falkland, Chillingworth, and Hales, in the earlier part of Charles I.'s reign, and

Jeremy Taylor at a later period, held a position not altogether unlike that of the modern school of liberal theologians; and though they do not appear to have had any decisive or even very powerful influence over the thoughts of their age, or to have been able to mitigate the fierce bigotry of its contending parties to any very considerable extent, their writings will always be entitled to respect and admiration, not only because of their inherent merit, but because, when they were written, they were unparalleled in any other Christian church, and because they first set the subject of religious controversy upon its true foundation. So severe a critic as Hallam, writing in the nineteenth century, could still feel himself compelled to say that Chillingworth's *Religion of Protestants,* and Bossuet's *Exposition de la foi catholique,* represented the utmost stretch of the human mind in opposite directions upon the great subject which they treated.

The genealogy of these celebrated works is easily traced. Hooker must be regarded as the founder of the school. The *Ecclesiastical Polity* is a vindication of the competency of reason to decide questions of Church government on grounds of expediency; and in the discharge of this task Hooker rises from time to time to a pitch of positive enthusiasm upon the powers — we might almost say the attributes — of reason. He speaks of it with an enthusiasm which in the present day would make him a suspected, not to say a dangerous, person.

Chillingworth was Hooker's greatest disciple. His great book is the most vigorous protest that has ever yet been written against that state of mind which pathetic and ingenious writers of our own day have made very prominent, and which flies to Popery as the only refuge from scepticism. The *Religion of Protestants* applies to the faith of individuals the very same principles which the *Ecclesiastical Polity* asserts in relation to Church government. Reason, says Hooker, is the guide of the legislator in ecclesiastical as well as in civil affairs. Reason, adds Chillingworth, is the organ by which individuals are certified of the truth of their religious creed.

Jeremy Taylor builds on these foundations, but he goes a step farther; for he adds to the principles of Hooker and Chillingworth the observation that the reason of different men tends to different results, even when exercised with the best intentions and with all possible industry; and thence he deduces the doctrine of general toleration—a doctrine which had a very long road to travel, after his day, before its truth was generally and fully recognised. It would, of course, be untrue to assert that any of these three eminent men taught the doctrines which we have ascribed to them nakedly, and without limitation. It is in the nature of such doctrines to be realised slowly, and only by the successive efforts of many minds. Of Hooker and Chillingworth we have already spoken. Taylor's work we will now proceed to examine more in detail.

The *Liberty of Prophesying* is by no means a philosophical book, as we understand philosophy in these days. It does not begin at the beginning, and build up a regular edifice of connected propositions. On the contrary, it takes theology in general for granted, and sets out to establish, by recognised means, a variety of particular results. Taylor's principles undoubtedly lead to the conclusion that every conceivable theological opinion, if held in good faith, is in itself innocent; but though, in consistency, he ought to have thought thus, in fact he did not. Such an opinion, indeed, is by no means generally held, and, as Mr. Lecky would say, 'realised' even in our own days.

Taylor does not go into the nature of faith and the grounds on which it rests, but assumes that there are some things which it is a positive duty to believe; and his first proposition is, that 'the duty of faith is completed in believing the articles of the Apostles' Creed.' He then inquires at length into heresy, which he seems to have considered—for his language throughout this chapter is vague and difficult to follow—as consisting in denying an article of the Apostles' Creed from corrupt motives. Consequently, according to Taylor, if a man rejected such an article from pride, he would be a heretic, but if he rejected it because in good faith he thought it false, he would not; and this, although the proud man and the humble man might both allege the very same intellectual grounds for their opinion. Taylor does not in so many words confine heresy to a direct denial of articles in the Apostles' Creed; but his reasoning implies it.

The rest of the book consists in arguments to show in detail that Scripture is obscure in matters not fundamental—*i.e.* not in the Apostles' Creed—and cannot be made an authority for anything else; that tradition is untrustworthy on a thousand grounds; that the Fathers contradict each other, and that the same is true of Councils and of Popes; besides which, it is altogether impossible to find any foundation upon which Popes and Councils can base their claims. Reason is the best judge of controversies. Its errors, if *bonâ fide*, are harmless, and we ought all to tolerate each other and permit a general 'liberty of prophesying.'

In order to illustrate the scope of his argument, he examines what in his day were the two extreme cases —the cases, namely, of the Anabaptists and the Roman Catholics. He goes with much minuteness into the question whether the doctrines of adult baptism and transubstantiation may be tolerated, and concludes that they may, inasmuch as both are capable of being held in perfect good faith, and neither can be shown to be in any respect injurious to the public. On the other hand, the opinions of the Anabaptists, and also those of the Roman Catholics, on the question of the civil government and the powers of the Pope, are not to be tolerated for an instant.

Nothing can be more peremptory than the way in which Taylor asserts the supremacy of State interest over all theological considerations whatever. 'Religion is to meliorate the condition of a people, not to do it disadvantage; and, therefore, those doctrines that inconvenience the public are no parts of true religion.' The Council of Nice may have appeared to condemn the use of arms, and Clemens Alexandrinus says that the secret tradition of the Apostles was to the same effect; but either these authorities are to be slighted, or to be made receptive of any interpretation, rather than the Commonwealth be disarmed of its necessary supports.'

Nay, the Sermon on the Mount is treated in the same way. 'Suppose there were divers places of Scripture which did seemingly restrain the political use of the sword; yet since the avoiding a personal inconvenience hath by all men been accounted sufficient reason to interpret Scripture to any sense rather than the literal, which infers an unreasonable inconvenience (and therefore the "putting out an eye" and the "cutting off a hand" is expounded by mortifying a vice and killing a criminal habit), much rather must the allegations against the power of the sword endure any sense rather than that it should be thought that Christianity should destroy that which is the only instrument of justice.'

Such is an outline of the argument of this memorable book. It is a curious instance of the lengths to which men will go, in what they themselves would regard as a heterodox direction, under the shelter of excuses which every one but themselves must see to be untenable. Jeremy Taylor would probably have been indignant at the imputation of holding that it is no sin to be a Mahometan, a Buddhist, a Deist, or an Atheist, so long as those opinions are held in good faith. He would have said, and with truth, that he held it to be a positive duty to believe the Apostles' Creed. Nothing, however, can be more certain than that his principles would justify disbelief in every article of the Apostles' Creed, upon grounds precisely similar to those by which he justifies doubts as to the articles decided on at Nice.

In a word, if the *Liberty of Prophesying* be taken as an attack upon the notion that there is any infallible guide at all to theological truth, and as an argument in favour of the moral innocence of all opinions whatever held in good faith, it is extremely powerful, and incomparably eloquent and persuasive. If it be viewed as a solution in any other sense of the great problem of religious toleration, it is altogether unsatisfactory.

This, however, is not the way in which so great a work should be criticised. In order to do it the most scanty justice, we must put ourselves, if possible, at the author's point of view, and try to see his subject as he saw it.

We must, then, remember, in the first place, that the whole aspect of theology, the way in which people viewed it, and its position amongst the various departments of human thought, were fundamentally different in Taylor's day from what they now are. It appears to have been viewed in a far more definite and positive light than that in which we, with our habits of thought, regard it. Its state might be compared, with a good deal of truth, to that of international law in our own time, or of English constitutional law in the last century.

'Is' and 'ought to be' were identical terms in its vocabulary, and Taylor's observation that 'those doctrines that inconvenience the public are no parts of true religion' must be taken as the key to a great part of his speculations and those of his contemporaries. Their object was strictly practical. It was not to investigate truth simply, but to supply a theory which should square as well as might be with established opinions, and should at the same time justify institutions to which the writer was attached, or measures of which he was the advocate.

Controversial theology, in short, is advocacy in that theoretical and general stage which is the indispensable preparation for the direct advocacy of specific measures and institutions. Its value, therefore, must in general be tested rather by its skill than its truth—by its cogency *ad homines*, and not by its instructiveness to all men at all times.

This remark enables us to understand Taylor's position with respect to the Apostles' Creed, which appears at first sight so weak that it is difficult to understand why so able a man took it up. It is indeed exceedingly weak as against those who deny the necessity of any dogmatic belief at all, but it is by no means weak as against those who contend for the necessity of a dogmatic belief, and extend its limits to what their adversaries consider an unreasonable extent.

The position, indeed, was not by any means

peculiar to Jeremy Taylor. It was the distinctive theory of a considerable school. Chillingworth insisted on it at length, and with his usual acuteness; and it is also maintained by Laud in his controversy with Fisher the Jesuit. The truth is, that the doctrine came in usefully at a particular stage of the Roman Catholic controversy, and must be considered in connection with that controversy.

It was in the nature of an answer made by the Protestant controversialist, to an objection raised by his antagonist, against an argument used by the Protestant to show that the Church of Rome had not the right to be a judge of controversy. To use the language of special pleading, it was a replication in a set of pleadings which may be thus stated:

A living judge of controversy is superfluous, inasmuch as all the necessary articles of Christian faith are clearly revealed in the Bible. One of the pleas in answer to this was, It is not certain what articles are necessary, and this has to be ascertained. The reply was, All necessary articles of faith are contained in the Apostles' Creed. The evidence in support of this reply was, that the Apostles' Creed was the oldest formal statement of the Christian faith; that it was probably older than the New Testament itself; and that, at all events, for the first three centuries, it was universally considered a sufficient profession of Christian belief.

We cannot enter at length into the subject, but any one who will view the writings of Taylor and his contemporaries in their true light, as *argumenta ad homines*, and who will read his chapter on the subject, will, we think, readily perceive that, whatever Taylor's argument may have been worth as against modern Liberals, it was no easy matter for those to whom it was addressed to answer it.

Taylor's view of heresy, as residing, not in the mistakes of the understanding, but in the misconduct of the will, won for him, amongst other things, the enthusiastic sympathy and admiration of Coleridge, who lavishes upon this part of the work a great amount of praise, conveyed in that mystical language of which he was so great a master. Considered in itself, it appears to us the weakest part of the book. It retains the words 'heretic' and 'heresy,' but defines them in such a manner that it makes them altogether superfluous. If heresy consists not in the opinions held, but in the motives for which men hold them, the motives and not the opinions constitute the sin; and thus heresy is only an alias for pride, sensuality, ambition, etc., actuating a man who turns his thoughts to religious subjects. There is, moreover, a sort of hesitation and confusion in the way in which the thought is worked out. The chapter conveys the impression that the author was reluctant, either from fear or from some other motive, to work out his meaning clearly and fully. If he had done so, and if, in order to do so, he had put something of a curb on the luxuriance of his language, it can hardly be doubted that he would have been brought to consider questions which lay straight before him, but which he probably wished to avoid.

If, however, the chapter on heresy is viewed practically, a very different criticism will be required. From that point of view, it may be put by the side of the liberal theories of the British Constitution, Erskine's Speeches upon the Law of Libel, or any other adaptation of an existing phraseology to a new and enlarged view of things.

Heresy, in the middle of the seventeenth century, was a word of terror. The writ *de hæretico comburendo* was still part of the law of the land, and men had been burnt for being Arians and Anabaptists within living memory. Such spirits cannot be exorcised roughly. They are a kind that cometh not forth but by accommodation and management; and though, from a purely speculative point of view, a great deal might be said against Jeremy Taylor's view of the nature of heresy, its practical value as an emollient and lenitive can hardly be exaggerated.

Nothing can be more unphilosophical than a contempt for air-cushions and swimming-bladders. In all political, moral, and theological matters they are practically indispensable. People must be led by degrees to unfamiliar conclusions. The innocence of error was in Taylor's day a startling and unfamiliar doctrine. To restrict the limits of heresy by definition was the way to bring people gently and by easy degrees to indifference to it, just as the gradual restriction of the law of libel to narrow limits by forensic discussion, gradually introduced practically unlimited freedom of political and religious discussion.

We do not mean to attribute to Taylor a conscious design to bring about this result. It is highly probable that he would himself have been alarmed at the full application of his own doctrines. We know, indeed, that after the Restoration he retracted, or at least modified, them, though we agree with Mr. Lecky in thinking that the *Liberty of Prophesying* must be taken to be the expression of his real sentiments.

The three destructive chapters are undoubtedly the most forcible part of the work. The impossibility of finding any infallible guide to truth, and the superiority of reason to all other guides, are insisted upon with extraordinary vigour, and with a profusion of learning which makes one feel thankful that the apology which Taylor makes in his preface for not multiplying quotations, because he had no library at hand, was necessary. If he had had a library to go to, the fuel would have interfered with the fire. In these chapters, a degree of liberty and independence of mind is shown, which, even in our day, is extremely rare amongst the clergy.

Indeed, many of the doctrines which a clerical writer of the present day would not dare to utter, unless he wrapped them up in a sort of honied mystical phraseology, are expressed by Taylor in the clearest and plainest words that he could find. Take, for instance, his doctrine that reason is the only rule of faith :—

'By *reason* I do not mean a distinct topic, but a transcendent that runs through all topics; for reason, like logic, is the instrument of all things else; and when revelation, and philosophy, and public experience, and all other grounds of probability or demonstration have supplied us with matter, then reason does but make use of them.'

Compare this plain-speaking with the passage in the *Essays and Reviews* about the 'verifying faculty,' which to many respectable people appeared an unheard-of monster, and we shall get a notion of the difference in vigour between the theologians of the seventeenth and those of the nineteenth century. Look, again, at the following passage about miracles, which Taylor considers as of use only to attract attention :—

'Although the argument drawn from miracles is good to attest a holy doctrine, which by its own worth will support itself, after way is a little made for it by miracles, yet of itself, and by its own reputation, it will not support any fabric; for instead of proving a doctrine to be true, it makes that the miracles themselves are suspected to be illusions if they be pretended in behalf of a doctrine which we have reason to account false. And, therefore, the Jews did not believe Christ's doctrine for his miracles, but disbelieved the truth of his miracles, because they did not like his doctrine. And if the holiness of his doctrine, and the Spirit of God by inspirations and infusions, and by that which St. Peter calls "a surer word of prophecy," had not attested the divinity both of his person and his office, we should have wanted many degrees of confidence which now we have upon the truth of Christian religion.'

It is impossible to put more forcibly and pointedly the very doctrines which in our day cause the ears of men to tingle, even when they are veiled in a haze of devotional language. The only really painful feeling experienced in reading our standard divines, arises from contrasts of this kind between the manliness of the past, and the affectation, timidity, and obscurity of the present. If any theological writer should arise with a gift of perfect plainness of speech, perfect distinctness and honesty of thought, and a due coldness of manner, he would be as welcome, perhaps not as flowers in May, but as a sharp frost after a November fog.

IX

JEREMY TAYLOR AS A MORALIST [1]

HARDLY any subject is so curious in itself, or has fallen so much into neglect, as what Roman Catholics call moral theology, which in our own time and country is better known by the highly unpopular title of casuistry. The reason why this subject has fallen into so much neglect in Protestant communities in general, and in England at least as much as elsewhere, is obvious enough.

Casuistry is the indispensable complement to the practice of confession, and when the tribunal by which the law is administered is closed it is but natural that the law itself should fall into oblivion. There can, however, we think, be very little doubt that, of the many forgotten departments of learning which contain curious matter of different kinds, few would give so rich a return, to the labour of any one adventurous enough to explore it, as the subject of casuistry.

[1] *Ductor Dubitantium; or, the Rule of Conscience.* By Jeremy Taylor. Vols. xi. xii. xiii. and xiv. of Heber's edition of Bishop Taylor's works.

We do not believe, for instance, that it will ever be possible to understand and appreciate the true character of some of the most characteristic doctrines of the Reformation without a better knowledge of the general bearings of casuistry than almost any one in the present day possesses.

It is highly probable, for instance, that if the various controversies about justification by faith, faith and works, and other such topics, were ever to be translated out of the scholastic dialect into modern forms of speech, it would be found that the existence of casuistry, the conception of a legal measure to which all human actions could be reduced, and of a spiritual tribunal established for the purpose of sitting in judgment upon every part of the conduct of all classes of human beings, had a great deal to do with the interest which the subject excited.

A theory which enabled men to dispense altogether with such a tribunal, and which was founded upon, and to a great extent identified with, the sentiment which in our own days would regard it as fundamentally immoral, would have immense attractions for a very large part of mankind. Whether the doctrine of justification by faith had anything—and if so, how much—to do with this sentiment, is a question on which we do not profess to offer anything more than a suggestion, which it may possibly be worth the while of those who have special knowledge of the question to consider.

Whatever may have been the general bearings and

connections of the subject, it is an indisputable truth that systematic treatises on morality, regarded from the theological point of view, were—in Protestant countries, and especially in our own—rare, in the age which immediately followed the Reformation.

Taylor himself says (xi. 346), 'For any public provisions of books of casuistical theology we were almost wholly unprovided, and like the children of Israel in the days of Saul and Jonathan, we were forced to go down to the forges of the Philistines to sharpen every man his share and his coulter, his axe and his mattock.'

He proceeds, after some severe criticism of the Romish casuists, to describe the character of his own book, which he regards (xi. 656) as 'an institution of moral theology,' a treatise, not intended to be used as a digest or 'exhaustive body of particular cases of conscience' (xi. 363), but as a statement of the theory of the whole subject. As to particular cases, he says, 'I find that they are infinite, and my life is not so. . . . I therefore resolved upon another way which, although no man before me hath had in writing cases of conscience, yet I cannot say it is new, for I took my pattern out of Tribonianus the lawyer, who, out of the laws of the old Romans, collected some choice rules, which give answer to very many cases that happen.'

His book may thus be regarded as an attempt, by a man of genius and of marvellous learning and industry, to extract from boundless heaps of material, not by any means unlike the contents of a library full of law reports, though arranged in a very different manner, the theory of the whole subject of casuistry.

He has not, however, confined himself by any means to the casuists. On the contrary, his book is filled with references to nearly every department of literature, for, to say nothing of the pleasure which he naturally took in the employment, not to say the display, of his wonderful learning upon all subjects, he obviously shared in the feeling which acted so strongly upon Grotius (to take a very prominent example), that it was desirable in all such inquiries, to confirm the results of abstract speculation by a continual appeal to the habitual sentiments of mankind, as displayed by the language of writers who might be supposed, from their popularity, to be specially well fitted to express them.

The general result is extremely curious. The *Ductor Dubitantium* is spread over four volumes of Bishop Heber's edition of Taylor's works, and fills 1707 very full octavo pages. It is by no means easy reading, nor can we honestly say that it repays the labour of being read straight through, still a good deal is to be learnt from that process, both as to the character of Taylor's own mind, and as to the nature of a system which for centuries exercised so vast an influence over human conduct, and which, to this very day, retains its power in many parts of the world, and over large and important classes, in a form which, if it differs to some extent from that under which Taylor knew it, still closely resembles it.

As to the light thrown by the *Ductor Dubitantium*

upon the mind of its author, it illustrates his intellect to perfection, though it affords comparatively little scope for the employment of the eloquence which was his most popular, and perhaps his most characteristic gift. He was a man of what, in these days, looks like incredible learning. He had very great ingenuity, and, as far as he went, remarkable independence of mind; but his independence was by no means thoroughgoing, and his ingenuity never went to the foundations of things. He was a great philosopher according to the notions of philosophy which were becoming old-fashioned even in his day, but he had not the remotest notion of what we in these days understand by philosophy. He does not even appear to have understood the existence of such questions as Hobbes, for instance, passed his life in debating.

But the best way of illustrating this will be to give some account of the contents of his book. Its length, and the peculiarity of its contents, make this a matter of some difficulty; but we propose on the present occasion to attempt to give some account of the elements into which Taylor's speculations may be resolved, and of the method on which they are conducted, reserving for a future occasion the task of attempting to translate into its modern equivalents his general theory of morality.

The book may be reduced to three principal elements. It is founded upon what, for want of a better name, must be called the scholastic or Aristotelian philosophy, as understood by writers of that age, and on this there is built a superstructure composed, in nearly equal proportions, of theological and legal authorities, the legal authorities being almost exclusively drawn from the civil law.

It is remarkable that of English law Taylor knew hardly anything. He refers to it very seldom, and when he does, not very correctly. But he quotes civil lawyers on all occasions, and with an odd tacit assumption, that the rules which they lay down, have about them some peculiarly fixed quality differing from the theories of more modern writers. He thus brings out at last a very odd result. His system is positive and precise enough, and is as coherent as any other; but it is impossible to say what it is worth. It neither enables us to affirm that a given act has a tendency to produce happiness, nor that it is agreeable to the civil law, nor that it is approved of by the canonists. It shows, in a word, nothing except the places of actions in a complicated and arbitrary system, compounded by Taylor himself out of these and some other authorities. To give an idea of the result, we will take separately some illustrations of the place occupied in his system by each of the three elements in question.

The first element to be examined is the scholastic philosophy by which every part of the book is pervaded, and from which, indeed, its whole method is derived. Every part of the book supplies illustrations of this, but perhaps as remarkable a one as any, is to be found in the distribution of the subject given (oddly enough) at the beginning of the fourth and last book. 'He that intends to consider anything fully and entirely, must consider it in all the four kinds of causes;' and he then points out that he has considered 'the formal cause, or essentiality, of good and evil;' which is, 'the doing it with or against conscience.' The 'material cause' . . . . 'which is the laws of God and man, by a conformity to which the action is good, and if it disagrees materially, evil;' and lastly he comes to the efficient 'and final causes' of all human actions. The will is the efficient cause. What we should call motive appears to be what Taylor calls the final cause; though, as we shall have occasion to observe hereafter, he explains himself on this head very obscurely.

This unnatural arrangement has the effect (for one thing) of throwing extreme obscurity over the whole book. It is studded throughout with distinctions about matter and form, and with phraseology which, in these days, hardly any one can understand. Take the following as specimens :—

'The external act is the occasion of the intending or extending the internal, but directly and of itself increases not the goodness or the badness of it. For the external is not properly and formally good or bad, but only objectively and materially; just as a wall cannot increase the whiteness unless the quality itself be intended by its own principle (xiv. 349). . . . For although in nature and logic time consignifies— that is, it does the work of accidents, and appendages, and circumstances, yet in theology it signifies and effects too; time may signify a substantial duty, and effect a material pardon (xiii. 189). . . . There is a double consent to a proposition; the one is direct, the other a reflex; the first is directly terminated upon the honesty or dishonesty of the object, the other upon the manner of it, and modality.'

Which, as appears from the context, is a way of saying that we sometimes have to act for the best without being sure of our facts. The point at issue is whether a priest was right in giving absolution upon evidence of repentance, supposed by some theologians to be sufficient, though his own view was that it was ambiguous, the penitent being at the point of death and unable to clear the matter up further.

It is generally possible to make out from the context what Taylor's meaning in such passages as these really was, and the question is rather one of expression than of substance; but his philosophy was as scholastic as his phraseology and this circumstance throws the greatest obscurity and confusion over large parts of his work. He appears to have been altogether unaware of the importance of having single and distinct meanings for fundamental terms, and the consequence is, that he uses them in a great variety of senses, meaning by the same word the most different things at different times.

He has no clear notion of the human mind and its various faculties, and of their relation to each other.

Great part, perhaps the greater part, of his language about the will and the conscience assumes that they are separate independent beings between whom definite relations exist. Take the following accounts of the will: 'The will is the mistress of all our actions, of all but such as are necessary and natural, and therefore to her it is to be imputed whatsoever be done' (xiv. 278); 'all other faculties are natural and necessary and obedient, this only is the empress, and is free, and mistress of the action' (*ib.* 285). So we are told elsewhere that 'the will may choose a less good and reject the greater' (xii. 75), and that it may cause the understanding 'to apply a general proposition to a particular case' (xii. 81) without proper grounds.

The language of which these expressions are a specimen, implies that will has a special independent existence of its own, that it is, so to speak, a subordinate man who governs the conduct of the whole of which he forms a part.

It is still worse with respect to conscience. The first words of the book (xi. 369) define conscience thus: 'Conscience is the mind of a man governed by a rule and measured by the proportions of good and evil, in order to practice—namely, to conduct all our relations and all our intercourse between God, our neighbours, and ourselves; that is in all moral actions.' The meaning of a mind governed by a rule and measured by proportions is not in itself by any means clear, but the explanation makes it ten times darker.

The greater part of the first book is a curious

mixture of rhetoric and scholastic logic, from which we learn that 'conscience is in God's stead to give us laws' (370); that it is God's 'vicegerent and subordinate' (xii. 18); that it is sometimes taken for 'the practical intellectual faculty,' sometimes for 'the habitual persuasion and belief of the principles written there,' and sometimes for 'any single operation and action of conscience' (372). That it is 'a conjunction of the universal practical law with the particular moral action' (382)—a definition (it is quoted by Taylor from Thomas Aquinas) which appears to treat conscience as the result of a logical process. This is explained to mean, in the next page, that conscience is a 'complication of acts'—the act, namely, of saying murder is wrong, and the act of affirming that to kill Uriah is murder. We afterwards (387) learn that 'the duties and offices of conscience are to dictate, and to testify or bear witness, to accuse or excuse, to loose or bind.' These phrases are rendered still more perplexing by the elaborate discussion which follows them, on the right or sure conscience, the erroneous conscience, the probable or thinking conscience, the doubtful conscience, and the scrupulous conscience.

We can discuss without much difficulty, or at least without much fear of being misunderstood, the cases of men who rightly believe given actions to be right, who wrongly believe given actions to be right, who doubt but decide to act upon one of the possible suppositions, who doubt without deciding, and who are too prone to doubt; but the whole subject is greatly perplexed by the introduction of a supposed entity called conscience, which is regarded as right, as confidently erroneous, as doubtful, or as scrupulous. This imperfect philosophical basis, and the awkward phraseology which is so closely connected with it, greatly diminish the value of Taylor's book to all modern readers, and make a large proportion of his discussions appear irrelevant or unintelligible.

Apart from this Taylor's book furnishes a good illustration of the endless perplexities which arise in practice from that form of the doctrine of innate ideas which was generally accepted in his time, and against which in the next generation Locke directed his vigorous attacks. The following passages are very distinct enunciations of this theory:—

'For those things which are first inspirated, which are universal principles, which are consented to by all men without a teacher, those which Aristotle calls κοινὰς ἐννοίας, those are always the last removed, etc. (xi. 417). . . . Our reason or understanding apprehends things three several ways; the first is called νόησις, or the "first notices" of things abstract and the *primo intelligibilia* such as are. The whole is greater than the half of the whole—good is to be chosen, God is to be loved. Nothing can be and not be at the same time, for these are objects of the simple understanding, congenite notices, encreated with the understanding' (xi. 440).

This crude and clumsy theory pervades the whole of the book. It assumes throughout that we have within us a sort of unwritten dictionary which enables us, by turning, for instance, to such a word as 'just' or 'justice,' to ascertain at once whether a given thing is just or not. It would be hard to suggest a better test, by which to ascertain whether or not a given writer is really philosophical, than that of considering whether he appreciates the importance of assigning precise meanings to common words, like 'just,' 'law,' 'right,' and 'wrong.' If not, whatever else he is, he is no philosopher.

The second of the elements of which Taylor's book is composed is the Canon Law, and the works of the casuists. He uses them in a very remarkable way. He clearly sees, on the one hand, that they were not laws properly so called in England; but, on the other hand, he entertains for them a sort of respect by no means unlike that which an English lawyer would feel for the American Law Reports.

The way in which he quotes them introduces his reader almost into a new world, and carries him back to a time when a state of things existed of which we see at present only the vestiges. They one and all imply the existence of an ecclesiastical measure of right and wrong, enforced upon individuals by the unrestrained use of the spiritual sanction, and modifying in the most curious way every one of the relations of life. Moral theology, as understood by the authors whom Taylor so freely quotes, can have been nothing less than a universal ethical system claiming to regulate all human conduct, and in so far as it prevailed constituting its authorised interpreters the moral sovereigns of the human race. Taylor appears to have accepted this system to a certain extent as a branch of that common law of the Christian Church to which, like his master Laud, he attached so much importance.

As instances of the immense importance of such a system, we may observe that such questions as the degree of moral authority belonging to the civil magistrate, the moral weight to be attached to human laws, and the right in particular cases to evade them, are all treated under this system as theological questions. Everything which relates to marriage in particular is treated in this way. Taylor, for instance, supposed that it was possible to say what was, and what not, a valid marriage by the law of nature apart from all positive human laws whatever, and to determine with exact precision all the moral duties arising out of such a conclusion.

Nothing can have a more singular effect upon a modern reader than the strange cross between law and morals thus produced. The sanctions of the rules are moral and religious, but the rules themselves have often all the harshness and disregard of special results, which could be found in the most technical system of law.

A single instance will illustrate this: 'Francisco Biretti, a Venetian gentleman, full of amours' . . . 'courts Julia, a senator's daughter, but with secret intent to abuse her, and so to leave her.' Julia's father forces her to consent to a contract with Biretti, who, still retaining his original intention, makes the contract, and takes advantage of it to seduce Julia. The law declares this to be a marriage, but Biretti marries another woman in the meantime, and Taylor says that the second marriage was good in conscience, although the law held the first transaction to be a marriage. 'Now the law presumes that after contract their congress did declare a marriage, for it supposes and presumes a consent, and yet without says if there was no consent there was no marriage.' Biretti knew that there was no consent, as his intention was seduction, and not marriage. He knew, therefore, that the presumption upon which the law proceeded to declare him to be Julia's husband was false in fact, therefore he is 'relieved in conscience' though 'condemned by the presumption.' The law did well to declare in favour of Julia, 'but Francisco, who knew that which the law could not know' (namely, the state of his own mind), 'was bound to make amends to Julia as well as he could, but to pursue the marriage with Antonia, and to dwell with her' (xiii. 283, 284). It would be difficult to give a better instance of the strange confusions into which casuists fell when they tried to solve absolutely every conceivable moral problem by putting together moral obligations, technical rules of evidence, and arbitrary matters as to the essence of marriage, which rest upon no other than a purely fanciful basis.

The last element worth noticing in the composition of Taylor's book is the purely legal one. He apparently knew little of English law, and cared less for it. He hardly ever refers to it except to quote the rule of the common law as to the effect of coercion by a husband in crimes committed by married women; and to sanction the vulgar error that 'a butcher is made incapable of being at the inquest of life and death' (xiii. 349). His deficiencies in this respect, however, are compensated by a positive passion for civil law. He regards it on every occasion in the light of a science, having an independent existence of its own hardly capable of being varied, and constituting a sort of philosophy of human actions from which no appeal can be admitted. It would be easy to fill any number of pages with illustrations of this; indeed, a great part of the book might be transcribed in illustration of it.

We must content ourselves with one or two. In discussing the question of the relation of the spiritual and temporal powers, Taylor says 'and here comes in that rule of the law "the accessory follows the nature of the principal" which hath been so infinitely mistaken and abused by the pretences of Romanists and Presbytery, for the establishing an empire ecclesiastical in things belonging to themselves, not to God.'

The soul was regarded as the principal, the body as the accessory, whence, of course, it followed that the temporal power was subservient to the spiritual. In order to meet this Taylor goes into a lengthy disquisition about the meaning of the rule, which he ascertains by introducing what amount really to nothing more than a variety of illustrations of the fact, that there are different senses in which the words principal and accessory may be used, and that some of these do, while others do not, apply to the case of the soul and the body. Many of these senses are mere arbitrary technicalities of the Roman lawyers. Taylor, for instance, says, 'A jewel set in gold is much better than the gold, but yet the gold is the principal, because it' (*i.e.* the jewel) 'was put there to illustrate and adorn the gold, according to that of Ulpian,' etc. (xiii. 573, 574). Another good illustration of the same thing occurs in the manner in which Taylor treats the whole question of the mutual rights and duties of parents and children (xiv. 182-199).

These are the three chief elements out of which the elaborate system of morals which fills the *Ductor Dubitantium* is made up.

X

JEREMY TAYLOR AS A MORALIST[1]

(Second Notice)

HAVING given some account of the different elements of which Taylor's great work on casuistry is composed, we propose, on the present occasion, to attempt to draw an outline of its contents, and to show its relation to subsequent and contemporary moral speculations.

The *Ductor Dubitantium* is divided into four books, which treat respectively of Conscience, its different kinds, and the general rules for conducting it; of the Law of Nature in general, and particularly as it is commanded and digested by Christ, and of the manner in which it is to be interpreted; of Human Laws, civil and ecclesiastical, and of the degree of obligation which they impose upon the conscience; and, lastly, of the Nature of Good and Evil, and

---

[1] *Ductor Dubitantium; or, the Rule of Conscience.* By Jeremy Taylor. Vols. xi. xii. xiii. and xiv. of Heber's edition of Bishop Taylor's works.

of Human Actions, and their efficient and final causes.

For reasons referred to in our former article, we will begin with the Fourth Book. Its subject is, 'The Nature and Causes of Good and Evil, their limits and circumstances, their aggravations and diminutions,' or, which Taylor regards as being the same thing, 'the efficient and the final causes of all human actions.' The efficient cause of human actions is the will—'the mistress of all our actions.' The will is free, and this liberty, 'agreeable to the whole method and purpose, the economy and design of human nature and being' (xiv. 281), is an imperfection.

In the whole book there is no more characteristic passage than the one in which this is explained. It is too long to quote, and in parts very eloquent; but the point of it is that our liberty is imperfect, and that liberty itself is an imperfection arising from the mixture of good and evil in ourselves and in the constitution of the world. The reason of this is shortly expressed as follows:—

'If we understood all the degrees of amability in the service of God, and if we could love God as he deserves . . . we should have no liberty left, nothing concerning which we could deliberate. . . . The saints and angels in Heaven, and God himself, love good and cannot choose evil, because to do so were imperfection and infelicity, and the devils and accursed souls hate all good without liberty and indifferency, but between these is the state of man in the days of his pilgrimage.'

He also says, 'In moral and spiritual things liberty and indetermination are weakness, and suppose a great infirmity of our reason and a great want of love.' In this theory Taylor, in effect, concedes all that a believer in the modern doctrine of philosophical necessity would contend for—namely, that what is commonly described as the consciousness of liberty, is nothing but the condition of a man who does not know his own mind. 'Liberty of will,' says Taylor, 'is like the motion of a magnetic needle towards the North, full of trembling and uncertainty, till it be fixed in the beloved point; it wavers as long as it is free, and is at rest when it can choose no more' (xiv. 286). Freedom, according to this, is only the sense of uncertainty of which we are conscious whilst we are employed in weighing motives.

There are, however, abundant indications in other parts of the chapter that Taylor did not perceive the full force of the line of thought towards which his rhetoric pointed; but it is needless to insist upon this. He goes on to point out (what no doubt is true) that voluntary actions only are moral, and he then proceeds to the question whether any voluntary acts can be indifferent (291, 292), and decides it in the negative; an idle word is a sin because it is idle, and conversely men are bound (Question ii. 297-305) to live in a manner 'fitted to the general design of a Christian's life,' and to adapt all their conduct to that end, so that every action of their lives may be in some degree actively good.

Next, he considers how the will may act, in respect of the immediate or remote character of its connection with its acts; and this involves him in most singular questions about ratification (305-309), 'a distinction known in the civil law between "mandatum" and "jussio"' (310), (instigation by an equal and the command of a superior) and the question how far silence gives consent (315-318), and whether in any case it is lawful to permit sin; as, for instance, when 'Pancirone, an Italian gentleman,' gave a German ambassador liquor enough to get drunk 'after his country fashion' (319).

He also discusses the question of the moral guilt of accessories and principals in the second degree, the question how far it is lawful to 'make or provide the instruments which usually minister to sin.' Acts, he says, 'which minister only to vanity and trifling pleasures are of ill fame.' A Christian is bound to do something profitable to the commonwealth and acceptable to God; but Taylor will not go so far as to say that a man who lives by juggling is to be 'directly condemned for this, and said to be in a state of damnation.' Still, 'if he comes near a spiritual guide,' he is 'to be called off from that which at the best is good for nothing' (325).

Card-making and dice-making he regards as lawful (324), because in certain cases (327-333) and subject to rules (333-344) it is lawful to play at cards and dice.

In the course of his disquisition upon this point a curious passage occurs which illustrates the state of knowledge of the time, and in particular the total absence in Taylor's mind of any just notions of chance or probability:—

'In these cases, I have heard from them that have skill in such things, there are such strange chances, such promoting of a hand by fancy and little arts of geomancy, such constant winning on one side, such unreasonable losses on the other, and these strange contingencies produce such horrible effects that it is not improbable that God hath permitted the conduct of such games of chance to the Devil, who will order them to where he can do the most mischief' (337).

From the question of principal and agent, Taylor passes to the question of intention, and of the degree of moral guilt which may be involved in it. There are six steps in the 'production of a sin'. (344)— 1, The inclination of the will; 2, The will arresting itself upon the tempting object; 3, The will being pleased with the thought of it; 4, Desiring to do it, but 'not clearly and distinctly, but upon certain conditions, if it were lawful,' etc.; 5, Desire to do it unconditionally; and, 6, Execution.

Having described these stages of guilt with much sagacity and ingenuity, he proceeds, by the help of odd scholastic phraseology about formal and material guilt (348-356), to consider how many sins are involved in the various mental stages through which guilt passes.

He gets here into the most singular refinements. 'If the course of the outward act' is interrupted and resumed, there is more than one sin or virtuous act. A man who brings up an orphan 'does often sleep and often not think of it, and hath many occasions to renew his resolution.' If he delights in it, and chooses *toties quoties*, he does so many distinct acts of charity. But each intention must produce some effect. 'Titius intends to give Caius a new gown at the calends,' but forgets. His first intention is thrown away; and if, upon a new intention, he does give him a gown at the calends, he is credited with only one act of charity, not two :—

'If a man against his will nod at his prayers, and awakening himself by his nodding, proceed in his devotion, he does not pray more than once, because the first intention is sufficient to point his prayer. But if he falls asleep overnight, and sleeps till morning, his morning prayer is upon a new account, and the will must renew her act, or there is nothing done.'

This is a good illustration of the absurd consequences which flow from the view which Taylor always takes of the will, as being a sort of subordinate man. It is followed by an inquiry into the cases in which an involuntary effect, proceeding from a voluntary cause, is imputed to the agent (356-367). By this Taylor means the case of a man who gets drunk, in order that when drunk he may sin without restraint, in which case he says the sin consequent on the drunkenness, as well as the drunkenness itself, is imputed. But it is otherwise if the consequence was not foreseen or designed, in which case the consequences of drunkenness have their moral effect as aggravations of the drunkenness, not as substantive offences (380-386); and so as to other cases of negligence.

This second part of the rule forms part of an inquiry into the effects of ignorance upon guilt. In relation to this matter, Taylor handles incidentally, as is his manner, very large questions. He begins by asking of what men may lawfully be ignorant (364). No man, he says, can be 'innocently ignorant of that which all the nations of the world have ever believed and publicly professed, as that there is a God—that God is good, and just, and true; that he is to be worshipped; that we must do no more wrong than we are willing to suffer,' etc. No Christian can be innocently ignorant of that which the Catholic Church teaches, but upon points on which Christians differ 'a man may innocently be ignorant' (365).

This gives a wonderfully wide license in such matters. He distinguishes ignorance as being invincible, probable (368), and vincible (372), and dwells at length upon the effect of infancy, in relation to which he makes a characteristic remark. We cannot tell exactly when children become responsible for their sins. Probably they are not punished so severely as men. 'When God does not impute their follies to damnation, it may be he will impute them so far as to cause a sickness or an immature and hasty death' (377).

One Anastasius Sinaita appears to have been better informed. He says, according to Taylor, 'Sometimes God imputes sins to boys from twelve years old and upwards.' He does not mention girls.

From the case of ignorance Taylor passes to that of fear and violence, and their effects upon contracts and other actions, as to which he says very little, at considerable length (389-398). The most characteristic of his doctrines is that a promise to a thief or bandit should be kept, 'because, he being an outlaw and rebel against all civil laws, and in a state of war, whatever you promise to him you are to understand according to that law under which then you are, which is the law of nature and force together.'

The rest of the fourth part of the book consists of an inquiry (398-414) into the final cause of human actions, the *summum bonum* or ideal by which all human conduct ought to be regulated, which, he says, is the glory of God. It is not, however, unlawful to add to this master motive 'temporal regards for ends of profit, pleasure, or honour,' though they must be kept in the second place. However, the love of God itself is not absolutely disinterested. 'There was no love of God ever so abstracted by any command or expressed intention of God as to lay aside all intuition of that reward' (411). This is a good instance of the spiritual and intellectual see-saw between various points of view which is one of Taylor's great characteristics.

Upon this part of the work we may observe in general that it is obscured and falsified throughout by a complete absence of true philosophy or real knowledge of the constitution of man, and that it is in fact nothing more or less than an elaborate attempt to apply legal conceptions to a subject-matter to which they have a very distant relation. Under Taylor's circumstances this was inevitable. The problem continually before him is, under what conditions will God punish men for sins of thought or act? and his constant tacit assumption is, that God will follow, at all events to a great extent, the principles of the civil law.

Nothing is more remarkable than the almost idolatrous admiration with which the leading writers of the sixteenth and seventeenth centuries regarded law, or than the manner in which they overlooked the defects inherent in all law, especially the great leading defect, that it involves the necessity of deciding for practical purposes what are in reality indeterminate and indeterminable problems. This is closely connected with the notion of innate ideas which Taylor held so strongly, and which was universal in his time. If you believe that a maxim like 'Contracts must be kept' is a first truth by which particular cases may be decided, you run of course into argumentations like the one quoted above about the robber. It is not till you have learnt that the general rule is only a summary mode of expression, generalised from a number of particular cases, that you can see that it throws no light upon cases which were not taken into account when it was formed, and that their solution must depend upon different principles.

Such is Taylor's view of the questions which lie at the root of ethics. We now pass to the body of his system. The First Book (xi. 369; xii. 190) is entitled 'Of Conscience, the Kinds of it and the General Rules of conducting them.' It treats successively of the rule of conscience in general (x. 369-427), of the right or sure conscience (xi. 427-511), the confident or erroneous conscience (xii. 1-31), the probable or thinking conscience (xii. 31-118), the doubtful conscience (xii. 118-172), and the scrupulous conscience (xii. 172-190). It is a most tedious inquiry, eloquent in the wrong places, abounding in distinctions which are of no real use, and above all, founded on no clear perception of the difficulties or nature of the questions to be discussed.

We have already referred to the definition of conscience, to the way in which it is personified, and to the different senses in which the word is used; but the observation may be extended to other faculties. Man, in Taylor's philosophy, is a being full of little men, named Will, Conscience, Reason, etc., each of whom has his own peculiar province and powers. It is obvious that any quantity of ingenuity can be displayed in settling the precedence between imaginary persons by the rules of the civil law, and in illustrating it by cases handled by casuists.

Simplifying the matter as far as possible, and translating Taylor into modern language, the substance of what he says appears to be as follows: As to conscience in general it is a fact that men judge of the moral character of their own and other people's actions, and have in their own minds rules by which they form those judgments. These rules are, in some sense or other, the voice of God to the soul, even when they are wrong. If the judgments founded on them correspond with 'the law of God or God's will signified to us by nature or revelation' (381), and known by various names, such as 'the law of nature, the consent of nations, right reason, the Decalogue, the Sermon of Christ, the canons of the apostles, the laws, ecclesiastical and civil, of princes and governors,' they are right. If not, they are wrong. In any event they regulate our conduct and influence our feelings, and so impose the powerful sanction of self-approval or self-condemnation upon every action of our lives.

These judgments form a 'right and true conscience' when they are right, and are known to be so; and they may be known to be right by reason, the operation of which is by three steps (439 *seq*.) In the first place, we have '"first notices" of things abstract, of principles, and the primo intelligibilia.' Next we have '"discourse," that is, such consequents and emanations which the understanding draws from the first principles.' Lastly, we have faith, which is the assent of the understanding to evidence.

In a word, conscience is our opinion of our own conduct, which is to be regulated by reason from which faith is derived. This is pure rationalism, but Taylor (*more suo*) narrows it by saying that, as geometrical propositions are not proved by moral philosophy, so revelation is not proved by a natural argument, but by 'principles proper to the inquisition.' What those principles are, or where or how they are to be got, he does not say.

This rationalism with stones in its shoes (442-449), weak for purposes of affirmation, strong for purposes of denial, is pre-eminently characteristic of Taylor, but he contrives, by a series of devices, and more or less adroit beggings of the question, to assign their usual provinces to faith and reason on grounds about as plausible as usual. Reason, however, gets a considerably larger share than is allowed to it by many writers.

A great deal of curious disputation follows as to the effect of knowing that a given thing is right. Two of the most characteristic arguments may be shortly referred to: (First), May you promote a true opinion by bad reasons? Is it lawful 'for a good end for preachers to affright men with panic terrors, and to create fears that have no ground; as to tell them if they be liars their faces will be deformed'? etc. (489). Answer: 'A preacher or governor may affright those that are under him, and deter them from sin, by threatening them with anything that may probably happen.' For instance, he may tell sacrilegious people that it is probable they will die childless, or 'be afflicted with the gout,' or 'have an ambulatory life,' etc.; but he must not threaten a judgment which implies a miracle, as, for instance, that if a sinner in England profanes the sacrament, 'a tiger shall meet him in the churchyard and tear him.' Moreover, he must not be 'too decretory and determinate,' and must only threaten and not prophesy, 'lest the whole dispensation become contemptible.'

(Secondly), How are you to act if you know the truth in one capacity and not in another? A judge knows a man to be innocent who, nevertheless, is proved to be guilty according to the rules of law. How is the judge to act? Taylor, in opposition as he says to the schoolmen, holds that he must acquit. He confines (499, etc.) this however to cases of life and death. In matters of property (510) a judge may give an unjust sentence, if the proof required by the law is produced; though again his knowledge that it is unjust may justify him in favouring the right side 'in all the ways that are permitted him.' It is worth observing that throughout the whole of this discussion, the judge whom Taylor has before him is an abstract judge, bound by abstract rules of evidence, more or less like those of the civil law. He does not perceive that the question cannot even be properly stated till you know specifically the nature of the procedure of which you are speaking, and the part assigned by it to the person vaguely called a judge.

The erroneous conscience is treated of next after

the right conscience. No chapter in the book shows so well as this the mischief of regarding conscience as a separate thing. The erroneous conscience binds, we are told, because it 'always has the same commission, as being the same faculty' (13). Throughout the chapter Taylor recognises three parties to the morality of an action — God, the conscience, and the man, who is bound to obey both God and his conscience. This, of course, produces inextricable confusion.

The following passages will illustrate this :—

'Conscience is God's creature, bound to its lord and maker by all the rights of duty and perfect subordination, and therefore cannot prejudice the right and power of its lord, and no wise man obeys the orders of a magistrate against the express law of his king, or the orders of a captain against the command of a general; and, therefore, neither, of conscience, which is God's messenger, against the purpose of the message with which God has intrusted it (xii. 7, 8). . . . The sum is this: God is supreme, and conscience is his vicegerent and subordinate. Now it is certain that the law of an inferior cannot bind against the command of a superior when it is known. But when the superior communicates the notices of his will by that inferior and not otherwise, the subject is to obey that inferior, and in so doing he obeys both. But the vicegerent is to answer for the misinformation, and the conscience for its errors, according to the degree of its being culpable.'

All such questions become simple enough, if we

remember that a man and his conscience are one, and not two, and that the case of an erroneous conscience is only another name for a *bonâ fide* error of judgment, as an excuse for crime or moral wrong. How much God and man will condemn a man for being mistaken, still more how much either or both ought to condemn him, and what 'ought' means in such a connection, are insoluble questions, which, however, Taylor seems to have been feeling after with a view to a solution.

The 'probable and thinking conscience' is next discussed. It means the case of a man who has to act upon probabilities. The most remarkable part of Taylor's treatment of it is the illustration which it gives of moral certainty. It is given in the shape of a statement of the historical evidences of Christianity, not altogether unlike the one which is inserted in the second part of Butler's *Analogy* (xii. 39-67). It is rhetorical and weak, giving the impression that Taylor had never met with any serious argument on the other side, and that he accordingly wrote off his own statement *currente calamo*. It contains at least one express contradiction within four pages. He says: 'What the histories of that age reported as a public affair, as one of the most eminent transactions of the world . . . that which was not done in a corner, but was thirty-three years and more in acting . . . is so certain that it was, that the defenders of it need not account it a favour to have it presupposed' (39, 40).

A little after, he says (43): 'This blessed person . . . was yet pleased for thirty years together to live an humble . . . a pious, and obscure life.' How then can the events of his life have been a 'public affair' . . . 'thirty-three years and more in acting'? It is worth notice that Taylor throughout this book regards the miracles as proof of the divinity of Christ. It does not appear to occur to him that the truth of the miracles is the very issue to be proved.[1] Few things would be more curious than to trace the gradual change of tone and topic which may be observed in the great evidential writers from Grotius through Taylor and Baxter to Butler, Lardner, and Paley, and so to the writers of our own day upon the same subject.

The rest of the discussion about the probable conscience (xii. 67-90) is a cumbrous and intricate way of saying that in the absence of certainty, probability should be followed, and that, where there are opposite probabilities, we must look to the specific consequences of the action, which may be of such a nature that it is wise to act upon a very slender probability.

The last part of this proposition is illustrated by an odd case. A man's wife is 'surprised by a Turk's man of war,' and said to have been killed. 'When the sorrow for this accident had boiled down,' the husband marries 'a maid of Brescia.' After some years the second wife hears that the first wife is alive at Malta, but before her

[1] In his *Liberty of Prophesying* as already pointed out he takes a diametrically opposite view.

husband hears of it, she hears again that the woman at Malta has died. 'The question now arises whether . . . it be required that the persons already engaged should contract anew. That a new contract is necessary is universally believed, and is almost certain, for the contrary opinion is affirmed by very few, and relies upon but trifling motives.' The woman, therefore, ought to get her husband to marry her again. 'But now the difficulty arises, for her husband is a vicious man, and hates her, . . . and wishes her dead,' and so is sure not to consent. In this case, says Taylor, 'it is lawful for her to follow that little probability of opinion which says that the consent of one is sufficient for the renovation of the contract.'

This appears to us a dishonest evasion of a superfluous technical difficulty. A person must be unwise who felt any hesitation, under the circumstances, about the moral innocence of continuing to cohabit, but if she did, it would clearly be her duty to act upon what was probably the right opinion. To act upon a slight probability because you have no better guide may be wise in certain cases, but to act upon a slight probability in opposition to a greater probability, because the slight probability is on the side of one's inclinations, is only a dishonest way of taking your inclinations as the guide of your conduct. It is characteristic of Taylor's disingenuity to miss this distinction.

The doubtful conscience (xii. 1-18) is next considered. It differs from the probable conscience, as far as we can understand, only in being rather more doubtful. Taylor's inquiry into it is divided into eight rules, such as 'a negative doubt binds only to caution and observance.' 'A privative doubt cannot of itself hinder a man from acting what he is moved to by an extrinsic argument or inducement that is in itself prudent or innocent.' What 'negative' and 'privative' doubts are is not explained.

There are other rules of a very technical and needlessly cumbrous kind. The only one which possesses much real interest is the last (140). 'When two precepts contrary to each other meet together about the same question, that is to be preferred which binds most.' This relates to such questions as whether a man may be advised to commit a less offence in order to keep him from committing a greater—to pick a pocket instead of committing robbery with violence. Under certain conditions Taylor thinks he may, and upon this question takes occasion to examine at length the question about doing evil that good may come.

It is a most remarkable and audacious passage, and deserves notice, both as an illustration of the occasional vigour of Taylor's rationalism, and as a specimen of the manner in which the most vigorous and audacious speculations might be reconciled with strict orthodoxy as formerly understood :—

'There can be no dispute' (says Taylor) 'that it is highly unlawful to do evil for a good end. St. Paul's words are decretory and passionate in the thing (xii. 158). . . . However, though this be clear and certain, yet I doubt not but all the world does evil that good may come of it, and though all men are of St. Paul's opinion, yet all men do not blame themselves when they do against it. . . . First, if we look in Scripture, we shall find that divines eminently holy have served God by strange violences of fact' (159).

He refers to David, Elijah, Jehu, and others. In government 'all princes knowingly procure their rights by wrong. . . . We make children vainglorious that they may love noble things (160). . . . Prescription doth transfer right, and confirms the putative and presumed in defiance of the legal and proper (161). . . . All princes think themselves excused if, by inferring a war, they go to lessen their growing neighbours (161). . . . Who will not tell a harmless lie to save the life of his friend? (162) . . . When the judges are corrupt, we think it fit to give them bribes to make them do justice' (162).

The most remarkable illustration of all, however, is given in these striking words :—

'The rules of war and the measures of public interest are not to be estimated by private measures, and therefore, because this is unlawful in private intercourses, it must not be concluded to be evil in the public. For human affairs are so intricate and entangled, our rules so imperfect, so many necessities supervene, and our power is so limited, and our knowledge so little, and our provisions so short-sighted, that those things which are, in private, evils, may be public goods' (163).

The line of thought thus vigorously taken leads obviously enough, straight towards the great question of morals, What, after all, is the real meaning of good and evil? It was not in Taylor's nature to face and work out to the bottom such a problem as this. He contents himself with a cloud of distinctions about 'evils in morality,' (164) and 'evils in nature' (165), 'evils properly and naturally,' evils 'by accident,' 'by our own fault,' 'by the faults of others,' the 'material part,' the 'formality of action' (168), and the like, and ends thus: 'The sum is this, whatsoever is forbidden by the law under which we stand, and, being weighed by its own measures, is found evil, that is in a matter certainly forbidden, not from any outer and accidental reason, but for its natural or essential contrariety to reason and the law of God, that may not be done or procured for any end whatsoever; but what is evil in some circumstances may be good in others, and what is condemned for a bad effect, by a good one may be followed.' All this is a mere fog of words until we assign a definite meaning to the word 'evil,' and hardly any passage in the whole book will better exemplify either the nature or the incurable weakness of Taylor's method.

The last variety of conscience which Taylor considers is the scrupulous conscience. The whole is summed up in a very pretty simile, which is a good illustration of Taylor's wit, and with which we will conclude this article:—

'A scrupulous conscience . . . is like a woman

handling of a frog or a chicken, which all their friends tell them can do them no hurt, and they are convinced in reason that they cannot, they believe it and know it, and yet when they take the little creature into their hands they shriek, and sometimes hold fast, and find their fears confuted, and sometimes they let go, and find their reason useless' (177).

XI

JEREMY TAYLOR AS A MORALIST [1]

(Third Notice)

THE Second and Third Books of the *Ductor Dubitantium* relate respectively to Laws Divine and Laws Human. The first of Divine Laws is the law of nature (xii. 190-280). Upon this point Taylor's views are substantially those of a much later generation. Properly speaking, he says, there is no such thing as a law of nature :—

'And this opinion Carneades did express but rudely, and was for it noted by Lactantius. He said there was no law of nature. But the Christians, who for many ages have followed the school of Aristotle, have been tender in suffering such expressions, and have been great promoters of Aristotle's doctrine concerning the τὸ φυσικὸν, 'the natural law.' But, indeed, Aristotle himself in this was various and indetermined' (193), as he proceeds to show.

---

[1] *Ductor Dubitantium; or, the Rule of Conscience.* By Jeremy Taylor. Vols. xi. xii. xiii. and xiv. of Heber's edition of Bishop Taylor's works.

The substance of his doctrine, which is expressed at great length and in a variety of forms, is almost identical with that of Mr. Austin. The law of nature is nothing but a collection of the maxims the observance of which natural reason deems to be essential to human society. These maxims are law, not on account of our natural inclination to them, or because of the consent of nations, or because they are prompted by reason, but because God has commanded them to be observed, and will enforce their observance by punishments here and hereafter.

Many passages in this inquiry anticipate, though in a cumbrous way, the doctrines of the Utilitarian school of the later part of the eighteenth century and of our own days, and they have in many places a considerable resemblance to Hobbes, to whom, however, Taylor never, so far as we know, directly refers. The following passage is an anticipation of much modern speculation :—

'From all which I conclude that the *jus gentium*, the law of nations, is no indication of the law of nature; neither, indeed, is there any *jus gentium* collectively at all; but only the distinct laws of several nations; and therefore it is to be taken distributively; for they are united only by contract or imitation, by fear, or neighbourhood, or necessity, or any other accident which I have mentioned' (207, 208).

He points out also that men 'can never agree in their enumeration of the natural laws' (220). Taylor, indeed, goes so far in this direction as to argue elaborately (224) that 'God cannot do an unjust thing, because whatsoever he wills or does is therefore just because he wills and does it,' and he reproves (221) Grotius for teaching that 'God cannot change the law of nature.' It is a singular instance of the differences which exist amongst theologians that Warburton regards this doctrine as atheistic.

The maxims of natural reason thus enacted into a law by God are, according to Taylor (228), the foundation and the measure of the obligation of all laws whatever; and, indeed, it is self-evident that a divine law, sanctioned by eternal happiness or misery, must, in the nature of things, be superior in its obligations to all other laws whatever. It is, however, curious to see upon what trifling grounds Taylor, who apprehends so clearly the true character of the law of nature, regards particular maxims as being articles of that law.

Austin's theory is that the principle of utility is the index to the will of God, so that conduct conformable to rules which tend to produce a maximum of happiness is agreeable to the law of God; but Taylor has no such test. He nowhere clears the matter up fully, but numerous passages in his book indicate the opinion that an intricate theory, founded rather on the civil law than on anything else, was the 'law of nature.' For instance, he argues at length upon the supposition that by the law of nature clandestine marriages are valid, and cannot be annulled, though they may be forbidden by the laws of particular nations (244, 245). It is, of course, an intelligible and imaginable thing that it might please God to make such a law; but why, in the absence of express revelation (which Taylor does not allege), it should be supposed that such was actually the case we cannot understand. It is equally difficult to comprehend why it should be said that 'by the law of nature every man hath power to make a testament of his own goods' (246).

Having thus described the law of nature and glanced at its provisions, Taylor proceeds to the question of sanctions, or, as he calls them, 'bands.' He does not see distinctly the necessity for defining or describing the nature of obligation, but in this passage (230) he approaches the question. 'Fear,' he says, 'is the band of all laws'; 'the stings of conscience and fear of the divine vengeance is this evil which naturally restrains us' (230); but he edges away from this by saying that the wise and good fear not so much punishment as sin. Their fear 'is natural, a fear produced from the congenite notices of things,' 'a fear of being a base person and doing vile things.' The second band of virtue is love; but as fear, the first band, is not to be taken simply, so neither is love. 'It is impossible a man should do great things or suffer nobly without consideration of a reward, and since much of virtue consists in suffering evil things, virtue of herself is not a beatitude, but the way to one' (237). These are excellent instances of the way in which Taylor always trims, and never embraces any view or adopts any principle in a thoroughgoing manner.

These speculations are followed by inquiries of a very technical and superfluous sort about the cases in which God or man can dispense with the law of nature, and the way in which the dispensation can be effected. God can dispense with the law of nature (260-270), but no human power can do so, although civil laws may so alter the circumstances as to vary the application of natural laws (272, 273), and though the rigour of the law of nature, as well as the rigour of human laws, may 'be allayed by equity, piety, and necessity' (278).

From the law of nature in general Taylor passes to the law of nature 'as it is commanded, digested, and perfected by our supreme lawgiver, Jesus Christ.' This is the least interesting part of the book. It refers to the abrogation of the Jewish law, in connection with which it discusses at length the question of prohibited degrees in marriage, and in particular the case of the marriage of first cousins (321-358); the question of image-worship (382-412); the question of the observance of Sunday (412-430). The last of these subjects is the only one which in the present day retains much interest. Taylor treats the institution of Sunday as merely ecclesiastical :—

'The question concerning particular works or permitted recreations is wholly useless and trifling, for "quod lege prohibitoriâ vetitum non est permissum intelligitur," but as for some persons to give themselves great liberties of sport on that day is neither pious nor prudent, so to deny some to others is neither just nor charitable' (429).

The most remarkable speculation in this part of the book is under Rule vii. (439-465). 'There is no state of men or things but is to be guided by the proportion of some rule or precept in the Christian law.' Taylor begins the exposition of this rule by setting out at length the necessity which exists for believing that the law of Christ 'must needs be absolute and alone, and unalterable, and perfect, and for ever.' As a general answer to the obvious difficulties of this view, he has the following characteristically beautiful, and not less characteristically fallacious, passage. It occurs amongst the 'cautions to be observed in civil permissions of an unlawful act or state':—

'As it is in the economy of the world, the decree of God doth establish the vicissitudes of night and day for ever; but the sun, looking on a point, not only signifies, but also makes the little portions of time and divides them into hours; but men coming with their little arts and instruments make them to be understood, and so become the sun's interpreters; so it is in the matter of justice, whose great return and firm establishments are made by God, and some rules given for the great measures of it; and we from His laws know just from unjust, as we understand day and night; but the laws of princes and the contracts of men, like the sun, make the little measures, and divide the great proportions into minutes of justice and fair intercourse; and the divines and lawyers go yet lower, and they become expounders of those measures, and set up dials and instruments of notice, by which we understand the proportion and obligation of the law and the lines of justice.'

This is a magnificent image, but its speculative worthlessness is shown by what follows:—

'Just and unjust, we love or hate respectively by our warrant from God; and from him also we are taught the general lines of it, as, Do what you would be done to, restore the pledge, hurt no man, rob not your neighbour of his rights, make no fraudulent contracts, no unjust bargains; but then, what are his rights and what not? what is fraudulent and what is fair? in what he hath power, in what he hath none, is to be determined by the laws of men. So that if a commonwealth permits an usurious exchange or contract, it is not unjust' (443).

The second part of the extract appears to me (as it appeared to Hobbes) to be perfectly true, but it stultifies the first part. If men decide specifically what is just and what is unjust, it is obvious that the general proposition 'Be just' is only a generalisation deduced from known laws, not a first truth from which other laws are deduced. The greatest of tyrants, the most unmerciful slave-owner, would not object to bind himself to respect his neighbour's rights if he were permitted to define them in the first instance as he pleased. If divines, lawyers, and legislators are to say what specific acts are murder, adultery, theft, false witness, and covetousness, it is obvious that they, and not the author of the Ten Commandments, are the real legislators. The Commandments are like the titles of the chapters of a book, and are highly useful as memoranda, but the best table of contents will not enable any one to dispense with the substance of the book itself.

The appreciation of this particular difficulty would have required a more distinct conception of the nature of generalisation than either Taylor or any other writer of his time possessed; but there is another difficulty in the way of his general estimate of the New Testament as a universal moral code, which he appreciated better, though he did not do much towards removing it. He says:—

'Against the doctrine of the rule many things may be objected; for there seem to be many things and great cases for which the laws of the holy Jesus have made no provision. I instance a very great one, that is, the whole state of war, and all the great cases and incidents of it' (446).

Some, he says, solve the difficulty by saying that all war is unlawful; but this, he observes, only introduces still greater difficulties. Others say that 'Christianity leaves that matter of war to be conducted by the law of nature and nations;' but this, he says, only 'entangles the whole inquiry.' For Christianity is a perfect digest of the law of nature, and if the law of Christ omits the case of war, so too must the law of nature. If we are to 'look for' the laws of nature on this matter 'in the tables of our own hearts,' we shall find that passion, interest, custom, and education are 'the authors of contrary inscriptions.'

The law of nations comes off still worse (448). There is no digest of it, no sanction to it; it is uncertain, and is 'admitted with variety and by accident'; and, in a word, by this rule 'the measures of war shall be the edicts of any single general, and nothing else.' Having stated his difficulties with his usual force, Taylor tries to remove them with his usual weakness. In the first place, 'if men be subjects of Christ's law they can never go to war with each other.' If they do go to war, they have got beyond the province of law. The injurious person has 'gone beyond all law into a state of things where laws are of no value.' The injured person can do whatever is necessary for his defence; and if it be asked, 'what is the measure of the actions which must be done in the conduct of the defence?' the answer is, he must observe the rules of justice like a private person, which rule of justice requires men, amongst other things, 'to keep themselves within the limits of a just defence,' which limits of a just defence prohibit people at war to hurt those who are not at war, 'except in a case of absolute necessity.' This is surely a very lame account of a matter of vital importance. It leads up to an elaborate inquiry into the value of Old Testament precedents (452-465), of which it is scarcely unjust to say that Taylor's rule is that they are to be used where they are applicable, otherwise not.

The concluding chapter of Book II (xii. 465 to end, xiii. 1-230) relates to the 'interpretation and obligation of the laws of Jesus Christ.' It is very long, and far from interesting. It is composed of twenty rules, several of which are little more than grammatical rules of interpretation. Thus the first rule is—'In negative precepts the affirmatives are commanded, and in the affirmative commandments the negatives are included.' Others are designed to fill up the extreme generality of the New Testament maxims so as to enable commentators to convert them into something approaching, at all events, to a general code of morals. Such are the following :—

'When anything is forbidden by the laws of Jesus Christ, all those things are forbidden also which follow from that forbidden action, and for whose sake it was forbidden. . . . The laws of Jesus Christ are the measures of the Spirit, and are always to be extended to a spiritual signification. . . . All those things also by which we come to a forbidden sin are understood to be forbidden by the same law. . . . Suppositive propositions ("When ye pray, stand not in the corners of the street," "when ye fast," etc., "when ye give alms," etc.) are always equivalent to a commandment.'

There is also an investigation of the difference between laws and counsels evangelical, a vindication at great length of the doctrine that the Christian law is fully contained in the Holy Scriptures, and some other matters of less importance.

We will confine ourselves to a very few observations on Taylor's treatment of these subjects. His rules of construction tacitly assume, if not what we should call in these days the verbal inspiration of the New Testament, at all events the exact preservation by the Evangelists of the very words and forms of expression used by Christ, for in many cases they attach consequences of the utmost importance to the negative or affirmative form into which a proposition is thrown. Notwithstanding, however, the sacredness which he attaches to the very words of the Gospels, Taylor is enabled by the maxims quoted to enlarge them to an extraordinary degree. A good instance of this is afforded by part of his chapter on Evangelical counsels. Although a counsel is not in itself a law, 'Yet there is also the *minimum morale* in it—that is, that degree of love and duty less than which is by interpretation no love, no duty at all.' Thus :—

'When we are commanded to love our neighbour as ourself, the least measure of this law, the legal or negative part of it, is that we should not do him injury; that we shall not do to him what we would not have done to ourselves. He that does not in this sense love his neighbour as himself has broken the commandment' (xiii. 60).

These illustrations are enough to show the manner in which Taylor provides means for converting the materials supplied by the New Testament into a complete moral code.

The 14th rule—that the whole Christian law is contained in the Scripture—is mostly controversial, and directed against the Roman Catholics, but incidentally it contains Taylor's theory of the uses of tradition, which is curious and singularly definite. Tradition, he says, 'is of great use for the conveying of this great rule of conscience, the Holy Scriptures of the Old and New Testament' (xiii. 114). There are also three doctrines, or rather 'rituals,' as Taylor calls them, which, 'although they have also great grounds in Scripture, yet, because the universal practice and doctrine of the Church of God in all ages, and in all Churches primitive, is infinitely evident and notorious, . . . may be placed under the protection of universal tradition, for they really have it beyond all exception.' These doctrines are—1, The observance of Sunday, especially Easter Sunday. 2, Episcopal government. 3, Offices ecclesiastical (*e.g.* public prayers and the administration of the Sacrament and other ceremonies), to be performed by ecclesiastical persons.

Upon the weakness of tradition, when stretched beyond these narrow limits, Taylor has some striking passages. Take, for instance, the following comment on 'Quod semper, quod ubique, quod ab omnibus':—

'No man now knows what the Catholic Church does believe in any question of controversy, for the Catholic Church is not to be spoken with; and, being divided by seas, and nations, and interests, and fears, and tyrants, and poverty, and innumerable accidents, does not declare her mind by any common instrument, and agrees in nothing but in the Apostles' Creed and the books of Scripture, and millions of Christians hear nothing of our controversies, and if they did, would not understand some of them.'

The last part of this rule (Ques. III. pp. 153-169) has some interest in these days. It is an inquiry into what we are so familiar with under the title of the doctrine of development, which Taylor opposes so strongly that he gives a very reluctant assent to the propriety of drawing up the Nicene Creed; 'and indeed the thing was very well if it had not been made an ill example . . . afterward the case was altered, and that example was made use of to explicate the same creed till, by explicating the old, they have inserted new articles' (163). He adds, 'All the world is not able to tell us how much is necessary and how much is not if they once go beside the Apostolic Creed' (167).

The Third Book relates to Human Laws, and is divided into six chapters, which treat respectively of human laws in general and their power over the conscience; of penal and tributary laws; of supreme civil powers and their laws; of the powers of the Church in canons and censures; of domestic laws enacted by parents; and of the interpretation, diminution (*i.e.* relaxation), and abrogation of human laws.

Certain chapters of this Third Book are much the

most interesting part of the whole work. The first chapter states, and vindicates at great length, the doctrine that human laws bind the conscience. This doctrine (234), says Taylor, has been greatly disputed, the opposite being believed 'by all the gentlemen and common people of Spain, the scholars only excepted.' Some also of the Calvinists, and Lutherans, and all the Anabaptists, were of the same way of thinking; and so were 'Almain, John Gerson, Felinus, Captan, and Navarre,' as far as concerned the civil laws of princes.

Taylor states eight grounds for their opinion, and elaborately answers them all. The sum of his argument is, that human government is of divine institution, and that the laws of God themselves are reduced to a certainty by the laws of man— *e.g.* (237) 'God forbade murder; but what is murder in England is not murder in Spain, and *vice versâ.*' We doubt (upon grounds already pointed out) whether Taylor appreciated the full importance of this remark. But it carries consequences of the very highest importance. It is difficult to overrate the practical importance of this controversy. The different views taken of the moral weight of law in England and in Ireland are a good illustration of it.

After an elaborate answer (250-261) to the eight arguments against his own view, Taylor gives an account of the differences between the obligations imposed by divine and those imposed by human laws (261-266). The principal points are that divine laws bind immediately, human laws mediately. We are bound not only to obey but to approve of divine laws, 'but human laws meddle not with the understanding, for that is a prince, and can be governed as he can be persuaded, but subject to the empire of none but God.' Divine laws are lasting. Human laws cease to bind by change of circumstances and lapse of time.

In subsequent parts of the chapter (rule ii. p. 266, rule iii. p. 274) immense deductions are made from the binding power of human laws. It is said that they do not oblige the conscience to an active obedience when there is imminent danger of death or of an intolerable or very grievous evil, but this is qualified characteristically by a proviso that if obedience is enforced, even at the risk of death, it must be yielded (272). It is also said generally that 'laws which are not just and good do not oblige the conscience' (274); but this again is qualified by five 'cautions' (281), two of which are to the effect that the inconvenience of the law to the republic must be so great as in the judgment of good and prudent men 'to be a sufficient cause of annulling the law,' and 'must reasonably outweigh the evil of material disobedience. Moreover, the inconvenience and injustice 'must be certain, notorious, and relied upon.' These are very slipshod directions. The great defect of the whole speculation is that Taylor never asks himself distinctly what he means by an obligation, and by such words as 'must' and 'ought.'

Of the remaining rules in this chapter one only

(rule vii. p. 296) deserves particular notice. It is 'that a law should oblige the conscience, and does not depend upon the acceptation of the law by the people.' The people at large, Taylor owns, may in certain cases have legislative power, though he is careful to say that such governments 'came in wrong' (296), but if they have not, their consent is not wanted. Upon this point he uses one of his fine images: 'Although a horse sometime cannot be ruled without strokings and meet and gentle usages, yet for all that his rider is his master' (279).

The chapter which relates to laws penal and tributary contains a great deal of trifling matter about the cases in which men may and ought to execute judgment on themselves. There are, however, three points in it which deserve express notice. The first is Taylor's vindication of a liberal use of the punishment of death, which he puts on the broad ground of general expediency, though he expressly admits that as to the criminal it frequently 'sends him to hell' (308). The following passage (311) is memorable in its way: 'If there were any other' (punishment) 'less than death, the galleys, and the mines, and the prisons would be nothing but nurseries of villains which, by their numbers, would grow as dangerous as a herd of wolves and lions.' Imagine a bishop of our own days advocating the wholesale extermination of the criminal classes as the best practical solution of the difficulties which they cause!

The second point is Taylor's discussion of the question of truth and falsehood which is suggested to him by considering whether a guilty person may lie to escape the penalty of the law (351-388). The discussion is elaborate and lengthy, but neither profound nor original. It allows of lying in the common cases, and shows a very unnecessary tenderness for equivocation, which, says Taylor, 'may upon less necessity and upon more causes be permitted than lying' (382). However, he adds, a man who equivocates 'had need be very witty to be innocent.' The greatest wit, indeed, will not always do, as we learn from an odd illustration—the case of the devil in the ancient oracles:—

'When he was put to it at his oracles, and durst not tell a downright lie, and yet knew not what was truth many times, he was put to the most pitiful shifts, and trifling equivocations, and acts of knavery which, when they were discovered . . . it made him much more contemptible and ridiculous than if he had said nothing or confessed his ignorance' (388).

Thirdly, with regard to the tributary laws, Taylor holds that people are bound in conscience to pay taxes (414), and that, whether they are demanded or not (420), and though this 'is to be understood of customs and tributes which are just,' yet most taxes are just, and 'let no merchant trust his own judgment' to the contrary, 'but the sentence of a wise spiritual guide, or of counsel learned in the law' (422). This assigns a remarkable province to casuists and counsel.

In the next chapter, Taylor proceeds to discuss the nature of States, and their laws, which he considers under eight rules (423-549). Though the inquiry is long, its result may be expressed shortly. First, as to the civil power in general, which is considered in the first four rules: Taylor agrees with Hobbes that 'the supreme power in every republic is universal, absolute, and unlimited' (423). This absolute power, however, 'is but an absolute power of government, not of possession; it is a power of doing right, but not a power of doing wrong' (427). The Sovereign is 'superior to the civil laws, but not wholly free from them'; but this rule 'hath been thrust into great difficulty.' 'Disputations in this case are not prudent or safe; but precepts and sermons and great examples, and the sayings of wise men, and positive affirmations in those particulars that be manifest' (435).

After much trimming and quoting of contradictory authorities, Taylor at last comes to the conclusion that the Sovereign is bound in conscience to keep the law, but that there is no remedy if he breaks it. The law is his guide, not his master. This is more fully explained in the next rule, which advocates the doctrine of passive obedience with extraordinary warmth of language :—

'I do not know any proposition in the world clearer and more certain in Christianity than this rule. . . . I have an ill task to write cases of conscience if such things as these shall be hard to be persuaded, for there are very few things in which any man is to hope for half so much conviction as in this article lies before him in every topic' (454).

It is needless to refer to his proofs of this proposition. They consist partly of the well-known texts of the Bible upon the subject, and partly of a passionate declamation on the evils of anarchy. Civil war is a universal evil, but as for a bad prince, 'let him be lustful, he shall not ravish the Commonwealth; and if he be bloody, his sword cannot cut off very great numbers; and if he be covetous, he will not take away all men's estates' (467).

No stronger proof can be given of the horrors of civil war than the fact that the recollection of it should lead such a man as Taylor to talk such degrading nonsense.

The last four rules of the chapter refer to the authority of the civil power in things ecclesiastical. It would be difficult for Hobbes himself to assert the royal prerogative much more vigorously:—

'It is necessary that the supreme power of kings or states should be governors in religion, or else they are but half kings at the best (475). The prince cannot rule without it (religion); he is but the shadow of a king, the servant of his priests; and, if they rule religion, they may also rule him' (479).

Religion, having a great influence over morals (479), and great power over individuals (480), the civil government must rule religion:—

'This course of forbidding new religions is certainly very prudent, and infinitely just and pious (484). . . . Against the law no man is to be permitted to bring in new religions, excepting those only who can change the law and secure the peace.'

The civil power, moreover, ought to legislate upon 'affairs of religion and the Church,' and that both in the punishment of sin as a crime (493), when it appears desirable, and also in all ecclesiastical matters 'which are directly under no commandment of God' (493). In case of a conflict between the temporal and spiritual powers the temporal power is to be obeyed unless its commands are opposed to the divine law, in which case the spiritual power is to be obeyed, not as a substantive authority, but as the interpreter of a divine command :—

'If the supreme civil power should command that the bishops of his kingdom should not ordain any persons that had been soldiers or of mean trades to be priests, or consecrate any knight to be a bishop; though the bishops should desire it very passionately, they have no power to command or do what the civil power has forbidden. But if the supreme should say there should be no bishops at all and no ordination of ministers of religion according to the laws of Jesus Christ,' then the bishops or others bound to ordain must do so (523), and give directions as to the circumstances. If, however, the spiritual power forbids what the civil power only permits—*e.g.* marriage in certain degrees of consanguinity or affinity—then the spiritual power binds the conscience unless the civil power has forbidden its exertion (527, 528). The civil power has jurisdiction over internal and spiritual, as well as merely ecclesiastical, causes. It may declare a doctrine to be heretical, as well as decide upon a right to present to a living :—

'If by excommunications the bishop can disturb the civil interest, the civil power can hold his hands that he shall not strike with it; or if he does, can take out the temporal sting that it shall not venom and fester. If by strange doctrines the ecclesiastics can alien the hearts of subjects from their duty, the civil power can forbid those doctrines to be preached. If the canons of the church be seditious, or peevish, or apt for trouble, the civil power can command them to be rescinded or refuse to verify them and make them into laws' (534).

In short, the maxim to be followed is, *ecclesia est in republicâ, non respublica in ecclesiâ* :—

'The church is not a distinct state or order of men, but the commonwealth turned Christian (536). . . . It is necessary that the supreme power should determine what doctrines are to be taught the people and what are to be forbidden' (540).

The utmost that can be said of the clergy is that they are advisers divinely constituted whom the Sovereign is bound in conscience to hear (543 *seq.*)

This vigorous exposition of the rights of the State over the Church, which carries out Hooker's theory to its extreme limit, is followed by a chapter on the power of the Church in canons and censures. He reduces it within very narrow limits, and, indeed, makes the power of the Church merely declaratory:—

'The use of the keys does differ from proper jurisdiction in this great thing—that if the keys be rightly used, they do bind and loose respectively; but if they err, they do nothing upon the subject, they neither bind nor loose. Now in proper jurisdiction it is otherwise; for, right or wrong, if a man be condemned he shall die for it, and if he be hanged he is hanged' (559).

As to excommunication, it 'operates only upon the will and understanding which can have no coercion; so that in effect it compels those who are willing to be compelled, that is, it does not compel at all, and therefore is but improperly an act of jurisdiction. . . . It must work wholly by opinion, and can affright them only that are taught to be afraid of it' (561).

So, of Church legislation, the bishop may command what God has already commanded, and nothing else. All that his command effects is to increase the guilt of the offender, but if, and in so far as, his command goes beyond God's command, it is of no effect at all (570).

The chapters relating to the power of priests, and to the 'diminution' of laws by equity or otherwise, contain some interesting points, but they are less interesting than those which we have attempted to describe. We have devoted much space to this work because it is seldom read, and also because it illustrates better almost than any other book in the language, a remarkable point in the history of speculation—the transition from moral theology to moral philosophy, from the text-books of the confessional to the works of writers on morals, regarded as a matter of ordinary speculation. The *Ductor Dubitantium* may be compared to a point of view from which we can look in two directions; backwards to the casuists whose names only are known to modern readers— Suarez, Sanchez, and scores of others, who are quoted by Pascal and his antagonists—and forwards to Paley and Bentham. It has something in common with both, and throws light upon both.

XII

HACKET'S LIFE OF ARCHBISHOP WILLIAMS[1]

Of the books from which we derive our knowledge of the early part of the seventeenth century, perhaps hardly any is so characteristic as Hacket's Life of Archbishop Williams. It is the life of one remarkable man by another, of a somewhat similar turn of mind. Both the author and the subject of his biography were members of that most interesting class, the deeply learned divines of the second period of the history of the Church of England—the period which intervenes between its full legal establishment and its suspension at the civil war. No book can give us a

[1] *Scrinia Reserata.* A Memorial offered to the great Deservings of John Williams, D.D., who some time held the places of Lord Keeper of the Great Seal of England, Lord Bishop of Lincoln, and Lord Archbishop of York. Containing a Series of the most Remarkable Occurrences and Transactions of his Life in relation both to Church and State. Written by John Hacket, late Lord Bishop of Lichfield and Coventry. 1693.

better notion of the general character and position of that class, and of some features of the time to which it belonged. Before entering upon the subject of Williams, it may be worth while to give, in a very few words, a summary of the life of his biographer.

Hacket was born in 1592, and was educated at Westminster School, and Trinity College, Cambridge. He was ordained in 1618; was made chaplain to Williams, then Lord Keeper, in 1621, and received from him two livings and a stall at Lincoln Cathedral. In 1631 he was made Archdeacon of Bedford. In 1642 he was made a canon of St. Paul's, and after considerable troubles during the civil wars was made Bishop of Lichfield in 1661. He died there in 1670, having rebuilt the cathedral at an expense of £20,000 out of his own pocket. He was also the builder of Bishop's Hostel at Trinity College, Cambridge.

His Life of Archbishop Williams, his old patron, was written under Cromwell's government, though it was not published till thirty-six years afterwards, in the year 1693, when it must have appeared nearly as much out of date, and nearly as old-world a production, as it does to ourselves. It is a folio volume in two parts, containing altogether nearly 500 pages, each of which reflects, as in a glass, the character both of the author and of the subject of the biography.

The book probably affords the latest specimen of the ancient, quaint, and learned style which was popular in the early part of the seventeenth century. It is learned as Burton's *Anatomy of Melancholy* (Burton was a contemporary of Hacket's) is learned. The author has nothing very profound to say, but for everything that he says he quotes some authority. The book, indeed, contains almost as much quotation as original matter, yet the quotations come in so naturally that the reader feels that they are not put in for display or out of affectation, but that they are the amusement of a man who had abundant leisure, enormous reading, a gigantic memory, and no considerable powers of original thought.

In a curious passage which fixes the date of the composition of the book, he says: 'That which my prayers and studies have long endeavoured, the dispatch of this labour, is come to pass by the good hand of God this 17th of February, 1657, which is some heartsease.' 'My scope is not so much to insist upon the memorable things of one man's life as to furnish them with reading out of my small store, that are wellwishers to learning in theological, political, and moral knowledge.' After which, in about a page, he proceeds to quote Plautus, Gregory Nazianzen, Cicero, Horace, Nazianzen again, Petrus Blesensis (a schoolman of the twelfth century), Valerius Maximus, Sidonius, Xenophon, and Manilius, of whom the Biographical Dictionary informs us that he was 'a Latin poet who lay buried in the German libraries, and never was heard of in the modern world till Poggius published him from some old MSS. found there about two centuries ago'—*i.e.* early in the seventeenth century.

These authorities add surprisingly little to the matter in hand. Indeed, Manilius is evoked from his long obscurity for the sake of an observation which I do not very distinctly understand. 'When I remember him I cannot but praise him—" Se quisque ut vivit et effert;" Manil. lib. 2.' If Manilius had nothing more important to say, Poggius might as well have left him alone. Strange and occasionally tedious as this inordinate display of learning is, the book is very pleasant reading, and gives a lively picture of the rapid growth of the last clerical Chancellor to the very summit of his fortunes, of the strange vicissitudes of his career, of the Court of James I., of the oppressions which preceded the civil war, and of the view taken of the war by the High Church divines.

John Williams was born on the 25th of March 1582, at Aber Conway, and was educated at Ruthin School, and St. John's College, Cambridge. He remained at the University from 1598 till about 1609, when he was ordained priest. His industry during this period was almost miraculous. Indeed, the account which Hacket gives of it is rendered credible only by the extraordinary exhibition of learning which he makes himself, and which proves that, at some time or other, he too must have gone through a similar course. 'From his youth to his old age he asked but three hours' sleep in the twenty-four to keep him in good health. This we all knew that lived in his family. It would not quickly be believed, but that a cloud of witnesses will avouch it, that it was ordinary with him to begin his studies at six of the clock, and continue them till three in the morning, and be ready again by seven to walk in the circle of his indefatigable labours.'

He learnt Greek and Hebrew; and, having 'fetched a great compass about theology in less than two years, he began to climb up higher upon the mountain of God.' He read the fathers and the schoolmen, and, in particular, studied ecclesiastical history with intense ardour. 'They are not the Divines of Magdeburg nor Baronius Annals (though twice read over by him) which furnished him with the tithe of his skill.' He had read all the originals. He knew all the Greek and Latin Canons. 'He carried in his mind an universal idea of all synods and convocations that were ever held in our land, of all our cathedrals, their foundations, conditions of alteration, statutes, revenues, etc. As he had spared for no travel to purchase this skill, so, to fill his vessel brim-full, he received all that Sir Harry Spelman, Sir Robert Cotton, and Mr. Holden, his dear friends, could pour into him.'

He was equally well acquainted with foreign history. 'There was not a corner of our history, sacred or secular, in any kingdom or state in Europe, which he had not pried into, and wherein he could not suddenly enlarge himself, whether they were their wars or leagues of amity; whether their laws, inheritances of their crowns and dignities, their lineages, marriages, or what not.'

He was a great man for university disputations

—the acts and opponencies which were then a real method of instruction, and of which the shadow lasted till our own time. Hacket gives some curious accounts of these performances, which put the old University strangely before our eyes. A certain Duke of Wittenberg passing through Cambridge was entertained with an act. Williams, then procter, was moderator, and by way of making himself all things to all men, 'to Dutchmen he became a Dutch philosopher, for all his conceptions he confirmed by quotations out of Julius Pacius, Goclenius, Keckerman, and others who had been professors within the districts of the German principalities.' This was 'unexpressibly acceptable' to the Duke of Wittenberg and his retinue.

Another act took place before the Elector Palatine, in which Williams and another great light of the day were set to argue the question whether clergymen might be in the service of distinguished persons with a view to Church preferment. The opponent 'somewhat frowningly' argued, 'Piscatores sumus hominum, non venatores munerum.' The respondent replied with a 'retorsion that had strength and sweetness like iron that is gilded. The end of theology is to gain souls. The end of the theologue subordinate to the first and architectonical end is for an honest maintenance and sustentation.' This, it is added, 'agrees with the mind of Seneca de Benef. lib. iii.,' and no doubt with the minds of many others.

Williams's accomplishments recommended him to the Chancellor, Lord Ellesmere, whose chaplain he was from 1610 to 1617, and through whose interest he obtained a fair share of ecclesiastical preferment and an introduction to King James I., who, shortly after the Chancellor's death, made him Dean of Salisbury.

He was a great favourite of King James's. 'He never met with any before, much less with any after, that loved him like King James at the full rate of his worth. His extraordinary learning enabled him to act as a sort of living commonplace book to the King, who delighted both in his reading and in his Toryism. He never would be pleased with anything new. 'His constant rule was, that old imperfections were safer than new experiments.' He could talk scholastic divinity every day, and all day long.

The King, however, was not everything. As Hacket observes, 'There was a pre-eminent pipe, through which all graces flowing from him were derived.' He was always 'clasping some one Gratioso in the embraces of his great love, who was unto him as a parelius.' The pre-eminent pipe in Williams's time was the Duke of Buckingham, on whom Williams contrived to confer a heavy obligation by converting Lady Catherine Manners from Popery, and smoothing various difficulties in the way of that lady's marriage with the Duke. For this service he was immediately rewarded by being translated from the Deanery of Salisbury to that of Westminster, and to the post of confidential adviser to the Duke. He seems to have advised him well, warning him of the danger of monopolies and other unconstitutional ways of raising money. 'Oh hearken not,' he says, 'to Rehoboam's earwigs.' 'An Englishman's tribute comes not from the King's exaction, but by the people's free oblation out of the mouth of their representatives.'

James and Buckingham gave way, and not only the monopolists but Lord Bacon fell before the anger of Parliament. After a good deal of doubt, Williams was made Lord Keeper, and at the same time was promoted to the Bishopric of Lincoln. By marvellous labour, and especially by the help of excellent advice, he managed not only to discharge the duties of his office creditably, but also to get through an immense multiplicity of business of other kinds.

He used to sit in the Court of Chancery from 6.30 to 8.30 A.M. He then went into the House of Lords till 12 or 1. He then dined and returned to the Court of Chancery, where he sat till 8 P.M. After this he went home, read papers, and prepared for the next day's business till late at night. He held his office till the beginning of the reign of King Charles; and Hacket gives many curious instances of his humour, his hot temper, and his wonderful quickness and industry. His occasional explosions were highly curious.

One of the oddest was as follows: He committed one Beeston for a contempt, who, 'loathing this captivity,' 'cries for mercy to the King, roars out that the Parliament might hear him, follows the Lord Buckingham with his clamours, who advised the Keeper to consider of it.' Williams gave the following characteristic reply: 'Decrees once made must be put in execution, else I will confess this Court to be the greatest imposture in the kingdom. The damned in hell do never cease repining at the justice of God; nor the prisoners in the Fleet at the decrees of Chancery. In the which hell of prisoners this one for antiquity and obstinacy may pass for a Lucifer I neither know him nor his cause, but 'as long as he stands in contempt he is not like to have any more liberty.' There is something eminently racy in this comparison, and it contrasts favourably with the strange harangues which Williams was accustomed to make on state occasions, which read almost like a caricature of pedantry.

It should also be observed that Williams's bark was worse than his bite. Hacket claims for him, apparently with justice, the praise of mildness in the Star Chamber. 'Many . . . said he was a friend to publicans and sinners, to all delinquents, and rather their patron than their judge.' . . . 'He never condemned an offender to be hanged, to be scourged, to have his ears cut.' One of the Lords 'complained against him to the King, that delinquents by his abatements were so slightly punished in their purse that the fees which came to His Majesty's enrichment would not give the Lords a dinner once a week, as the custom had been, nay hardly once a term'—a curious glimpse into the old Court.

The great event of Williams's term of office as Chancellor was the negotiation about the Spanish marriage and about the extrication of Prince Charles and Buckingham from the difficulty into which their famous journey had thrown them. It is a terribly long and intricate history, and in Hacket's hands it becomes doubly wearisome. The result to Williams was that he gave mortal offence to Buckingham, who took occasion to revenge himself on the first opportunity.

Incidentally, the story brings out one or two curious points. The Spanish Court had made a great point of obtaining a repeal of the penal laws as a condition of the marriage, and a rumour got abroad that James meant to grant their wish. When the match was broken off, James called a Parliament, in opening which he treated this imputation as scandalous and wicked. 'It hath been talked of my remissness in maintenance of religion and suspicion of a toleration. But as God shall judge me I never thought or meant it, nor ever in word exprest anything that favoured of it.'

The nation, as is well known, was vehemently anxious, on this and other grounds, for a war with Spain. James steadily refused, and his reasons for refusing are given with delightful simplicity by his Minister. He would have to ask for supplies, and this would make him dependent on his Parliament, who ''twas likely would ask the change of the Church, of the laws, of the Court Royal, the displacing of his officers, the cashiering of his servants.' This remark shows a vivid consciousness on the King's part of the degree to which his whole system of government was unpopular, and the correctness with which he appreciated the strength of the Parliament.

Though he offended Buckingham and Charles by his management of the Spanish affairs, Williams retained his power with James till his death. He obviously had a real affection for the kind old man whom Hacket represents in a pleasanter and more respectable light than that in which he is generally viewed. He had the great merit of clearly understanding the limits tacitly imposed on him by the Constitution, and though he certainly talked as big as a man well could, he acted soberly and indulgently, though beset by contending bigots.

Hacket's book is full of illustrations of the fierceness of feeling between the Protestants and Catholics, of the monstrous claims of the one and the eagerness to persecute of the others. The Roman Catholics actually went so far at one time as to 'put a paper into my Lord of Buckingham's hands, to assist them for the erection of titulary Popish prelates in this Kingdom.' The Protestants, on the other hand, appear to have looked on toleration as the great abomination of all abominations.

At the end of James's reign Williams had a long conference with the French ambassador about the policy of the English towards the Roman Catholics. He goes into the matter at great length, arguing in a manner which makes it clear that the penal laws were due entirely to political reasons and to the strength of the popular feeling. It seems very improbable that genuine fanaticism exercised much influence on the Government in the matter. He says, 'The Protestants receive a benefit of some toleration in your realm to stop the mischief of civil wars, and to settle a firm peace among yourselves. . . . But such a toleration in this Kingdom would not only destroy peace, but with great probability dissolve it.'

Hacket gives a definite notion of the nature of that learning for which James is still famous. He says, 'Take him for a scholar, and he had gathered knowledge to astonishment; and was so expert to use it, that had he been born in a private fortune he might have deserved to be a bishop of the highest promotion.' He gives proofs of this, one of which is very curious. He used to pass most of his time at Royston and Newmarket in study. 'I have stood by his table often when I was about the age of twenty-two years, and from thenceforward, and have heard learned pieces read before him at his dinners, which I thought strange; but a chaplain of James Montague, Bishop of Winton, told me that the bishop had read over unto him the four tomes of Cardinal Bellarmine's controversies at those respites when His Majesty took fresh air, and weighed the objections and answers to that subtle author; and sent often to the libraries at Cambridge for books to examine the quotations.'

James died on the 22d March 1624, and in the following October, after the dissolution of the first Parliament of Charles, Williams was dismissed from his place as Chancellor. He remained for many years entirely out of Court favour, and passed his time almost exclusively in the discharge of his duties as Bishop of Lincoln.

Hacket's account of his way of life in that capacity is very interesting. He must have been a very splendid prelate. He had two palaces, one at Bugden in Huntingdonshire, and the other at Lincoln; and he laid out vast sums in improving and adorning them. At Bugden 'he turned a ruinous thing into a stately mansion. The out-houses . . . were the greatest eye-sore. These he plucked down to the ground and re-edified with convenient beauty. These were stables, barns, granaries, houses for doves, brewing and dairies, and the outward courts which were next to them he cast into fair allies and grass plats. Within doors the cloisters were the trimmest part of his reparations; the windows of the square beautified with stories of coloured glass, the pavement laid smooth and new, and the walls on every side hung with pieces of exquisite workmen in limning, collected and provided for long before. He planted woods. He fenced the park and stored it with deer. He provided for good husbandry and bought in the leases. . . . He loved stirring and walking, which he used two hours or more every day in the open air if the weather served.' . . . 'It would amount to an error that he should bury so much money in gardens, arbours, orchards, pools for waterfowl, and for fish of all variety, with a walk raised three foot from the ground of about a mile in compass, shaded and covered on each side with trees and pales.' . . . All the nurseries about

London for fair flowers and choice fruits were ransacked to furnish him. Alcinous, if he had lived at Bugden, could not have lived better.' His palace at Lincoln was 'built for none but the ancient Bishops of the See that had four-and-thirty rich manors belonging to them' . . . 'besides a vast jurisdiction of great profit derived into other channels. This palace, fit for the pomp of the great potentates, was formidable to their poor successors that could not keep it warm with the rent that remained.' Still though 'workmen did ask so much, yet in three years he brought it on and up to as much strength and comeliness as when it was first inhabited.'

His way of life was as splendid as his houses. He spent from £1000 to £1200 a year in charity. Many of the sons of the nobility were educated in his house; 'the sons of Marquis Hartford, of the Earls of Pembroke, Salisbury and Leicester, with many others of the gentry of the same tender age to bear them company.' He looked diligently after their education, and upon some points instructed them himself.

He was blamed for two things each of which in these days may be regarded as merits. First, he was very tolerant about the theological disputes of his day, 'indulging his favours and preferment' impartially to Calvinists and Arminians. 'Many, that think the Bishop not the worse patron for this neutrality, blame him that he gave hospitality, showed equanimity, afforded kindness and sufferance to Puritans.' His other fault was that he 'admitted, in his public hall, a comedy once or twice to be presented before him exhibited by his own servants for an evening recreation.'

Though the account of Williams's behaviour in his see is rather long and sufficiently pedantic (it contains amongst other things a digression to prove that the Sibylline verses were not genuine), it gives a striking picture of the courtly, splendid, liberal-minded, and charitable bishop, which sets his character and that of the party in the Church and State which he represented in a very amiable light.

Williams was forbidden to attend the second Parliament of Charles (1626), and an attempt was made to prevent him from attending the Parliament of 1628, which passed the Petition of Right. He attended, nevertheless, and manfully supported the petition. He 'went on to show that the contents of the petition were suitable to the ancient laws of the realm ever claimed and pleaded, expedient for the subject, and no less honourable for the King, which made him a king of men and not of beasts, of brave-spirited freemen and not of broken-hearted peasants.'

On this occasion he was partially reconciled to the King; but after Buckingham's assassination Laud became vehemently jealous of him, and did his very utmost, with only too much success, to ruin him. He laboured at this task throughout the whole of the interval between the Parliament of 1629 and the Long Parliament. Hacket's account of Laud's malignity, extracted from Laud's own journals, is extremely humorous. 'The undoing of his brother and colleague in dignity did so run in his mind that it never was out of his dreams, to be seen in the notes drawn with his own hands in Mr. Prynne's breviate. He dreamt the Lord Keeper was dead, 23d Oct. 1623—that is, being interpreted, in the Duke's affections. 14th June 1626, he dreamt the Bishop of Lincoln came he knew not with whom with iron chains, but returning freed from them, he leapt upon a horse and departed, neither could he overtake him. 17th Mar. 1627, Mr. George Wright whispered in his ear in his sleep that he was the cause that Lincoln was not admitted again into favour in the Court. 13th July 1633, he dreamt at Anderwick that this Bishop came and offered to sit above him at the Council Table ('Quæ Deus in melius crudelia somnia vertat'); that the Earl of Holland came and placed him there.'

This summary of the dreams is grotesque enough, but Hacket's comment is still odder. He quotes upon the subject, Jeremiah xxix. 8, Eccl. v. 3, Salmasius Clymact, p. 789, Isaiah xxix. 7, Plutarch's *Life of Dion*, Acts ii. 17, Eph. iv. 22, Machiavelli's *Prince*, c. 26, Quintus Curtius, Book vii., and Cicero's *Epistles*, iii. 37.

Laud, however, did something more than dream. He instituted three prosecutions against Williams in the Star Chamber. The first was in 1628, and was so absurd that Noy, 'a man of cynical behaviour, but of honest heart to his friends and clients,' refused to go on with it after it had dragged on for two years. It was taken up by a miserable creature called Kilvert, a pettifogging attorney, whose insolence towards the judges, (he threatened to procure the Chief Justice of the Common Pleas 'to be turned out of his place for his forwardness') and iniquity towards the accused, are related at length by Hacket, but seem scarcely credible in these days.

The suit went on till 1636, the Bishop having refused to compromise it by paying £8000 down to the King in 1635. The charge was, that in the former suit the Bishop had tampered with witnesses. He was convicted in July 1636, and sentenced to pay a fine of £10,000, to be imprisoned during pleasure in the Tower, and to be suspended during pleasure from his office as Bishop. Laud pressed 'for the degradation of his brother Bishop, and his deportation God knows where.' The Lord Keeper Finch said, 'That if it had liked others he would have laid some ignominy on the Bishop's person,' . . . 'it was conceived he meant the cutting off his ears.' The Bishop was hereupon committed to the Tower, where he was confined for four years, whilst the wretched Kilvert plundered his property at his own discretion, under pretence of raising the fine. 'He killed up the deer of the Park ; settles in Bugden house for three summers with a seraglio of *quædam*, sells an organ that cost £120 for £10, pictures that cost £400 at £5, books he filched what he would,' etc. etc.

Even this, however, was not enough to satisfy Laud's inveterate malice. He got up a third prosecution for what he called a libel, the libel being supposed to be contained in some letters which the Bishop probably never received, written to him by Mr. Osbaldeston, Master of Westminster School. On this absurd charge he was fined £8000 more, and Charles I. offered to pardon him if he would resign his preferment, and take an Irish bishopric instead. A more disgraceful attempt at extortion and more brutal tyranny have seldom been displayed. Laud owed his original preferment to Williams, and Charles was under great obligations to him.

The Long Parliament restored the Bishop to liberty, the proceedings against him were soon afterwards cancelled, and when it became clear that he would be wanted, he was received into favour. His conduct in the Long Parliament was very characteristic. He was anxious to save Strafford. 'He would have gone through fire and water' to do so; still, 'this being now a thing beyond wit and power,' he joined with three other prelates, Usher, Morton, and Potter, 'to propound how the tenderness of the King's conscience might wade through this insuperable difficulty.' Nothing in the whole of that striking history is more characteristic than the necessity which Charles's conscience felt for a sop, the readiness which the Bishops showed to find one, and the entire efficacy for its purpose of the device which they invented.

Not very long after Strafford's execution, Williams became Archbishop of York, and within a year after his liberation from the Tower he was sent there again by the Parliament (in December 1641) for the famous protest which he, with eleven other bishops, drew up against all legislation which should take place in their enforced absence. He was again released in about a year, and joined the King at York. He afterwards held Conway Castle for the King, and though he joined with a Parliamentary officer to retake it, after a royal officer had dispossessed him, he was devotedly loyal throughout the civil war. Charles's execution broke his heart. He spent the last few years of his life in strict retirement in his native county, and died on his sixty-eighth birthday, 25th March 1650.

The latter part of Hacket's book is taken up with denunciations of the Parliament, and lamentations over Charles, which, to a reader fresh from his details of the cruelties of the Star Chamber, produce a singular effect. Utterly forgetting the twelve years between 1629 and 1641, he reproaches the Parliament bitterly for not trusting the King, and, as Clarendon did, claims for him perfect honesty. 'They would trust him with nothing. An affront of deep indignity! Dare not they trust him that never broke with them? And I have heard his nearest servants say that no man could ever challenge him of the least lie.' He admits that Charles was not popular —'The common people's love to him was cold and lazy.' He makes nothing of Ship-money and the Star Chamber. 'Wherefore so much outcry for Peccadilloes, and verily occasioned by the undutifulness of former Parliaments and subsequent necessities?'

As for the prominent persons in the popular party, Hacket cannot express his feelings about them. 'What a venomous spirit is in that serpent Milton, that black-mouthed Zoilus that blows his viper's breath upon' the Eikon Basilike—'a petty schoolboy scribbler'; 'Get thee behind me, Milton.' In fairness to Hacket it should be remembered that at this time Milton was known principally as a political writer. 'Cromwell, that imp of Satan, compounded of all vice and violence, and Titan-like courage, devoid of all pity and conscience.' . . . 'The Scotch at Newcastle . . . sold their master as Judas did his to the Jews, to the race of New England, the Independent Salvages: oh barbarous! perfidious! mammonish! sacrilegious! to make bargain and sale of him that sate in God's stead over them :—

> Nomen erit pardus, tigris, leo, quicquid adhuc est
> Quod fremat in terris violentius.—Juv. *Sat.* 8.

'I roar it out to all people and languages, are you not astonished at it?' and the good Bishop has to ease his mind by quoting Habakkuk i. 5, Valerius, Lib. vi., Florus, iv. 8, Manilius, ii. (He must obviously have just bought Manilius.) And at last, after raging and shrieking through many other authors, he concludes with this remarkable quotation about Cromwell: 'If I had ever met with a more odious passage than that in St. Basil, ep. 246, I would afford it him κατάβρωμα τοῦ διαβόλου—a morsel fit for the devil's stomach.'

We have done our best to give a notion of the

contents of this curious book. It is of necessity a very imperfect notion, as the book contains much which our space will not permit us to notice; but we have said enough to give some sort of indication of its multifarious contents. Probably no book gives such a full-length portrait of a first-rate divine of the seventeenth century, learned in all the learning of his age and profession, and endowed with abilities, and above all with industry, which must have put him in the front rank in any age and any profession.

The general character of the portrait is surely an attractive one. There was no superstition (unless his passionate loyalty deserved that name) about Williams, and no fanaticism. His fault lay in his slyness, but he appears on the whole to have been a bold, magnanimous, high-bred man, with all the instincts of a scholar, a gentleman, and a statesman, and with none of the characteristic vices of a churchman. He was full of the contracted liberalism which marks the infancy of the reformed Church of England. His view of the Church appears to have been that it was a vast and ancient body, with a complex system of laws and maxims to be learnt by intense study of history and antiquity.

This explains the price which the divines of that day set upon learning, and the enormous mass of quasi-scientific apparatus with which they thought it necessary to be equipped. They were practically their own Popes, and their characters show much of the magnanimity of those who are engaged in the task of constructing a great scheme of ecclesiastical polity out of materials of almost infinite extent and variety. Their view of their opponents shows this feeling. To them the Papists are audacious impostors, supporting a system of priestcraft by misrepresenting history and Scripture. The Puritans are narrow-minded bigots, idolising the letter of Scripture, and afflicted with consciences in a state of chronic hysterical weakness. It has always appeared to us that there was much more contempt than fanaticism in their persecution; though, as against the Roman Catholics, the popular feeling forced them to be fanatical as well as contemptuous. Their loyalty was their romance. Williams and Hacket are striking instances of this. They could see no serious faults in Charles, they could sanction no real precautions against him, they could not even admit to their own minds the undoubted fact that he was thoroughly fraudulent and insincere.

On the whole, the position which they filled was, and still is, eminently characteristic of the Church of England. Its weakness and its strength always have lain, and always will lie, in the fact that it is a Church specially adapted to the rich, the powerful, the learned, and those who combine a strong tinge of scepticism with a genuine dash of devotional feeling.

Hacket's book is very interesting to students of language. It contains many words which have died out in the struggle for existence, and some which strike the eye as modern in the seventeenth century. Thus we read, 'Men that are sound in their morals are best reclaimed when they are *mignarised* and stroked gently.' 'The chief *minerval* which he bestowed was . . . a library, the best in Cambridge.' 'Their *platform*' (in the American sense—the word is common also in Hooker) 'comes so near to the old Protestant Church of England,' etc. 'He put this *dodgery* strongly upon those at London.' 'He gave the Spaniard *the dodge.*' 'The *dodges* of the Prince of Parma.' 'The *exequies* of the dead'—the correct form of the absurd word 'obsequies.' 'As for the Duke, his domestic *creatures*'—for servants simply, with no unfavourable sense. Eliot calls himself Buckingham's 'creature.' '*Novelists*' for innovators. 'It was heard of long ago in the *middle ages*,' occurs in a sermon of Williams about the year 1630. The most curious of all is, 'When they found he was not *selfish* (it is a word of their own'—*i.e.* the Puritans'—'new mint').

XIII

CLARENDON'S
'HISTORY OF THE REBELLION'[1]

THOUGH Clarendon's *History of the Rebellion* is not only a well-established classic, but is also one of the leading authorities upon the most interesting and best-known period of our history, it is probable that the number of well-educated men who can honestly say that they have read it through is not very large. It is the fate of standard books to pass by slow degrees out of circulation. They furnish materials for writers whose works in their turn undergo the same fate; and thus, after a time, they influence readers through four or five different removes.

Hume had hardly any other authority for the reign of Charles than Clarendon. Hallam's *Constitutional History* put Hume's theories of the Stuart times out of sight. Lord Macaulay's review of Hallam is better known to many persons in the

[1] *The History of the Rebellion and Civil Wars in England.* By Edward, Earl of Clarendon.

present day than Hallam himself; and it is to be hoped that Mr. Forster's curious and learned investigations into the reign of Charles I. have given to a still newer generation of readers more accurate notions on the subject than they could well have derived from any earlier source.

This is not to be regretted. If knowledge is to be kept within any sort of compass, original authorities must be gradually sifted, and laid on one side after their main results have been extracted. Still it is interesting from time to time to recur to them, even for other purposes than those of special study of the matters to which they refer. We have, no doubt, the means of understanding the history of the reign of Charles I. far better than Clarendon understood it; but the history of great events by a great man rather gains than loses in interest by the acquisition of a point of view, and of a set of thoughts, different from and wider than those under which he wrote.

The first thing that strikes a modern reader of Clarendon is the utter absence, from every part of his book, of anything approaching to what, in the present day, would be considered a philosophical or general view of his subject. The civil war appears to him, in the full sense of the words, an impious, wicked, unnatural rebellion. From first to last he views it with as much astonishment as horror. He cannot, or will not, understand how or why it could have happened. All his careful study of individual character, all his keen insight into the outrageous folly, wickedness, and selfishness of a great number of the King's adherents, do not appear to enable him to sympathise in the very least degree with the Parliamentary leaders. Charles himself could hardly have taken a more simple and decisive view of the perfect justice of his own cause, and the perfect wickedness of. that of his opponents, than was taken for him by his zealous Chancellor of the Exchequer.

This is a singular contrast to the style of the present day. Any book with the faintest pretensions to rise above the rank of a collection of dates would contain some view as to the general causes of the civil wars—some account of the principles represented by the two contending parties, and of the degree in which those principles rose out of, or were suggested by, the ancient institutions of the country. Indeed, we should be apt to regard it as a merit if the author observed any moderation in such reflections.

Their total absence, and the absence of any notion of the very possibility of making them, produces as disagreeable an effect in Clarendon as an affected profusion of them often produces in our own times. It has for, one thing, the disadvantage of making the story unintelligible. Why, the reader asks again and again, did a quiet, orderly, loyal people rush into civil war? The only explanation suggested by Clarendon is that they waxed fat and kicked, that, being puffed up by peace and prosperity, they took to cutting each other's throats —a simply childish notion. ·The explanation that their liberties both were, and were felt to be, in real danger, and that the circumstances of the time rendered this almost unavoidable, never strikes Clarendon even when he is on the brink of it.

For instance, after describing, probably with truth, the years between 1630 and 1640 as times of great plenty and riches, he actually adds:—'All these blessings could but enable not compel us to be happy. . . . The country full of pride, mutiny, and discontent; every man more troubled and perplexed at that they called the violation of one law [such a violation, for instance, as the forced loans, ship-money, or arbitrary imprisonment for things said in Parliament] than delighted or pleased with the observation of all the rest of the charter; never imputing the increase of their receipts, revenue, and plenty to the wisdom, virtue, and merit of the Crown, but objecting every small imposition to the exorbitancy and tyranny of the Government.'

The fact that, for one reason or another, the Royal power on the one hand, and the popular appreciation of liberty on the other, had been increasing for ages, and that their collision was altogether inevitable sooner or later, never seems to have occurred to Clarendon, though the whole nation felt it, no doubt, more or less obscurely.

This want of speculative power, however, applies only to general views of history and morals. There is in Clarendon's history a good deal of philosophy of a certain kind; that is to say, the book contains isolated reflections upon particular circumstances which show that it was not from want of ability that its author did not take general views of what we should now call the philosophy of history, but because that philosophy or science was not then invented.

Many of our readers will, no doubt, remember with very mixed feelings the famous but dreadfully difficult chapters (iii. 82, 83, 84,) which contain the reflections of Thucydides on the massacre at Corcyra. In the 7th book of Clarendon's *History* there is a passage, suggested by the quarrels in the Privy Council at Oxford, which in some ways so much resembles them that it is by no means unlikely that it is a conscious imitation. It is an essay of four or five pages on the nature of Councils, and on the sort of character and conduct which fits men to succeed in them. It is most characteristic of the man and of his mind. It is throughout a refutation of depreciatory commonplaces, and a vindication of truths which, though they may look commonplace, are constantly forgotten and disregarded. Debates in council, he says, are by no means merely formal, nor are they, as rash observers are apt to consider, useless. Men are often 'in this particular argument unskilful, in that affected, who may seem to have levity or formality or vanity in ordinary conversation, and yet in formal counsels, deliberations, and transactions are men of great insight and wisdom.' The objections to them are founded on ignorance of their practical working, and of the way in which affairs are of necessity conducted; and the way to succeed in them is to attain a certain even temper of mind, hard to be learnt, but absolutely essential :—

'There is not a more troublesome passion, or that often draws more inconveniences with it, than that which proceeds from the indignation of being unjustly calumniated and from the pride of an upright conscience; when men cannot endure to be spoken ill of if they have not deserved it.'

This summary of the temper of mind necessary for public life, and the way of conducting public affairs, is very like the speculation of Thucydides (referred to above) on the temper of mind produced by, and successful in, revolutions. The tone and reach of the two speculations is similar, though their comparative importance differs.

The descriptions of character on which the fame of Clarendon as a writer principally depends are much upon the same intellectual level as this speculation. Each of them shows how closely and with what searching curiosity he examined and revolved in his mind any fact which interested him. Every one, his dearest friend, his bitterest enemy, the objects of his deepest contempt and of his highest admiration, are all passed through the same crucible. He looks into them with all the curiosity of a modern novelist, and gives in a few phrases a summary which in the present day would, by the invention of characteristic illustrative instances, be made to fill the constitutional three volumes of a novel.

The best, to our taste at least, are the characters

of the men with whom he lived, and who were upon the same sort of level with himself. There is, for instance, an admirable character of Lord Cottington, who was his fellow-ambassador from Charles II. to the Court of Spain in 1650. He was a very old man, who passed the greater part of his life in diplomacy, and changed his religion three or four times. This is Clarendon's summary of his gifts :—

'He was of excellent humour and very easy to live with, and under a grave countenance covered the most of mirth, and caused more than any man of the most pleasant disposition. He never used anybody ill, but used many very well for whom he had no regard; his greatest fault was that he could dissemble and make men believe that he loved them well when he cared not for them. He had not very tender affections, nor bowels apt to yearn at all objects which deserved compassion; he was heartily weary of the world, and no man more willing to die; which is an argument that he had peace of conscience. He left behind him a greater esteem of his parts than love to his person.'

It would be hardly possible in so few words to give a livelier picture of an upright, amiable, rather cold-hearted man of the world with a great sense of humour. In the original, which is too long to extract, these generalities are borne out by a well-selected and well-told set of anecdotes and particulars which make the man live again before those who read them.

Clarendon was not so happy in describing his antagonists. He could not understand a Puritan at all. His character of Cromwell, for instance, represents, not a man, but a monster made up of contradictions. He describes him with great honesty, and was obviously struck deeply by his wonderful genius and force of character; but there is not a touch of sympathy in the whole description. He supposes, apparently, that, from the very first, Cromwell meant to be a usurper, and acted accordingly.

That a man could really believe in such principles as he held, that he could honestly act upon them, that his strength was derived from the fact that he clearly understood what he wanted and steadily pursued it, and that what he did want was by no means entirely bad, or even bad in the main—all this is utterly incredible to Clarendon. He arrives at the result that Cromwell was a living contradiction: 'In a word, as he had all the wickednesses against which damnation is denounced, and for which hell-fire is prepared, so he had some virtues which have caused the memory of some men in all ages to be celebrated, and he will be looked upon by posterity as a brave bad man.'

Perhaps a still better instance of Clarendon's inability to enter into the feelings of a Puritan is to be found in a much less conspicuous case, which shows that to him it was a horrible mystery that the Puritans should be anything else but a crew of unnatural villains. In 1651 a Presbyterian, named Love, was executed for treason against the Commonwealth.[1]

[1] See his trial in 5 S. T., iv. 267, *et seq.*

He died like a martyr. Clarendon observes upon this :—

'It is a wonderful thing what operation this Presbyterian spirit had upon the minds of those who were possessed by it. This poor man Love, who had been guilty of so much treason against the King from the beginning of the rebellion as the pulpit could contain, was so much without remorse for any wickedness of that kind he had committed that he was jealous of nothing so much as of being suspected to repent.'

He then describes the 'marvellous undauntedness' of his language, and the 'inward joy' which his behaviour showed, and, after giving some of his dying words, concludes thus :—

'And in this raving fit without so much as praying for the King otherwise than that he might propagate the covenant, he laid his head upon the block with as much courage as the bravest and honestest man could do on the most pious occasion.'

The very essence of Clarendon's mind, and of the spirit of the age in which he lived, is in these words. The great lesson which the book, fairly read, would appear to teach is, that the whole war was a lamentable, but, as far as we can see, an inevitable mistake, the result of ignorance and narrowness of mind on each side, though no doubt Charles himself was more deeply to blame for it than any other person.

Clarendon contrives to obscure the incidents connected with its outbreak, and, as Mr. Hallam truly observed, he (if he were the author of Charles's State papers) got much the best of the written controversy with the Parliament; but the true nature of the case is plain beyond all dispute.

After his conduct in the early part of his reign, and after the attempt to arrest the five members (which we agree with Mr. Forster in considering as an abortive *coup d'état*), it was impossible to trust the King without security, and that security he never would give. In a word, it was necessary to depose him, at least for a time. The Parliament wished to do this gently, and without disturbing the forms of the Constitution; and those forms, of course, implied that the King was still to be King. This gave Clarendon an immense controversial advantage, for it was easy for him to show that their proposals amounted virtually to deposition, though they abounded in expressions of humility and duty; and this gave occasion for an inexhaustible supply of charges of hypocrisy and falsehood—charges which were well founded only on the supposition that there are to be no such things as constitutional fictions, and that a King of England ought to consider every phrase which the law uses about his office, as investing him individually with the full amount of the power which the literal sense of the words professes to convey.

On the other hand, it cannot be denied that some at least of the views of Charles and his principal advisers were what we should in the present day describe as far more liberal than those of their opponents. Perhaps the most remarkable passage in Clarendon's works is a part of his Life in which he describes the society in which he used to pass his leisure during his youth in London.

His account of the friends who used to meet at Lord Falkland's house near Oxford is charming, and there can be no doubt that some of them—Falkland, Hales, and Chillingworth, for instance—were at once the most learned and the most liberal-minded men in England. Of these, Falkland and Chillingworth lost their lives in serving the King, and Hales received preferment from Laud.

There can be little room for doubt that Charles I., Clarendon himself, and Lord Falkland were really and deeply attached to the Church of England, and as really and deeply opposed to the Church of Rome; and there is as little question that they, or at least that Charles and Clarendon, were opposed on every ground to the cruel laws then in force against the Roman Catholics, which it was one object of the Parliament to have strictly executed.

It is also matter of fact that by far the most liberal theological book of that age (Chillingworth's *Religion of Protestants*) expressed the tone of opinion and sentiment prevalent amongst Clarendon's friends. It was dedicated to Charles, and was greatly admired by Laud. There are few more curious problems in English history than that which these facts suggest. Why was it that religious liberalism in the seventeenth century was allied with political Toryism, whilst the most bigoted and narrow views of religion were held by the founders of our political liberties? We cannot at present enter upon this inquiry; but, in order to understand Clarendon, it is necessary to be aware of its existence, and to know that, though the highest of high Tories, he was anything but a bigot.

One or two of the sentences in which he refers to John Hales (who earned the epithet of the Ever Memorable) are very characteristic upon this point. He describes with manifest sympathy some of his opinions, then viewed as dangerous novelties:—

'He therefore exceedingly detested the tyranny of the Church of Rome more for their imposing uncharitably upon the consciences of other men, than for the errors in their own opinions; and would often say that he would renounce the religion of the Church of England to-morrow if it obliged him to believe that any other Christians should be damned; and that nobody would conclude another man to be damned who did not wish him so.'

This foundation of highmindedness and liberality went admirably with the devotion of Clarendon to his sovereign, and with that passionate belief in him which blinded perhaps the keenest critic of character in all England to the most patent, as it was the most fatal, of all Charles's defects. Clarendon actually begins his character with these words: 'He was if ever any the most worthy of the title of an honest man,' and this he says though not many pages before he had given a full account of the secret treaty between Charles and the Presbyterian Commissioners from Scotland, which, says Clarendon himself, the King signed on the representation 'that the treaty was only made to enable them to engage the Kingdom of Scotland to raise an army . . . but when that army should be entered into England . . . there would be nobody to exact all those particulars.' In other words, he agreed to it only because he believed it to be a gross fraud.

Such blindness in our own days is scarcely conceivable, but we cannot estimate the power of personal loyalty as it then was. A king of England was to Clarendon both a temporal sovereign and a pope; and nothing more clearly shows the danger of this blind personal devotion to a single man than the fact that so wise and great a man as Clarendon was should have been converted by it into an instrument of tyranny and an enemy to the best interests of his country.

The general temper of Clarendon's mind, when he wrote his History, is discernible enough. The foundation of the whole, as we have said, was a stately, highminded conception of things human and divine; but this conception was twisted, by his distaste for the narrowness and other faults of the Puritan party, in such a manner, as to lead the man who held it to a blind admiration for a party, not really more exalted than the one which he hated, and by no means so useful.

Falkland, Chillingworth, and others, no doubt, had a stately and noble view of an English king, but the stately view of the subject was by no means the only one. Every page of the History of the Civil War and of Charles's exile is filled with instances of meanness, brutality, cruelty, and debauchery amongst the King's adherents, which fully justify the bad opinion held by the Puritans of the Court and its party.

The history of the war in the West of England, where Lord Goring and Sir Richard Grenville were the King's principal officers, is full of instances of brutality and cruelty. Speaking of the Prince of Wales's own quarters, Clarendon says: 'The troops were without any discipline, and the country as much exposed to rapine and violence as it could suffer under an enemy.' Charles 'drew out his garrison from Cambden House which had brought no other benefit to the public than the enriching the licentious governor thereof, who exercised an illimited tyranny over the whole country, and took his leave of it, in wantonly burning the noble structure where he had too long inhabited, and which not many years before had cost above £30,000 the building.'

When Leicester was taken, 'the conquerors pursued their advantage with the usual license of rapine and plunder, and miserably sacked the whole town without any distinction of persons or places; churches and hospitals as well as other places were made a prey to the enraged and greedy soldier.' Sir Richard Grenville hanged as a spy an attorney who had been engaged against him in law proceedings, and his general course of proceeding is thus described. He used to summon men to attend him; if they failed to come, he sent to arrest them. 'If the persons were taken, they were very well content to remit their stock to redeem their persons; for the better disposing them whereto he would now and then hang a constable, or some other poor fellow,' etc. By these means this thief and robber 'had a greater stock of cattle of all sorts upon his grounds than any person whatsoever in the West of England.'

The book is full of misfortunes occasioned by the habitual drunkenness of the King's officers. Lord Wilmot 'drank hard and had a great power over all who did so, which was a great people.' When Lord Essex's army was surrounded in Cornwall, near Fowey, his cavalry escaped because Goring was drunk and disorderly ('the notice and orders came to Goring when he was in one of his jovial exercises') when he ought to have been on duty. Nothing can exceed the scene of petty, dirty intrigue which was constantly going on at the Court, and the impression left by the whole story is that, though Clarendon and a very few others were of a noble and magnificent character, the general hatred against Charles and his government was by no means ill-founded.

The natural result of this state of things upon a highminded, enthusiastic, decorous man, whose temper was naturally hot and keen, was to turn him to grave but fierce humour, and his book is full of illustrations of this. Its style is too well known to call for description. Every one who has ever looked into it knows the endless sentences, the involutions, the strange constructions, which make it wearisome to modern readers. The qualities to which it owes its reputation are not so apparent but they may be traced by an attentive reader who will take the trouble to discard the historical tenses and to modernise the stops.

The following passage is a fair specimen of the defects and the energy of Clarendon's way of writing. It is part of a manifesto on the commission to the Earl of Essex against the King:—

'It was not possible that a commission could be granted to the Earl of Essex to raise an army against us, and for the safety of our person, and preservation of the peace of the kingdom, to pursue kill and slay us and all who wish well to us, but that in a short time inferior commanders by the same authority would require our good subjects for the maintenance of the property of the subject to supply them with such sums of money as they think fit upon the penalty of being plundered with all extremity of war and by such rules of arbitrary power as are inconsistent with the least pretence or shadow of that property it would seem to defend.'

A few verbal alterations will convert this clumsy sentence into the style of the most cutting leading article or review. For instance: 'You issue a commission to the Earl of Essex to raise an army against us, and for the safety of our person and the preservation of the peace of the kingdom to pursue, kill, and slay us, and all who wish well to us. Inferior commanders will soon learn the same lesson. They will require our subjects, for the maintenance of the property of the subject, to supply them with such sums of money as they please, and those who refuse will be plundered with all extremity of war. You thus erect, for your protection, an arbitrary power which in its very nature is inconsistent with the existence of the rights which you say you mean it to protect.'

The following is, as it stands, as powerful as it can be:—

'By this rule if a member of either house commit a murder you must by no means meddle with him till you have acquainted that house of which he is a member, and received their direction for your proceeding, assuring yourself he will not stir from that place where you left him till you return with their consent; should it be otherwise it would be in the power of every man under the pretence of murder to take one after another and as many as he pleaseth and so consequently bring a parliament to what he pleaseth when he pleaseth. If a member of either house shall take a purse at York (he may as probably take a purse from a subject as arms against the King) you must ride to London to know what to do, and he may ride with you and take a new purse at every stage, and must not be apprehended, or declared a felon till you have asked that house of which he is a member; should it be otherwise it might be in every man's power to accuse as many members as he would of taking purses, and so bring a parliament and so all parliaments to nothing. Would these men be believed?'

A very little attention to the rules of composition now generally understood, will show that Clarendon might, with hardly an effort, have made his book as brilliant as it is impressive, nor need it have lost any of its weight in the process. Indeed, its weight arises from the gravity of the author's thoughts, and by no means from the cumbrousness of his style.

It is full of humour. Numerous instances might be given, but we must content ourselves with a few. Cromwell's 'physicians began to think him in danger, though the preachers who prayed always about him *and told God Almighty what great things he had done for him and how much more need he still had of his service* declared as from God that he should recover.' Strafford's great fault was pride, which was punished 'in that he fell by the two things he most despised, the people and Sir Harry Vane.' Montrose refuses to be prayed for by the Presbyterian ministers because he knows how they would have prayed, thus: ' "Lord vouchsafe yet to touch the obdurate heart of this proud incorrigible sinner this wicked perjured traitorous and profane person who refuses to hearken to the voice of thy Kirk" and the like charitable expressions.' Lord Berkshire's 'affection for the Crown was good; his interest and reputation less than anything but his understanding.' Lord Salisbury 'was a man of no words except in hunting and hawking, in which only he knew how to behave himself. In matters of state and council he always concurred in what was proposed for the King and cancelled and repaired all those transgressions by concurring in all that was proposed against him as soon as any such propositions were made.'

Undoubtedly the most remarkable of Clarendon's gifts was his occasional eloquence. With one specimen of this we must conclude. It may be doubted whether the language contains a nobler passage of the kind. The very negligence of the composition heightens its dreary pathos. The desolation of the church, the smallness and sadness of the company, the 'fellow from the town' who alone happened to know where lay 'King Harry VIII. and Queen Jane Seymour,' the Governor locking up the place, 'which was seldom put to any use,' when all was over, are marvellous accompaniments to the funeral of an English king who had died the death of a traitor.

The superiority of this passage over Mr. Wolfe's poem on Sir John Moore's funeral shows how impossible it is for the finest imagination and the most elaborate choice of words to equal the concentrated emotion which colours the language of a man who is writing of that which touches the very core of his heart :—

'Then they went into the church, to make choice of a place for burial. But when they entered into it, which they had been so well acquainted with, they found it so altered and transformed, all tombs, inscriptions, and those landmarks pulled down, by which all men knew every particular place in that church, and such a dismal mutation over the whole, that they knew not where they were; nor was there one old officer that had belonged to it, or knew where our princes had used to be interred. At last there was a fellow of the town who undertook to tell them the place, where, he said, "there was a vault in which King Harry the Eighth and Queen Jane Seymour were interred." As near that place as could conveniently be, they caused the grave to be made. There the King's body was laid without any words, or other ceremonies than the tears and sighs of the few beholders. Upon the coffin was a plate of silver fixed with these words only—*King Charles.* 1648. When the coffin was put in, the black velvet pall that had covered it was thrown over it, and then the earth thrown in; which the Governor stayed to see perfectly done, and then took the keys of the church, which was seldom put to any use.'

XIV

LORD CLARENDON'S 'LIFE'[1]

LORD CLARENDON'S Life is partly supplementary to, and partly a continuation of, his more famous work, and throws a good deal of additional light on the character of the author and on the age in which he lived. There are three principal periods which the memoirs illustrate. First, the early part of his life, down to the meeting of the Long Parliament (birth, 18th February 1609, to November 1640). Secondly, some parts of the history of the Long Parliament and the Civil War, and of the residence of Charles II. abroad (1640-1660). Thirdly, the Restoration, the early years of Charles II.'s reign (1660-1667), and the six years which

---

[1] *The Life of Edward, Earl of Clarendon, Lord High Chancellor of England, and Chancellor of the University of Oxford.* Containing, 1. An Account of the Chancellor's Life from his Birth to the Restoration in 1660; 2. A Continuation of the same, and of his History of the Great Rebellion from the Restoration to his Banishment in 1667. Written by Himself. Oxford: 1761.

Clarendon passed in banishment, until his death on 9th December 1673.

The first period is much the most entertaining. Clarendon was not industrious in his youth. He learnt very little at college, where indeed he was a mere boy; and his life as a law student 'was without great application to the study of the law for some years, it being then a time when the town was full of soldiers. . . . And he had gotten into the acquaintance of many of those officers, which took up too much of his time for one year.' He read some 'polite literature and history,' however, and, as he remarked in his old age, 'lived *cautè* if not *castè*.' He had, however, the means of seeing good society. He was connected by marriage with the family of the Marquis of Hamilton, and he was brought very early in his career into business of importance. In particular, he vindicated before the Privy Council the rights of the merchants of London, in a dispute which affected the revenue; and, in consequence of his management of the case, he was introduced to Archbishop Laud. His professional success and distinction put him in very pleasant circumstances. 'He grew every day in practice, of which he had as much as he desired; and, having a competent estate of his own, he enjoyed a very pleasant and a plentiful life, living much above the rank of those lawyers whose business was only to be rich, and was generally beloved and esteemed by most persons of condition and great reputation.'

His account of these pleasant days is by far the most interesting passage of his writings. It is composed of characters of Ben Jonson, Selden, Sir Kenelm Digby, May the historian of the Long Parliament, Lord Falkland, Waller the poet, Sheldon, afterwards Archbishop of Canterbury, Hales, Chillingworth, and some others of less note. The accounts of Falkland and Chillingworth are memorable passages in English literature, and deserve to be described as portraits of the highest excellence. The other characters are rather collections of remarks than pictures.

Clarendon's History and his Memoirs are full of interest, but their interest is that of the conversation of an experienced public man, who was, besides, one of the strongest of all conceivable partisans. It is not the interest of a work of art. Moreover, his extreme gravity and stateliness, though it allowed him to be sarcastic and occasionally humorous, prevented him from devising any of those pointed vigorous expressions which, as Mr. Carlyle says of some of Mirabeau's, make a complete portrait in three scratches and a dot. This renders his portraits far less amusing than they would otherwise have been, and in some respects less instructive.

That Clarendon's partisanship continually blinded his judgment is painfully obvious. This appears strikingly in the worship which he lavished on Charles I.; but he partially redeems his fault by his views of the Stuart family in general, and of Charles II. in particular. His account of him and his brother is an admirable specimen of the sarcastic vein which he sometimes indulged :—

'It was the unhappy fate of that family that they trusted naturally the judgments of those who were as much inferior to them in understanding as they were in quality. . . . They were too much inclined to like men at first sight, and did not love the conversation of men of many more years than themselves, and thought age not only troublesome but impertinent. They did not love to deny, and less to strangers than to their friends; not out of bounty or generosity, which was a flower that did never grow naturally in the heart of either of the families—that of Stuart or the other of Bourbon—but out of an unskilfulness and defect in the countenance; and when they prevailed with themselves to make some pause rather than to deny, importunities removed all resolution, which they knew not how to shut out nor defend themselves against, even when it was evident enough that they had much rather not consent. . . . If the Duke seemed more fixed and firm in his resolutions, it was rather from an obstinacy in his will than from the constancy of his judgment.'

A delightful character, from the most faithful servant and most zealous partisan that ever any family had.

We get, however, from Clarendon a very pleasing notion of his early friends. Perhaps the most characteristic point about them is their great intellectual activity, and the extraordinary degree of learning that some of them attained to.

Falkland appears to have formed a kind of centre for the whole party, when he was little over twenty; and the well-known passage in which his pursuits are described is so beautiful that we transcribe it:—

'His whole conversation was one continued *convivium philosophicum* or *convivium theologicum*, enlivened and refreshed with all the facetiousness of wit and good humour, and pleasantness of discourse, which made the argument itself (whatever it was) very delectable. His house, where he usually resided (Tew or Burford, in Oxfordshire), being within ten or twelve miles of the University, looked like the University itself, by the company that was always found there. There was Dr. Sheldon, Dr. Morley, Dr. Hammond, Dr. Earles, Mr. Chillingworth, and indeed all men of eminent parts and faculties at Oxford, besides those who resorted thither from London; who all found their lodgings there as ready as in the colleges; nor did the lord of the house know of their coming or going, nor who were in his house, till he came to dinner or supper, where all still met; otherwise there was no troublesome ceremony or constraint to forbid men to come to the house, or to make them weary of staying there; so that many came thither to study in a better air, finding all the books they could desire in his library, and all the persons together whose company they could wish, and not find in any other society. Here Mr. Chillingworth wrote and formed and modelled his excellent book against the learned Jesuit Mr. Knott, after frequent debates upon the most important particulars.'

Lord Falkland's own studies were remarkable :—

'There were very few classic authors in the Greek or Latin tongue that he had not read with great exactness; he had read all the Greek and Latin fathers, all the most allowed and authentic ecclesiastical writers, and all the Councils, with wonderful care and observation; for in religion he thought too careful and too curious an inquiry could not be made amongst those whose purity was not questioned'—and whose authority was appealed to on both sides. The sentence meanders on for thirteen lines more, which we spare our readers; but this is what it comes to.

This passage — to which other well-known facts correspond — as, for instance, the prodigious learning of Selden, and the curiously minute acquaintance with all the details of English history which was shown in the great Parliamentary debates of the period, and of which Mr. Forster's *Life of Eliot* supplies numerous illustrations—raises the question whether men in those days were more energetic and industrious than in our own. To discuss it at length would lead us far from our present subject, but Clarendon's Life throws some light upon the matter.

There would seem to have been hardly any light literature in those days, plays excepted; and the common subjects of education were fewer than at present. Falkland, for instance, who was carefully educated at Dublin, knew no Greek till he taught it himself long afterwards. Clarendon learnt French only during his second exile, 'not,' he says, 'towards speaking it, the defect of which he found many conveniences in, but for the reading any books.' A man might get through a great deal of reading if there were no circulating library works, no periodical literature, and only one language besides his own, or at most two, which he had any occasion to understand.

Next to his own immediate friends, the most interesting personages described in the early part of Clarendon's Life are Archbishop Laud and Clarendon himself. He was very fond of Laud; he 'had so great an affection and reverence for his memory' that he 'believed him to be a man of the most exemplar virtue and piety of any of that age.' Laud took notice of him as he was just rising into large business at the Bar, and when life in general must have looked very bright to him; and probably some of the rays of that brightness fell upon the Archbishop. The only fault that he could, or would, see in him was the roughness of his manner.

Clarendon probably secretly liked him all the better for defects which he was conscious of not sharing, though he had a certain tendency towards them, corrected by education. Of Laud he observes, in a well-known passage :—

'It is the misfortune of most persons of that education (how worthy soever) that they have rarely friendships with men above their own condition, and that their ascent being commonly sudden from low to high, they have afterwards rather dependants than friends, and are still deceived by keeping somewhat in reserve to themselves even from those with whom they seem most openly to communicate, and, which is worse, receive for the most part their informations and advertisements from clergymen who understand the least, and take the worst measure of human affairs of all mankind that can write and read.'

It is easy to trace in this celebrated passage the inward satisfaction with which Clarendon contrasted his own social advantages with the somewhat narrow education of Laud. His own temper apparently had something of the same sort of roughness in it, for he continually boasts of his habitual plainness of speech.

The following account of himself is one of the oddest passages that ever were written:—

'He was in his nature inclined to pride and passion, and to a humour between wrangling and disputing, very troublesome; which good company in a short time so much reformed and mastered, that no man was more affable and courteous to all kinds of persons; and they who knew the great infirmity of his whole family, which abounded in passion, used to say he had much extinguished the unruliness of that fire. That which supported and rendered him generally acceptable was his generosity (for he had too much a contempt of money), and the opinion men had of the goodness and justness of his nature which was transcendent in him, in a wonderful tenderness and delight in obliging. His integrity was ever without blemish, and believed to be above temptation. He was firm and unshaken in his friendships; and though he had great candour towards others in the differences of religion, he was zealously and deliberately fixed in the principles both of the doctrine and discipline of the Church.'

Few men have sung their own praises with such calm assurance. Has any other writer said in so many words: 'Upon mature reflection, I pronounce myself to be a man of transcendent goodness and justice, wonderful tenderness, unblemished integrity, a firm friend, and as candid as I am strict in my religious views'? In every part of his autobiography Clarendon shows a solid, deliberate admiration of himself, which it seems hardly fair to call vanity, because it is so calm and grave.

The great blemish of the early part of the Memoirs is that they throw very little light either upon the history of Clarendon's earlier opinions or on the nature of his change. Perhaps the most plausible guess—for, after all, it is little more that can be made—as to his frame of mind, is that he was one of the very few who clearly understood the nature of the struggle between the King and the Parliament, and took part emphatically and passionately for the King; and this although, in the earlier part of his career, he was as well aware as any one of the existence of great abuses which required a remedy.

All study of that period leads to the conclusion that the real question was the question of sovereignty. Was the King or the Parliament to be the substantive or the adjective? Clarendon took the royal side, perhaps, all the more warmly because he had sufficient faith in it to wish to reform collateral abuses, like the Courts of the Earl Marshal and those of the President of the North, and the Council of Wales. He appears really and honestly to have believed that it was an everlasting divine decree that the King and the Bishops should direct, substantially and really, all the temporal and spiritual affairs of the nation, and that it was in the highest degree morally wicked, and even impious, to try to alter this arrangement.

Nothing is more difficult for us, at this distance of time, to realise, than the view which in those days a man like Clarendon took of a man like Hampden. What Hampden thought of Clarendon we do not know, but Clarendon obviously considered Hampden as a wicked man, a rebel, a traitor, and a hypocrite.

In a curious summary of his own experience of life with which the book concludes, he says, in language too ample for quotation, that he began by 'so great a tenderness and love towards mankind' that he believed every one to be virtuous, but that his Parliamentary experience soon taught him that men 'upon whose ingenuity and probity he would willingly have deposited all his concernments of this world' were 'totally false and disingenuous'; that 'religion was made a cloak to cover the most impious designs, and reputation of honesty a stratagem to deceive and cheat others who had no mind to be wicked.' It is true that he adds that the Court was 'as full of murmuring, ingratitude, and treachery against the best and most bountiful master in the world as the country and the city'; but scores of passages might easily be quoted from his works which show that he was utterly unable to believe that the Parliamentary party could have any conscientious belief at all in their own principles.

This intense zeal is the more difficult to explain because he stood almost alone in it. Falkland, for instance, was obviously in great doubt as to the course which he had taken; but perhaps the most curious case was that of Sir Edmund Verney, the standard-bearer. On the march to Edge Hill he complimented Hyde on his cheerfulness, adding that, for his own part, he could not be cheerful :—

' "You," said Verney, "have satisfaction in your conscience that you are in the right; that the King ought not to grant what is required of him . . . but for my part, I do not like the quarrel, and do heartily wish that the King would yield, and consent to what they desire. . . . I will deal freely with you. I have no reverence for the Bishops for whom this quarrel subsists." '

Clarendon's intense partisanship for the King and the Bishops, wherever he got it, certainly went a very long way, for it made him thoroughly disingenuous in his subsequent account of the transactions in which he was concerned. No one would ever guess from his writings that he had voted for Strafford's attainder, or for the Bill for perpetual Parliaments. Other instances of great forgetfulness or deceitfulness have been exposed elaborately by Mr. Forster in his *Life of Eliot*. It ought, however, to be observed that both his History and his Life are exceedingly imperfect. He omits many matters which ought to have found a place in his writings. For instance, he does not even allude to the Act for abolishing feudal tenures.

In the second stage of his life—the Civil War, and the years of exile which followed it—the autobiography adds little to the *History of the Rebellion* except a certain number of personal anecdotes. The most interesting relate to his residence at Jersey, where he employed himself, between 1646 and 1648, in writing his History. As usual, he commends his own industry with that grave, measured self-esteem which was peculiar to him :—

'He seldom spent less than ten hours in the day' (amongst his books and papers), 'and it can hardly be believed how much he read and writ there; inasmuch as he did usually compute that during his whole stay in Jersey, which was some months above two years, he writ daily little less than one sheet of large paper with his own hand.'

Creditable enough, but nothing to make a marvel of, one would think.

The third part of Clarendon's Life stands alone, relating as it does, to a period subsequent to the termination of his History. It relates to the first years of the reign of Charles II. It is a good deal occupied with Clarendon's own personal affairs, which have now fallen much out of date. He finds it necessary, for instance, to go with extreme minuteness into most of the points on which his impeachment was grounded, and to show, step by step, how unreasonable they were, and how hardly he was used. This he does successfully enough, but at wearisome length to a modern reader.

One only of the personal scenes of the book is curious enough to be worth particular reference. It is the one in which he describes his behaviour on hearing of his daughter's private marriage to James II. When informed of the fact by the Marquis of Ormond and the Earl of Southampton, at the desire of Charles II., he behaved in a manner which it takes him two pages to describe, the nature of which is sufficiently indicated by the marginal notes which illustrate them. 'The Chancellor struck with it to the heart' is the summary of about half a page; 'and breaks out into a very immoderate passion' is the summary of the remainder. It is a most appropriate one, for the concluding sentences, the stately style of which is in strange contrast to their character, are :—

'He hoped their Lordships would concur with him that the King should immediately cause the woman to be sent to the Tower, and to be cast into a dungeon, under so strict a guard that no person living should be committed to come to her; and then that an Act of Parliament should be immediately passed for the cutting off of her head, to which he would not only give his consent, but would very willingly be the first man to propose it; and whoever knew the man will believe that he said all this very heartily.'

He also observed 'that he had much rather his daughter should be the Duke's whore than his wife,' as, in the first case, he might turn her out of doors, and have done with her; whereas, in the second, his duty as a loyal subject, and as first Minister of the Crown, would be to get her head cut off. This story is often told as a proof of the passionate, bigoted loyalty of Clarendon. We agree with Lord Campbell in thinking that his lordship did protest too much, and that in truth he was by no means so angry as he professed to be.

The worst part of his whole character—and the fault is illustrated in endless ways—is his frequent insincerity. No doubt the events of his life afforded much excuse for it, but it shows itself continually, and almost always in the same form. He keeps continually saying, almost in so many words, but at all events indirectly, 'I am a rough, honest, passionate, plain-spoken man, proud of my sincerity, perhaps too secure in my good conscience. My frank harshness of manner was the cause of all my misfortunes.' The slyness which lurks under this sort of roughness is the slyest thing in the whole world.

The general view which the later part of the Life

affords of the state of the country at the Restoration is exceedingly interesting. When attentively read, it shows what an immense change had been made by the Civil War in the position of Royalty, notwithstanding the eagerness with which Charles was welcomed back in the first instance.

It has been usual to represent Clarendon as the grave Mentor, the partisan of decency and order, who was driven into exile by the gross ingratitude and wickedness of a King who could not bear his own vices to be reproved, and of a Court which was the natural enemy of all decency and gravity. In all this there is a good deal of truth, but it is not the whole truth. There are many indications which it is impossible to mistake, though it would be difficult to exhibit them at full length in a moderate compass, that, apart from and over and above the offence given by Clarendon's well-deserved rebukes of Charles and his vices, Charles perceived that he did not enter into the spirit of the times, but belonged to a different age. Throughout the whole of his book he speaks of the Presbyterian party in a tone of rancorous moral condemnation. They had, he says in one place, no title to their lives except the King's mercy.

All his policy was in the same direction. He never could look upon any of the doings of the Long Parliament with toleration. For instance, the Triennial Act was then as much a part of the law of the land as any other; yet Charles said, in so many words, apparently with the full concurrence of his

Chancellor, that he would never permit a Parliament to assemble under its provisions, because they were derogatory to the Royal power.

So Clarendon continually tried to get the King to dissolve the Parliament elected after his return—the second Long Parliament, as it was called. This seemed, and perhaps in some respects actually was, a constitutional measure, but Charles's reasons for not doing so show what the real issue between himself and his Chancellor was. He refused to dissolve the Parliament because he thought he could govern through it. His other counsellors told him 'that he would never have such another Parliament, where he had near one hundred members of his own menial servants and their near relations, who were all at his disposal.' Clarendon would, no doubt, have liked the Parliament to have greater purity and less power. Charles felt that the Parliament could never again recede to the position which it had occupied in the early part of the century, and that the only chance of maintaining his power was by the use of influence. The honester man of the two was less favourable to freedom than the other.

A remarkable summary of Clarendon's own views is given in the latter part of the book:—

'He did never dissemble from the time of his return with the King, whom he had likewise prepared and disposed to the same sentiments, whilst His Majesty was abroad, that his opinion was that the late rebellion never could be extirpated and pulled up by the roots till the King's regal and inherent power and prerogative should be fully avowed and vindicated, and till the usurpations in both Houses of Parliament, since the year 1640, were disclaimed and made odious; and many other excesses which had been affected by both before that time, under the name of Privileges, should be restrained or explained.'

This was the leading idea of all his policy, and it is to be traced, in a variety of minute ways, in all that he has to say on the management of public affairs. He could not forgive Charles for being less of a Tory than himself:—

'The King had in his nature so little reverence or esteem for antiquity and did, in truth, so much contemn old orders, forms, and institutions, that the objections of novelty rather advanced than obstructed any proposition.'

There are a good many incidental remarks in Clarendon's Life which throw light on the manners of the age which he describes.

He gives an account, for instance, of his way of spending his time when he began to get business at the Bar—*i.e.* at some period being between 1630 and 1640. How he spent his mornings does not appear; but he saw his friends at dinner, in the middle of the day. The afternoons 'he dedicated to the business of his profession,' and he read 'polite learning' at night. 'He never supped for many years before the troubles brought in that custom.' His vacation he passed in study, except two months in the summer, when he went out of town. He afterwards speaks of the House of Commons rising at four as a 'disorderly hour,' and refers to dinners given by the popular leaders after the House had risen. Probably this is what he means by the troubles bringing in the custom of supping.

During the Civil War there was a rapid transport of despatches, 'when gentlemen undertook the service, which they were willing enough to do,' between London and York. Letters went out at twelve on Saturday night and the answer returned at ten on Monday morning. Clarendon, too, gives us the first notice of newspapers:—

'After he' (the King) 'had read his several letters of intelligence, he took out the prints of diurnals, and speeches, and the like, which were every day printed at London.'

After the Restoration, he speaks of bankers as 'a tribe that had risen and grown up in Cromwell's time, and never were heard of before the late troubles, till when the whole trade of money had passed through the hands of the scriveners.'

He thinks it necessary to explain the word 'million' as often as he uses it, by adding, in a parenthesis, 'Ten hundred thousand.'

In a notice of Clarendon's *History of the Rebellion*, we gave a specimen of his occasional eloquence. We will conclude this notice of his Life, which is far from being an eloquent book, with a specimen of the wonderful clumsiness into which he habitually allowed himself to slide when he wrote under no special excitement.

'The Earl of Falmouth and Mr. Coventry were rivals who should have most interest in the Duke, who loved the Earl best, but thought the other the wiser man, who supported Pen (who disobliged all the courtiers), even against the Earl, who contemned Pen.'

Here are five 'who's' in one sentence, and each refers to a different antecedent, namely, 1, Falmouth and Coventry; 2, the Duke of York; 3, Coventry; 4, Pen; and 5, Falmouth. The translation of the passage is as follows: 'The Earl of Falmouth and Mr. Coventry were rivals in the pursuit of interest with the Duke of York. The Duke liked Lord Falmouth best, but thought Mr. Coventry the wiser man. Coventry supported Pen even against Lord Falmouth, who contemned Pen. Pen on the other hand disobliged all the courtiers.'

END OF FIRST SERIES

www.ingramcontent.com/pod-product-compliance
Lightning Source LLC
Chambersburg PA
CBHW030258240426
43673CB00040B/997